PEARSON　　　　　　　　　　　ALWAYS LEARNING

Positive Behavior Support, Communication & Social Skills for Students with Moderate/Severe Disabilities

Custom Edition for National University

SPD 646

Taken from:
Instruction of Students with Severe Disabilities, Sixth Edition
by Martha E. Snell and Fredda Brown

*Curriculum and Instruction for Students with Significant
Disabilities in Inclusive Settings,* Second Edition
by Diane Lea Ryndak and Sandra Alper

Taken from:

Instruction of Students with Severe Disabilities, Sixth Edition
by Martha E. Snell and Fredda Brown
Copyright © 2006, 2000, 1993, 1987, 1983, 1978 by Pearson Education, Inc.
Published by Merrill Prentice Hall
Upper Saddle River, New Jersey 07458

*Curriculum and Instruction for Students with Significant Disabilities
in Inclusive Settings*, Second Edition
by Diane Lea Ryndak and Sandra Alper
Copyright © 2003, 1996 by Pearson Education, Inc.
Published by Allyn & Bacon
Boston, Massachusetts 02116

This special edition published in cooperation with Pearson Learning Solutions.

All trademarks, service marks, registered trademarks, and registered service marks are the property of their respective owners and are used herein for identification purposes only.

Pearson Learning Solutions, 501 Boylston Street, Suite 900, Boston, MA 02116
A Pearson Education Company
www.pearsoned.com

Printed in the United States of America

1 2 3 4 5 6 7 8 9 10 V036 16 15 14 13 12

000200010271285403

SB

ISBN 10: 1-256-50219-7
ISBN 13: 978-1-256-50219-7

Contents

4

Nonsymbolic Communication   88

ELLIN SIEGEL AND AMY WETHERBY

5

Teaching Functional Communication Skills   130

ANN P. KAISER AND JOAN C. GRIM

Note: Every effort has been made to provide accurate and current Internet information in this book. However, the Internet and information on it are constantly changing, so it is inevitable that some of the Internet addresses listed in this textbook will change.

Chapter 1 taken from: *Curriculum and Instruction for Students with Significant Disabilities in Inclusive Settings,* by Diane Lea Ryndak and Sandra Alper.

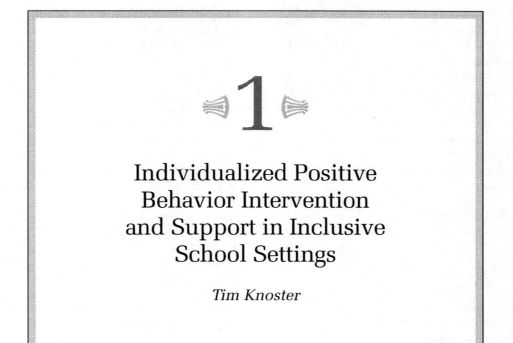

1

Individualized Positive Behavior Intervention and Support in Inclusive School Settings

Tim Knoster

Objectives

After completing this chapter, the reader will be able to:

1. Define student-centered positive behavior support (PBS).
2. Define school-wide PBS.
3. Describe the relationship between student-centered and schoolwide PBS.
4. Define and describe the problem-solving process known as functional behavioral assessment (FBA).
5. Describe and outline the various elements of a comprehensive, student-centered behavior support plan.
6. Describe important aspects of monitoring an individual student's progress.
7. Describe an efficient process to design student-centered behavior support plans based on hypotheses generated through an FBA.
8. Describe strategies to address two primary factors that can inhibit application of student-centered PBS.

Key Terms

Antecedents (fast triggers)
Array of tools/procedures
Aversive interventions
Behavior intervention/support plan
Collaboration
Child-centered
Community-based
Consequence strategies
Contextual fit
Continuum of approaches
Coping and tolerance skills
Crisis management
Culturally competent
Databased decision-making
Durable behavior change
Experimental analysis
Family-centered
Focus student

General skills
Global hypothesis
Individual student system
Informant method
Integrated assessment procedures
Intervention and support
Least restrictive/intrusive
Long-term prevention
Life style enhancements
Monitoring student progress
Multi-component behavior support plan
Normal deviance
Observation
Person-centered planning
Positive behavior support
Prevention
Quality of life
Reactive strategies
Reinforcement
Replacement skills
School-wide PBS
Setting events (slow triggers)
Specific hypothesis
Student-centered behavior support team
Student-centered PBS
Systems change
Teaching alternative skills
Wraparound process

One of the more perplexing challenges that schools face today is effectively educating students with problem behavior in typical school, work, and community settings. In particular, students with disabilities who have histories of problem behavior often find themselves at great risk for exclusion and devaluation at school and by society at large. Further, students with significant disabilities and problem behavior are typically the last group of students in even the most progressive schools to receive a Free Appropriate Public Education (FAPE) within the Least Restrictive Environment (LRE). Although there are many reasons as to why this occurs, one clear inhibitor to providing inclusive educational programs for this population of students is the capacity of school systems to support teachers in providing student-centered, positive behavior support (PBS).

This chapter will highlight the core component parts and processes associated with providing student-centered PBS within inclusive school settings. In particular, the practices highlighted will describe an approach to designing interventions and supports that is portable to general education settings. The chapter begins by providing definitions of a) schoolwide PBS and b) student-centered PBS. Next, the PBS process is described using practical terms and illustrations that are relevant to inclusive schools. In a larger sense, student-centered programs are contextualized within broader schoolwide prevention and early intervention approaches highlighting the application of the problem-solving process known as functional behavioral assessment (FBA). Assessment and intervention procedures are presented as occurring along a least-to-most intrusive continuum. Further, FBA procedures are reviewed in concert with a description of a process for designing comprehensive, student-centered behavior support plans for particular students. Specifically, key components of student-centered behavior support plans are described (that is, prevention, teaching alternative skills, consequence strategies, lifestyle intervention and support). Further, practices relevant to monitoring student progress are highlighted, along with a description of an efficient process to design student-centered programs in general education settings. Finally, strategies are provided to facilitate application of student-centered PBS within inclusive settings.

PBS

PBS is an applied science that places emphasis on changes in practice to enhance the quality of life of stakeholders and to reduce problem behaviors. As Carr et al. (2002) notes, PBS initially evolved within the field of developmental disabilities and emerged from three major sources: applied behavior analysis, the normalization and inclusion movement, and person-centered values. Although components of PBS may be found in other approaches, PBS uniquely interweaves a number of key features, including a comprehensive lifestyle perspective, stakeholder participation and social validity, flexibility in application, and implementation of evidence-based practice with individual students and entire schools.

An Overview of Schoolwide PBS

In addition to being successfully employed across a broad range of individual students and settings, PBS has been extended to a systems-level intervention approach for entire schools (Colvin, Kameenui, & Sugai, 1993; Taylor-Green et al., 1997; Todd, Horner, Sugai, & Sprague, 1999). Acknowledging the fact that many children (and specifically not just students with disabilities) come to school with learning histories that set the stage for increasing behavioral problems, schools (in general) have responded to student problem behavior in a variety of ways. Unfortunately, evidence suggests that many aspects of traditional school discipline practices exacerbate and, in some instances, contribute to children and youth's patterns of problem behavior (Lewis & Sugai, 1999). In response to this dilemma, efforts to build schoolwide PBS have been gaining national attention (Dwyer, Osher, & Warger, 1998). Schoolwide PBS is, first and foremost, a teaching approach. As such, emphasis is placed primarily on identifying and defining behavioral expectations, teaching those expectations, and systematically reinforcing performance of the behavioral expectations with all students in the school (not just those who have a history of problem behavior). For example, a given school might identify three school expectations, such as, be on time, be respectful, and be responsible. They would next define those expectations across routines/settings (for example, classroom, cafeteria, or playground). In turn, a system for acknowledging student performance of these expectations would be put in place and implemented by a majority (if not all staff) to "catch kids being good." Data would be collected relevant to student behavior over time and used to design, adapt, or modify strategies to further reinforce acquisition and demonstration of the behavioral expectations by all students.

Although variation exists among schools implementing schoolwide PBS, they share a number of essential features (key themes according to Horner & Sugai, 2000) that enable them to realize positive changes in school environments accompanied by sustainable reductions in student problem behavior (for example, reductions in discipline referrals). Applying a systems approach (that is, broadening the focus from a given student's program to programs for all students) supports the application of positive prevention and early intervention in schools with the entire student body that emphasizes teaching and acknowledges appropriate student behavior. A systems approach at the school-building level provides for a continuum of PBS practices (see Figure 1–1) in which prevention is emphasized and intensity of problem behavior and context are considered.

Introduction to Student-Centered PBS

PBS is a general term that refers to the application of positive behavioral interventions and systems to achieve socially important behavior change (Sugai et al., 2000). Socially important behavior change for an individual student includes skills that are necessary to increase the likelihood of success and personal satisfaction in typical school, work, home, and community settings. The primary goal of student-centered PBS is to assist a student's lifestyle to evolve in a direction that enables all relevant stakeholders (for example, teachers, employers, parents, friends, and the focus student) to have the opportunity to perceive and to enjoy an improved quality of life (Carr et al., in press). An important, but secondary, goal of this approach is to decrease a student's problem behavior by helping students to learn to meet their needs in a socially acceptable manner (for example, asking for help or a break as opposed to crying and screaming in the classroom) and through environmental changes (for example, making changes in how we teach). Student-centered PBS initially emerged in practice as an alternative to aversive interventions used with students with significant disabilities. More recently, the approach has been successfully used with a wide range of students in a variety of school settings (Carr et al, 1999; Horner, Albin, Sprague, & Todd, 1999). PBS represents the application of a behaviorally-based systems approach to building the capacity of schools, families, and communities to design conducive environments for learning that improves the match between research-proven practices and naturally occurring routines. Interventions and supports that are designed through the process reflect culturally competent approaches that take into account the unique and personal learning experiences (histories) of all relevant stakeholders (for example, the student with problem behavior, his/her family and friends, and teachers).

PBS and Student-Centered Programs

The process of designing and implementing comprehensive student-centered behavior support is comprised of five major steps that include: 1) conducting a functional behavioral assessment, 2) developing hypothesis statements, 3) designing and implementing the behavior support plan, 4) monitoring student progress and evaluating the effect of the behavior support plan,

FIGURE 1–1

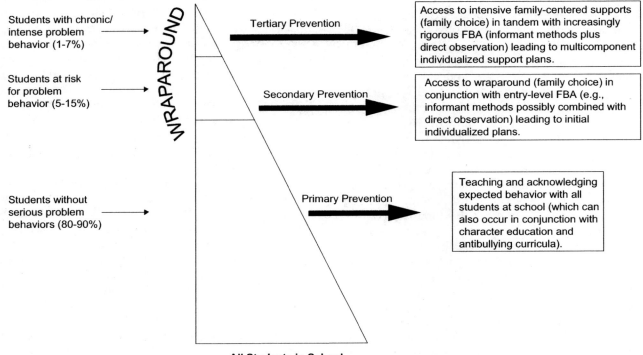

Continuum of behavior support

Source: Adapted from Eber, in press; and Sugai et al., 2000.

and 5) modifying the support plan as needed. This five-step process places great emphasis on determining the function of student problem behavior and identifying factors that may be contributing to the student's problem behavior in order to develop and provide effective intervention and support. The five-step process of designing and providing student-centered behavior support is most effective when employed by student-centered teams.

Step One: Conducting a Functional Behavioral Assessment (FBA)

FBA serves as the foundation for the design and delivery of positive behavior support. In particular, student-centered, school-based teams educating students with disabilities who present behavior that impedes learning have the responsibility of conducting FBAs as stip-

ulated in the Individuals with Disabilities Education Act (IDEA). The regulations state the following:

> *Either before or no later than 10 business days after either first removing the child for more than 10 school days in a school year or commencing removal that constitutes a change in placement under section 300.519 .... If the LEA did not conduct a functional behavioral assessment and implement a behavioral intervention plan that resulted in the suspension described in subparagraph (a), the agency shall convene an IEP meeting to develop an assessment plan.*

Acknowledging this requirement coupled with an understanding of the IDEA (in total), a case can be made for the application of FBA in a proactive manner by Individualized Education Plan (IEP) teams in providing educational services and programs. In light of the practical utility of FBA coupled with legal requirements, it is important to understand that the true utility of FBA is not simply the adoption and documentation of its use, but as a process that leads to desired outcomes (Reid, 2000).

FBA is a problem-solving framework that leads to student-centered intervention and support (Knoster & McCurdy, 2002; Repp, Karsh, Munk, & Dahlquist, 1995; Tilly et al., 1998). The process of coming to an understanding about why a student engages in problem behavior and how student behavior relates to the environment (both internal to the student and external in terms of settings and routines) is referred to as FBA. There are three common approaches to collecting functional assessment information, the first two of which are very applicable in general education settings. The first commonly employed approach in general education classrooms is referred to as informant methods, which involve record reviews and talking with the student of concern as well as people who have direct contact with the student. The second approach that can also be efficiently used in typical classrooms is direct observation (in its various forms), which involves systematic observation of the student within typical settings and routines over time. The third approach, which is not typically required or employed in general education classrooms, is experimental analysis (that is, analog functional analysis), which involves the manipulations of variables that are hypothesized as being related to the student's problem behavior.

The process of FBA can best be understood as a continuum of integrated assessment procedures that may involve an array of data collection tools and procedures (Tilly et al., 1998, 2000). In this sense, the continuum for FBA is consistent and analogous to the array of integrated assessment procedures that general education teachers use in assessing academic progress of students. Student-centered teams, in determining the amount of resources and precision necessary to design an effective behavior support plan, should make decisions on a case-by-case basis (for example, initial use of informant methods alone or in combination with some form of direct observation). Decisions should be made in relation to the need for immediate behavior change (for example, urgent behaviors, such as self-injury versus what has been described as excessive or nuisance behaviors that reflect "normal" deviance as described by Meyer & Evans, 1989). In addition, it is important to also consider resource

and capacity issues in the school program (for example, available time and competencies of staff).

After a student-centered team decides to conduct an FBA, these information-gathering approaches are used in a least-to-most resource intensive manner to collect two types of information that is ultimately summarized into hypothesis statements (Bambara & Knoster, 1995, 1998). First, the team gathers broad contextual information about the student: skills and abilities, preferences and interests, general health, and quality of life. Next, the team gathers specific information that pinpoints the conditions that are regularly associated with occurrence and nonoccurrence of problem behavior. When viewed together, these two types of information can enable the team to see the proverbial "forest and the trees" as it pertains to the student of concern.

To illustrate, most mild problem behaviors in general education classrooms can be efficiently assessed through informant methods (for example, infrequent acts such as one child occasionally raising his/her voice toward other children during activities to resolve conflicts). Contrarily, an educational team confronted with a student who engages in extreme problem behavior will likely need to combine informant methods with direct observation (for example, a student who frequently bites his hands and scratches his face in a variety of settings when upset). In addition, this may require a comprehensive record review, which could lead to a medical assessment concerning physical health factors (for example, history of a dry skin condition) that may be contributing to the student's problem behavior. Further, the team may see fit to conduct this record review within the context of a person-centered planning process (Kincaid, 1996; Knoster, 2000) and/or in tandem with a wraparound approach (Eber, in press).

Person-centered planning describes a range of techniques for identifying a person's wants and needs (Kincaid, 1996). The team-facilitated process helps team members learn more about the student and emphasizes planning for a more positive future as defined by the student and his or her family. Person-centered planning processes include Lifestyle Planning (O'Brien, 1987), Personal Futures Planning (Mount, 1987; Mount & Zwernick, 1988), the McGill Action Planning System (Forrest & Lusthaus, 1987; Vandercook, York & Forest, 1989), Framework for Accomplishment/Personal Profile (O'Brien, 1987), and Essential

Lifestyle Planning (Smull & Harrison, 1992). Each of these processes can result in gaining a deeper understanding of the student with a disability and can help guide the student-centered team to design interventions and supports that facilitate the realization of self-determined life goals and objectives.

The wraparound process has emerged from the system of care concept that uses a community-based approach to provide comprehensive and integrated services and supports in collaboration with families. More specifically, wraparound is a philosophy of care with a defined planning process that results in a uniquely designed individual plan through a partnership with the child and family to achieve a set of outcomes that reflect the voice and choices of the child and his or her family (Eber, in press).

Step Two: Generating Hypothesis Statements

The culminating activity of an FBA is the team developing hypothesis statements. Hypotheses summarize assessment results by offering a logical explanation for problem behavior (O'Neill et al., 1997; Tilly et al., 1998, 2000). Specifically, hypotheses summarize the function of and factors identified as contributing to the student's problem behavior. Specific and global

hypotheses serve as the foundation from which student-centered interventions and supports are designed (Bambara & Knoster, 1995, 1998). An example of a specific and global hypothesis is provided in Table 1-1.

As shown in Table 1-1, important information is contained in both the specific and global hypotheses. The support team in this example would design interventions and supports for Joshua in his general education classes based on the specific hypothesis (for example, teaching him how to get a break in a more socially acceptable manner) as well as take into account the broader information associated with Joshua's general health and well-being as highlighted in the global hypothesis (for example, desire/need for expanded relationships with others).

Step Three: Designing and Implementing Behavior Support Plans

Although the use of hypotheses should increase the likelihood of success, it is unlikely that any one intervention or support will be sufficient by itself to realize durable behavior change for students with complex needs (Horner & Day, 1991; Horner, Day, & Day, 1997). Therefore, student-centered teams should design comprehensive support plans that involve multiple inter-

TABLE 1–1
An Example of Specific and Global Hypotheses

Joshua

Specific Hypothesis Statement
When Joshua is presented with instructions of more than a few words that are not paired with pictures/symbols, passive and/or independent tasks that last more than three minutes, and/or he did not get an ample amount of sleep the night before (i.e., less than six hours), he disrupts the classroom through verbal outbursts (e.g., making shrieking sounds), destroying property (e.g.. flipping the desk at the workstation), or leaving his work area and invading the physical space of the teaching staff (e.g., sometimes grabbing the teacher's arm when ignored) in order to stop the task and/or activity (i.e., get a break).

Global Hypothesis
Joshua is a 12-year old student who is identified as having a significant language delay and mental retardation. He appears interested in social relationships with peers his own age and enjoys listening to country music (especially with other kids). Joshua is a physically active boy who loves gym class. Joshua uses a picture communication system (limited to about 20 key words/phrases). He enjoys physical activities. His greatest difficulties have been increasingly noted in traditional academic settings. As Joshua started attending his local middle school this year (he previously attended a special education class in a neighboring school district), he is familiar with some of the students at school who live in his neighborhood. He has not (to date) established what might be viewed as any real close friendships. Joshua's mother and brother both report that Joshua wants and needs some friends to "hang around with." Joshua lives with his mother and older brother John. His father moved to another state following a divorce three years ago, and Joshua rarely sees his father (about one time per year when he comes back to town). John goes to visit his father about three times a year. Joshua's mother reports that Joshua tends to be irritable when his brother is away visiting his father.

---

vention strategies. Comprehensive plans are sometimes referred to as multicomponent plans, which is a technical way of saying that the team is going to provide a variety of interventions and supports within a close time proximity in an agreed upon manner. Bambara and Knoster (1995, 1998) describe four component parts in multicomponent support plans that include 1) prevention, 2) teaching alternative skills, 3) consequence strategies, and 4) life-style intervention and support.

Preventative strategies can have a powerful and fast effect on a student's behavior as a result of addressing antecedents (fast triggers) and setting events (slow triggers) associated with problem behavior. In Joshua's case, this could include the teacher(s) minimizing non-activity-based independent tasks and lessening demands on days when he is tired (that is, did not get a good night's sleep of at least six hours). However, it is unlikely that any given general education classroom setting will lend itself to completely engineering the entire school day for any particular student. Additionally, even if this were possible, it would not be desirable because the student in such circumstances is not being taught new skills to help him or her function independently. Therefore, it is necessary to combine the use of preventative strategies with teaching alternative skills (Meyer & Evans, 1989).

Alternative skill instruction can be classified into a few domains (Bambara, Mitchell-Kvacky, & Iacobelli, 1994; Dunlap & Kern, 1996; Meyer & Evans, 1989). Specifically, Bambara and Knoster (1995, 1998) describe these domains as teaching a) replacement skills, b) general skills, and c) coping and tolerance skills. Replacement skills operate as a one-for-one substitute for the student that will serve the exact same function as the problem behavior. In Joshua's case, having him cue the teacher with a picture card that he needs a break from the current situation could serve as a substitute for his problem behavior because it would serve the same function as the problem behavior (that is, to get a break). General skills are broad skills that constructively alter problem situations and help to prevent the need for problem behavior. For Joshua, helping him to more effectively use his communication system across all settings would likely enhance his ability to interact with others and therefore help to minimize the likelihood of problem behavior in the future. Coping and tolerance skills are things that the student learns to do when he or she is faced with difficult situations. For

Joshua, teaching him how to calm himself down when he is upset in order to communicate that he needs a break from the stressful situation by using his picture card for "break" serves as an example of a coping skill.

It is necessary for student-centered teams to employ consequence strategies in concert with antecedent/setting event modifications and the teaching of alternative skills. For example, a child's teacher (or peers) may use consequence strategies to reinforce the acquisition and use of alternative skills. In Joshua's case, this could simply include the teacher or classmates responding to his cues (signaling "break") when he needs a break. In a further example, the classroom teacher might provide negative feedback to reduce the effectiveness of problem behavior should it continue to occur (much like any basic redirection procedure used with any child in a typical classroom setting). For Joshua, this might include the use of verbal redirections and loss of special extra privileges for disruptive behavior. The goal of consequence strategies is to teach the student that his or her use of alternative skills is a better way to address his or her needs (that is, more acceptable, more effective, and more efficient [Horner & Day, 1991]). For student-centered teams concerned about a child with significant disabilities and a history of behavioral challenges in the general education classroom, consequence strategies may also be used to de-escalate crisis situations and to protect the child, others, and property from harm. A four-step approach should be considered in developing crisis management plans (Knoster, 2000). First, carefully define what constitutes a crisis. Second, describe intervention procedures to employ and who will implement the procedures. Next, identify resources needed to implement the plan. Finally, agree on documentation procedures. Crisis management plans should be developed to address the escalation, eruption, and de-escalation phases of the crisis and should never be used as an isolated approach to addressing a student's problem behavior (Bambara & Knoster, 1995, 1998; Meyer & Evans, 1989).

Finally, lifestyle intervention and support should be designed and implemented by the team in conjunction with the other previously described components. Lifestyle refers to the typical ebb and flow of the student's life across routines and settings. Lifestyle interventions and support will be most directly influenced by the team's global hypotheses and will result in general improvement in the student's quality of life (for example, friends, access to events or activities of interest, personal choice, and power over age-appropriate life decisions). In the case of Joshua, lifestyle support could employ strategies that would increase Joshua's participation in peer-mediated activities at school with others of his own age in tandem with increasing access to preferred community-based experiences. Lifestyle interventions and support are important for three reasons. First, a student's dissatisfaction with his or her circumstances may likely contribute to problem behavior. Second, students are more likely to learn new skills in contexts that are enjoyable and desired. Lastly, lifestyle interventions and supports allow for ongoing, long-term support for the student over time (for example, the evolving parameters of social/sexual relationships from adolescents through adulthood).

In total, individualized plans of intervention and support are uniquely tailored to each student's needs, preferences, and long-range goals (Hansen, 1999). Comprehensive intervention in the general education classroom is a multifaceted approach to prevention and early intervention. Effective support plans take into consideration the perspective of the student and his or her family and the feasibility of interventions in the plan (that is, contextual fit per Albin, Lucyshyn, Horner, & Flannery, 1996). This is accomplished by involving the student along with his or her family, staff members, and other relevant parties in designing interventions and support to best ensure a good fit across typical settings and routines.

Step Four: Monitoring Student Progress and Evaluating Effects

Effective student-centered PBS focuses first on improvement in quality of life and then on reduction in problem behavior. Meaningful outcomes leading to an improved quality of life include lifestyle improvements, such as participation in community life, gaining and maintaining satisfying relationships, expressing personal preferences and making choices, and developing personal competencies (Meyer & Evans, 1989). Such improvements in quality of life are facilitated by establishing a positive long-range vision with the student and his or her family and by mobilizing natural supports through effective teamwork (Kincaid, 1996).

IEP teams educating students who exhibit problem behavior are required to monitor student progress. Deciding what information to collect and analyze will be guided by the specific goals in the student's behavior intervention plan in the IEP. As such, assessment procedures employed during the initial FBA may be used to monitor student progress (that is, informant procedures used during the initial FBA may be used to monitor the effect of the student's program). Table 1–2 illustrates progress-monitoring procedures that may be used by Joshua's IEP team.

Step Five: Modifying the Support Plan as Needed

Student-centered support teams will need to make modifications in support plans for a variety of reasons. Based on the information that the team collects, the team will need to reevaluate components of the plan, strengthen support strategies, or expand the plan beyond its current scope (Bambara & Knoster, 1998).

Obviously, intervention and support changes may be warranted if the student of concern is not demonstrating progress within a reasonable amount of time. Examples of situations that may warrant concern by the support team include: limited to no acquisition and use of socially acceptable alternative skills following teaching despite some reduction in problem behavior; limited to no reduction in problem behavior despite increases in the acquisition and use of socially acceptable alternative skills; and/or limited acquisition and use of socially acceptable alternative skills in combination with little decrease in problem behavior. In such circumstances, student-centered support teams should revisit their original hypothesis statements and expand their information sources relevant to the functional behavioral assessment.

In an instance in which a student's support plan appears effective, the team will likely note acquisition and use of socially acceptable alternative skills in tandem with reductions in problem behavior. However, even under such positive circumstances, support teams should be thinking into the future (for example, asking the question "what is next?"). It is not uncommon for the needs, interests, and desires of children, adolescents, and young adults to change over time. As such, it is important for student-centered support teams to keep looking forward into the future with the student and his or her family (for example, person-centered plans can help guide the team in their endeavors to modify support plans in a manner consistent with long-range personal goals).

TABLE 1–2
Progress Monitoring Procedures—Joshua's Support Team

Desired Changes	How to Gather Information	What to Do with Information
Increases in alternative skills: • Joshua holds up picture card to signal he needs a break. • Joshua will use his picture communication system (including his use of "break card") across school, home, and community settings. • Joshua will use deep breathing procedures and listen to his country music on his portable CD when upset.	• At the end of each class period, the teacher will score Joshua's use of his picture card (for break) as either 1) appropriately used, 2) inappropriately used, or 3) not applicable. • Throughout the course of the week, Joshua's circle of friends and teachers will record Joshua's use of picture communication system by placing a penny in a coin jar every time he initiates contact with a peer using his system. Total of pennies will be calculated daily and cashed in on a monthly basis for a pizza party, with friends. • At the end of each class period, the teacher will score Joshua's use of deep breathing when frustrated as either successful, unsuccessful, or not applicable.	Data will be summarized on paper and circulated among team members on a weekly basis. The team will convene (at a minimum) once a month to review data. The team will convene more frequently as needed to problem solve. Further, all information will be summarized quarterly in context of report card cycle and summarized for annual educational reevaluation meetings and will be incorporated into future IEP planning as relevant.
Decreases in problem behavior: • Joshua will decrease his use of shrieking sounds, property destruction, and invading others' space at school.	• During each class period, Joshua's teacher will keep a frequency chart of incidents.	
Enhancements to quality of life: • Joshua will increase his successful interactions with others at school. • Joshua will expand his circle of friends beyond school. • Joshua will successfully travel and visit with his father along with his brother John.	• Throughout the course of the week, Joshua's circle of friends will record the number of successful interactions that Joshua initiates that last at least one minute, by dropping a nickel into a coin jar. • Total of nickels will be calculated weekly and cashed in on a monthly basis as noted previously. • Once a month, in context of circle of support meeting, a circle of friends-map will be developed. • Mom will report when Joshua accompanies his brother John to visit his father.	

An Efficient Process to Design Student-Centered Programs

It is not uncommon for student-centered teams to be composed of people with diverse perspectives. In reality, this diversity is natural and can be helpful to providing PBS for an individual student. In order to increase the likelihood of successful outcomes, a structured process should be used to identify and select strategies and interventions across component parts of the support plan in light of the student-centered team's hypotheses (Knoster, 1998, 1999, 2000). The student's support team may proceed in the following manner repeating the process across the four components of the support plan as depicted in Figure 1–2 (that is, prevention, teaching alternative skills, consequence strategies, and lifestyle intervention and support). First, the team brainstorms possible interventions and supports with the goal being to generate the greatest number of potential options for

FIGURE 1–2

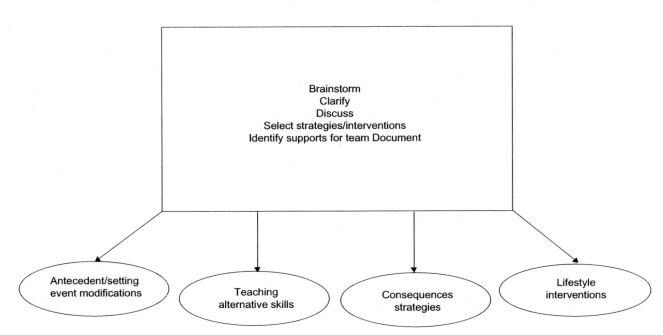

Design process of support plans
(Knoster, 1998)

Brainstorm
Clarify
Discuss
Select strategies/interventions
Identify supports for team Document

Antecedent/setting event modifications

Teaching alternative skills

Consequences strategies

Lifestyle interventions

Source: Adapted from Knoster, 1998.

strategies within a set time frame (for example, within four minutes). Second, team members clarify strategies should questions arise at the end of the set time for brainstorming. Third, the team discusses the appropriateness of interventions and supports in terms of the match with the hypotheses and feasibility of implementation. Fourth, the team prioritizes interventions and supports. Next, the top two to four priorities per program component are selected along with identifying the types of supports that team members will need to implement the selected interventions and supports. Finally, the selected interventions and supports (including the necessary supports for team members) are documented in the student's support plan (and/or IEP).

Factors that Can Inhibit Student-Centered PBS

Effective student-centered teams accomplish two primary objectives: 1) They accomplish important tasks, and 2) they maintain relationships among team mem-

bers. These two objectives are particularly important for student-centered teams working with students who have histories of problem behavior. In particular, collaborative problem solving concerning the problem behavior of a student with disabilities in a general education classroom may be inhibited by a number of factors. Specifically, a sense of helplessness or hopelessness on the part of team members as a result of past adverse experiences coupled with the personal (emotional) stress that can be created when confronted with the need to change practice can essentially freeze some teams in space and time.

Factor One: Past Experiences

We are all influenced by our past experiences. This can be a particular problem in the instance in which team members have experienced prolonged negative interactions with the student as well as among stakeholders in team meetings (for example, faculty, staff, and family). In Joshua's example, this could include numerous class disruptions over the course of the school year coupled with negative experiences among the team members in failed attempts to problem-solve (for example, emergency team meetings in response to problem behavior). In light of the potential impact that past experiences will likely have on team functioning, it is important to proactively structure collaboration by 1) establishing a common set of ground rules for meetings; 2) attending to the process of interactions so that all team members feel that their perspective is heard; 3) using conversational language to the greatest extent possible, and where impossible, defining terms and jargon; 4) agreeing to a shared set of goals and objectives prior to rushing headstrong into identifying interventions and supports; 5) reaching consensus (not majority voting) on which interventions and supports to employ; and 6) documenting a plan of action to which all team members commit.

Factor Two: Personal (Emotional) Aspects of Change

Volumes upon volumes of helpful books, articles, videotapes, and audiocassettes have been published on the process of change in schools and other organizations. One common theme (a common denominator, so to speak) throughout these resources is the realization that change is a highly personal experience that can be emotionally unsettling. This can be particularly the case when confronted with the need to change our operating assumptions and procedures under highly stressful circumstances, such as being confronted by a student who engages in serious problem behavior (for example, Joshua uses increasingly disruptive behavior in his general education classes). Such circumstances can be even further compounded when the problem behavior of concern can become dangerous to the safety of the child or others in the classroom. In order to address this inhibiting factor effectively, student-centered teams are encouraged to attend to the support needs of individual team members as a part of the process of designing and implementing behavior support plans. The need for support by each team member will likely vary over time and may include different forms of support. In the case of Joshua, supports for team members may include providing in-service training for his teacher, altering staffing patterns for a short time frame in the general education classrooms where Joshua is experiencing greatest difficulty, or simply providing team members with a sympathetic ear to listen to their story or a shoulder to cry on after a really tough day.

Summary

Successfully including students with significant disabilities that include problem behavior can be challenging. The focus of this chapter has been on the approach known as positive behavior support (PBS). The chapter provides a description of student-centered and school-wide PBS. In particular, a team process to designing and implementing individualized student-centered support plans based on functional behavior assessment is described. In addition, guidance is provided concerning factors (practical matters) that can inhibit initiation and sustained implementation of student-centered PBS within inclusive school settings.

References

Albin, R. W., Lucyshyn, J. M., Horner, R. H., & Flannery, K. B. (1996). Contextual fit for behavior support plans. In L. K. Koegel, R. L. Koegel, & G. Dunlap (Eds.), *Positive behavioral support: Including people with difficult behavior in the community* (pp. 82-98). Baltimore: Paul H. Brookes Publishing Co.

Bambara, L. M., & Knoster, T. (1995). *Guidelines: Effective behavior support.* Harrisburg, PA: Pennsylvania Department of Education, Bureau of Special Education.

Bambara, L. M., & Knoster, T. (1998). *Designing positive behavior support plans.* Washington, D.C.: American Association on Mental Retardation.

Bambara, L. M., Mitchell-Kvacky, N. A., & Iacobelli, S. (1994). Positive behavioral support for students with severe disabilities: An emerging multicomponent approach for addressing challenging behaviors. *School Psychology Review; 23*, 263-278.

Carr, E. G., Dunlap, G., Horner, R. H., Koegel, R. L., Turnbull, A. F., Sailor, W., Anderson, J., Albin, R. W., Koegel, L. K., Fox, L. (2002). Positive behavior support: Evolution of an applied science. *Journal of Positive Behavior Interventions, 4*, 4-16.

Carr, E. G., Horner, R. H., Turnbull, A. P., Marquis, J. G., McLaughlin, D. D., AcAtee, M. L., Smith, C. E., Ryan, K. A., Ruef, M. B., & Doolabh, A. (1999). *Positive behavior support for people with developmental disabilities: A research synthesis.* Washington, D.C.: American Association on Mental Retardation.

Colvin, G., Kameenui, E. J., Sugai, G. (1993). Reconceptualizing behavior management and school-wide discipline in general education. *Education and Treatment of Children, 16*, 361-381.

Dunlap, G., & Kern, L. (1996). Modifying instructional activities to promote desirable behavior: A conceptual and practical framework. *School Psychology Quarterly, 11*, 297-312.

Dwyer, K. P., Osher, D, & Warger, W. (1998). *Early warning, timely response: A guide to safe schools.* Washington, D.C.: U.S. Department of Education.

Eber, L. (in press). Blending process and practice to maximize outcomes: Wraparound and positive behavioral interventions and supports in the schools. *Journal of Emotional and Behavioral Disorders.*

Forrest, M., & Lusthaus, E. (1987). The kaleidoscope: Challenge to the cascade. In M. Forrest (Ed.), *More education/integration* (pp. 1–16). Downsview, Ontario, Canada: G. Allan Roeher Institute.

Hansen, M. (1999). *Writing effective treatment plans: The Pennsylvania CASSP model.* Harrisburg, PA: Pennsylvania CASSP Training and Technical Assistance Institute, Pennsylvania Department of Education.

Horner, R. H., & Day, H. M. (1991). The effects of response efficiency on functionally equivalent competing behaviors. *Journal of Applied Behavior Analysis, 24,* 719–732.

Horner, R. H., & Sugai, G. (2000). School-wide behavior support. *Journal of Positive Behavior Interventions, 2,* 231–232.

Horner, R. H., Day, H. M., & Day, J. R. (1997). Using neutralizing routines to reduce problem behaviors. *Journal of Applied Behavior Analysis, 30,* 601–614.

Horner, R. H., Albin, R. W., Sprague, J. R., Todd, A. W. (1999). Positive behavior support. In M. E. Snell and F. Brown (Eds.), *Instruction of students with severe disabilities (5th ed., pp. 207–243). Upper Saddle River, NJ: Merril/Prentice-Hall.*

Kincaid, D. (1996). Person-centered planning. In L. Kern-Koegel, R. L. Koegel, & G. Dunlap (Eds.), *Positive behavioral support: Including people with difficult behavior in the community* (pp. 439–465). Baltimore: Paul H. Brookes Publishing Co.

Knoster, T. (1998, Spring). Positive behavior support in schools. *Tri-State Consortium on Positive Behavior Support Newsletter, 1,* 1–3.

Knoster, T. (1999). Effective support for students with dual diagnoses who have histories of challenging behavior at school. *Journal of Positive Approaches.* 15–20.

Knoster, T. (2000). Practical application of functional behavioral assessment in schools. *The Journal of The Association for Persons with Severe Handicaps, 4,* 201–211.

Knoster T., & McCurdy, B. (2002). Best practices in functional behavioral assessment. In A. Thomas & J. Grimes (Eds.), *Best practices in school psychology: Vol. 4.* (pp. 1007–1028). Bethesda, MD: National Association of School Psychologists.

Lewis, T. J., & Sugai, G. (1999). Effective behavior support: A systems approach to proactive school-wide management. *Focus on Exceptional Children, 31*(6), 1–24.

Meyer, L. H., & Evans, I. M. (1989). *Non-aversive intervention for behavior problems: A manual for home and community.* Baltimore, MD: Paul H. Brookes Publishing Co.

Mount, B. (1987). *Personal futures planning: Finding directions for change* (Doctoral dissertation, University of Georgia). Ann Arbor, MI: UMI Dissertation Information Service.

Mount, B., & Zwerniek, K. (1988). *It's never too early. It's never too late: A booklet about personal futures planning.* St. Paul, MN: Metropolitan Council.

O'Brien, J. (1987). A guide to lifestyle planning: Using The Activities Catalog to integrate services and natural support systems. In B. Wilcox & G. T. Bellamy (Eds.), *A comprehensive guide to The Activities Catalog: An alternative curriculum for youth and adults with severe disabilities* (pp. 175–189). Baltimore: Paul H. Brookes Publishing Co.

O'Neill, R. E., Horner, R. H., Albin, R. W., Sprague, J. R., Storey, K., & Newton, J. S. (1997). *Functional assessment and program development for problem behaviors: A practical handbook.* Pacific Grove, CA: Brookes/Cole.

Reid, D. H. (2000). Enhancing the applied utility of functional assessment. *Journal of The Association for Persons with Severe Handicaps, 4,* 241–244.

Repp, A. C, Karsh, K. G., Munk, D., & Dahlquist, C. M. (1995). Hypothesis-based interventions: A theory of clinical decision-making. In W. O'Donohue & L. Krasner (Eds.), *Theories of behavior therapy: Exploring behavior change* (pp. 585–608). Washington, D.C.: American Psychological Association.

Smull, M. W., & Harrison, S. B. (1992). *Supporting people with severe retardation in the community.* Alexandria, VA: National Association of State Mental Retardation Program Directors.

Sugai, G., Horner, R. H., Dunlap, G., Hieneman, M., Lewis, T. J., Nelson, C. M., Scott, T., Liaupsin, C., Sailor, W., Turnbull, A. P., Turnbull, H. R., Wickham, D., Wilcox, B., & Ruef, M. (2000). Applying positive behavior support and functional behavioral assessment in schools. *Journal of Positive Behavior Interventions, 2,* 131–143.

Taylor-Green, S., Brown, D., Nelson, L., Longton, J., Gassman, T., Cohen, J., Swatz, J., Horner, R. H., Sugai, G., & Hall, S. (1997). School-wide behavior support: Starting the year off right. *Journal of Behavioral Education, 7,* 99–112.

Tilly, W. D., Knoster, T. P., & Ikeda, J. J. (2000). Functional behavioral assessment: Strategies for positive behavior support. In C. Telzrow & M. Tankersley (Eds.), *IDEA amendments of 1997: Practice guidelines for school-based teams* Bethesda, MD: National Association of School Psychologists Publications.

Tilly, W. D., Knoster, T. P., Kovaleski, J., Bambara, L., Dunlap, G., & Kincaid, D. (1998). *Functional behavioral assessment: Policy development in light of emerging research and practice.* Alexandria, VA: National Association of State Directors of Special Education.

Todd, A. W., Horner, R. H., Sugai, G., & Sprague, J. R. (1999). Effective behavior support: Strengthening school-wide systems through a team-based approach. *Effective School Practices, 17*(4), 23–37.

Vandercook, T., York, J., & Forrest, M. (1989). The McGill Action Planning System (MAPS): A strategy for building the vision. *Journal of The Association for Persons with Severe handicaps, 14,* 205–215.

2

Positive Behavior Support for Individuals with Severe Disabilities

Robert H. Horner
Richard W. Albin
J. Stephen Newton
Anne W. Todd
Jeffrey Sprague

In this chapter, we provide an introduction to positive behavior support, a description of the core procedures that make positive behavior support effective, and examples of how this approach is applied with individuals who have severe disabilities. Throughout the chapter, we refer to two students, Maya and Isha, and to the activities that their support teams conducted to illustrate the various features and procedures that constitute individualized student behavior support. Some terms used and procedures described in these examples may be unfamiliar and new to some readers. Bear with us; by the end of the chapter, all these terms and procedures will be explained and described. To start, meet Maya.

Maya

Maya is 12 years old, lives at home with her family, and has Down syndrome and moderate to severe intellectual disabilities. Maya lives with her two high school–age brothers and both birth parents and recently entered sixth grade at her neighborhood middle school. She enjoys fish, has a fish aquarium, and hopes to work at a fish or pet store in the future. Maya takes care of most of her dressing and personal care needs and enjoys cooking and listening to music with peers. She reads at a first-grade level; follows step-by-step directions by reading words, icons, and photos; adds and subtracts single-digit numbers; identifies numbers 1 to 10; and copies two- to three-word

---

Development of this chapter was supported by a grant from the Office of Special Education Programs, with additional funding from the Safe and Drug Free Schools Program, U.S. Department of Education (H326S030002). Opinions expressed herein are those of the authors and do not necessarily reflect the position of the U.S. Department of Education, and such endorsements should not be inferred. For additional information regarding the contents of this chapter, contact the first author (robh@uoregon.edu)

phrases. Maya also engages in problem behaviors that are becoming increasingly intense and currently threaten her continued participation in regular school settings. The major concern is that in situations where Maya is not receiving social attention from peers, she will yell at her peers and then sometimes hit them. Maya's behavior can escalate to dangerous levels. She also has a history of sticking her tongue out, spitting, and throwing objects when she has had very little peer attention.

Twenty-five years ago, Maya most likely would have been placed in a segregated school with a minimalist curriculum and behavior support that included the delivery of aversive events (e.g., physical punishment, restraint, and isolation). Today, the Individuals with Disabilities Education Act (U.S. Department of Education, 1997) and current U.S. Department of Education standards (Shavelson & Towne, 2002) require research-validated strategies that provide Maya with access to the least restrictive environment and help her meet her individual education plan (IEP) goals.

Positive behavior support (PBS) is about the redesign of environments to produce both decreases in problem behavior and increases in basic lifestyle goals such as improved learning, access to social networks, employment, and involvement in the full range of community activities. PBS builds directly from a powerful science of human behavior (Bijou & Baer, 1961; Bijou, Peterson, & Ault, 1968; Catania, 1992), advances in biomedical support (Reiss & Aman, 1998), and the strong values base provided by advocates of normalization (Nirje, 1969; Wolfensberger, 1983), self-determination (Wehmeyer & Schwartz, 1997), and person-centered support (Kincaid, 1996; O'Brien, O'Brien, & Mount, 1997).

At its core, PBS is the values-driven application of applied behavior analysis, biomedical supports, systems change, and education (Carr et al., 1999; Carr et al., 2002; Fox & Dunlap, 2002; Horner et al., 1990; Koegel, Koegel, & Dunlap, 1996; Sugai et al., 2000). The values of the focus individual and his or her family and advocates shape the outcomes that define successful intervention and the array of intervention options that are acceptable.

The science of human behavior defines the array of intervention options that are likely to result in desired effects. The organizational and social systems establish the foundation for sustainable effects. This blending of values, science, and organizational systems gives PBS strong promise as a viable approach for addressing the real and difficult challenges posed by problem behaviors such as defiance, self-injury, aggression, property destruction, noncompliance, and withdrawal.

The goal of PBS is to invest in understanding the vision and strengths of each individual and to use this information to craft an environment that promotes socially adaptive behaviors while simultaneously making problem behaviors irrelevant, inefficient, and ineffective. This represents a significant shift in perspective from a vision of behavior support as a process that "changes the person," or emphasizes delivering consequences that will guide a person toward adapting to an established setting (e.g., classroom, residential setting). Within the PBS approach, consequences (both positive and negative consequences) remain important, but a major focus is placed on the redesign of the setting to *prevent* problem behaviors (Carr et al.,1994; Durand, 1990). This focus on prevention is seen in the emphasis given to removing stimuli that promote or evoke problem behavior (e.g., changing activity schedules, tasks, and social contexts associated with problem behavior) and to investing in teaching new skills, such as communication and social skills, that can replace problem behavior (Dunlap, Foster-Johnson, Clarke, Kern, & Childs, 1995; Dunlap, Kern-Dunlap, Clarke, & Robbins, 1991).

Carr (1994, 2000) offered an important insight into PBS when he encouraged those who design support to focus as much or more on what happens *between* bouts of problem behavior (e.g., when the person is doing well) as they do on what is happening during a bout of problem behavior. Using information about situations where the person is successful can provide valuable guidance for identifying how to organize support in more difficult situations. To illustrate the implications of this idea, meet our second student, Isha, described next.

Isha

Isha is a 15-year-old young woman with autism and severe intellectual disabilities who was at risk of being excluded from her school because she would scream, pull at her own hair, and scratch at staff when she was asked to shift from one activity to another. Isha has some speech but primarily uses a symbol communication system for much of her "formal" communication. Isha does not like

change or new situations. She also is allergic to grass and tree pollens, which contributes to her challenges during parts of the year. Earlier efforts to "address her autism" and provide clear positive and negative consequences (e.g., token economies, dense schedules of reinforcement) had been ineffective. Isha's team decided to try a PBS approach. Her teachers looked carefully at the situations where she behaved well and considered the differences between situations where she was successful and those that were difficult for her. In Isha's case, a process of functional behavioral assessment (described in detail later in this chapter), a central feature of PBS, made it clear that when her day followed highly predictable routines, she did well. When she was asked to shift from her routine (even to preferred activities), she found the process highly aversive and engaged in dangerous behaviors. Her problem behaviors maintained over time because periodically Isha was successful in getting her predictable routine reinstated. Isha's behavior support plan emerged as a combination of schedule redesign to prevent problem situations, teaching her new ways to request predictability, systematic consequences to prevent problem behaviors from being rewarded, and

clear rewards for moving through her daily events. To provide predictability without succumbing to the trap of continually repeating a narrow daily routine, the staff taught Isha to use a picture communication system to review current activities and label what activity would come next (Flannery & Horner, 1994). New activities could be introduced as long as they had a picture, were reviewed in advance, and were to be followed by a preferred activity. The staff also learned to give Isha precorrection prompts (Colvin, Sugai, & Patching, 1993) 1 to 3 minutes before an activity change. Finally, staff made sure that Isha received her allergy medication during the spring and early summer pollen season. Together these efforts resulted in an 85% reduction in her problem behavior, the opportunity to remain in her neighborhood school, and the ability to sustain important social relationships with peers.

Cascading Model of PBS

In many ways, the process of PBS is a cascade of steps, each step building from its predecessor. Figure 2–1 offers an overview of this process and provides the organizing structure for describing the specific practices and organizational systems for each step. We begin with a review of the whole process and then provide more detailed implementation recommendations and supporting research for each step.

FIGURE 2–1
Cascading Structure of Behavior Support

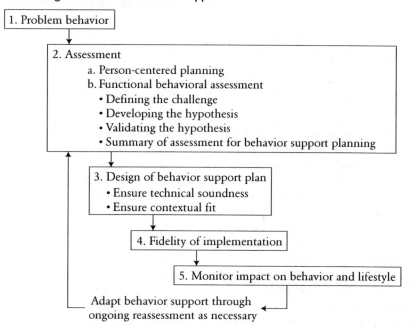

Step 1: Problem behavior. The cascade of activities begins when a problem behavior (or set of problem behaviors) is identified. If the problem behavior is of sufficient severity to require a formal plan of support, then an assessment is conducted. Note that from the beginning, problem behavior is (a) defined as problematic because it serves as a barrier to important lifestyle goals, including health, safety, and inclusion; (b) clustered into classes of behavior maintained by the same consequence (e.g., obtain attention, allow escape from an aversive activity); and (c) organized according to daily routines when it is most likely to occur (e.g., transitions, meal time, toileting, reading period), so the challenge shifts from simply reducing problem behavior to providing the support needed so the person is successful within daily routines. PBS focuses not just on reducing problem behavior but also on building the skills that result in success within routines that are difficult for the individual.

Step 2: Assessment. The assessment needed to guide PBS includes a *person-centered plan* that defines the personal goals and preferences of the individual and his or her family and a *functional behavioral assessment* that provides a clear statement defining (a) exactly what the problem behavior(s) looks like, (b) when it is most and least likely to occur, and (c) why the problem behavior keeps occurring. This information is obtained from review of the student's history; from active interviews with advocates, the student, and those who support the student; from direct observation; and, on occasion, from formal functional analysis.

Step 3: Design of support plan. The assessment information is used to construct a plan of support. In fact, a major feature of PBS is that the unique knowledge gleaned from the assessment process should directly guide the content of the support plan. A process known as "competing behavior analysis" (described later in this chapter) has been useful in moving from assessment results to a formal plan. PBS plans resulting from this process are characterized by (a) clear, operational definitions of the problem behavior(s); (b) a formal summary of the assessment outcomes; (c) specific strategies for altering the environment to prevent problem behaviors; (d) teaching objectives to build the desired skills that replace problem behaviors; (e) strategies for ensuring that desired behaviors are rewarded;

(f) strategies for minimizing the rewards associated with problem behaviors; (g) negative consequences for problem behaviors (if necessary); (h) strategies for minimizing the danger caused by severe problem behaviors (if necessary); and (i) formal procedures for assessing and adapting the plan over time.

Step 4: Fidelity of implementation. To increase the likelihood that behavior support plans are implemented as written, emphasis is placed on (a) clear description of the implementation process (who will do what, when) and (b) consideration of contextual fit, that is, the extent to which those individuals who are expected to provide support have the skills, resources, and support to be successful (Albin, Lucyshyn, Horner, & Flannery, 1996).

Step 5: Monitor and adapt support to achieve problem behavior reduction and lifestyle impact. For PBS to have substantive impact on not just problem behavior but also the options available for a desirable lifestyle, attention is needed for ongoing adaptation and sustainability. The vision of PBS is not that a brief intervention will "fix" or "correct" a person but that *ongoing* support may well be needed. Effective plans of support incorporate procedures for monitoring and adapting support strategies over time.

In the following sections, we will follow Maya through the cascade of PBS steps, with more detailed descriptions of the specific procedures that result in effective support. This example helps highlight the relevance of each step in the cascade of PBS steps.

Problem Behavior

The individualized student PBS process begins when a student is identified as having problem behavior(s) that requires more attention and support than is provided for the vast majority of students within the broader contexts of schoolwide and classroom behavior support systems (Sugai, Horner, & Gresham, 2002). In particular, PBS is used for students whose behavior raises concerns regarding the health and safety of the student, peers, school staff, or others; whose behavior interferes significantly with the student's educational program or the education of others; or whose behavior places the student at risk for loss of an inclusive educational placement and placement into a more restrictive or segregated setting. Consider Maya, who was entering a regular middle school but whose problem behavior put her at risk for exclusion from that school because of concerns about Maya's and other students' safety.

Maya had a history of engaging in problem behavior that the middle school staff knew from her history and files and from the transition process that was implemented to facilitate Maya's move from elementary to middle school. Middle school staff was concerned about Maya's serious problem behaviors, which included hitting other students, spitting, and yelling, in addition to the annoying behavior of sticking her tongue out at other students. There also was concern that Maya's behaviors were becoming increasingly intense and that sometimes her behavior escalated out of control. From the very beginning of the school year, staff were alerted to Maya's behavior, and behavioral incidents in the hallways did occur and were noted. If Maya was to be supported successfully in her new middle school, it was clear to Maya's teachers that an individualized behavior support plan (BSP) would be needed. A behavior support team was created for Maya, and the process of designing and implementing a BSP was initiated.

Assessment for Behavior Support Planning

Before a BSP can be developed for a student who is experiencing problem behavior, an assessment process is initiated. In supporting students with disabilities, it is advisable that two types of assessment be completed: person-centered planning and functional behavioral assessment.

Person-Centered Planning

In recent years, there has been growing recognition that the outcomes of behavior support should include not just the elimination or reduction of problem behavior but also an improvement in adaptive behavior and overall quality of life (e.g., Koegel et al., 1996; Meyer & Evans, 1989; Newton & Horner, 2004; Schalock & Alonso, 2002). To be successful, the outcomes of behavior support must be referenced to the personal values of the student receiving support and his or her family.

This focus on quality of life, personal values, and outcomes has resulted in people with disabilities, their

families, and teachers and other professionals working to create processes for defining a person's values and desired lifestyle and for rallying the support required to achieve that vision. For example, the many varieties of person-centered planning (see Holburn & Vietze, 2002; Kincaid, 1996; Mount, 1994) are designed to ensure that the person and those closest to the person both (a) define a high-quality lifestyle from their personal perspectives and (b) discuss and develop broad strategies for creating the conditions that will enable that lifestyle. Person-centered planning assists support teams to identify a "vision" for the focus student and to place behavior support into the broader contexts of the student's life and personal goals.

The design of behavior support for Maya began with her support team conducting a Personal Futures Plan meeting (Kincaid, 1996; Mount, 1994). The team that participated in the Personal Futures Plan was led to the greatest degree possible by Maya and included Maya's family, three middle school staff, Maya's fifth-grade teacher, the middle school behavior specialist, two friends, Maya's aunt, and Maya's longtime home care provider. This group of people met and then developed the following goals for Maya: (a) high school graduation; (b) living in an apartment with a friend; (c) employment in a fish or pet store; (d) skill development in cooking, clothing care, basic household chores, money management, personal care, and time management; (e) joining a community group; and (f) maintenance of good physical health through diet and exercise. These goals provided Maya's support team with a common vision for Maya and for what they wanted and needed to accomplish with a BSP.

Teachers and others providing support to students with disabilities will want to be mindful that the development and implementation of any BSP should occur within the context of broader lifestyle considerations that have emerged from previously completed person-centered planning processes. It is recommended that person-centered planning occur on a regular basis, given that students' aspirations may change across time, particularly as the onset of their postschool lives approaches. When students have the kinds of lives they want and deserve, their problem behaviors may decrease, and PBS can be initiated to address "residual" problem behaviors. In dealing with such problem behaviors and in supporting a student in the quest to obtain a more desired life, the initiation of functional behavioral assessment will be vital (Holburn, Jacobson, Vietze, Schwartz, & Sersen, 2000).

Functional Behavioral Assessment

Functional behavioral assessment (FBA) is a central feature of PBS. FBA is a process for gathering information about problem behavior and the environmental conditions that predict and maintain it (Crone & Horner, 2003; O'Neill et al., 1997). The goal of FBA is to improve the effectiveness and efficiency of the BSP. The process of FBA involves gathering information about the problem behavior, the situations where problem behavior is most and least likely to occur, and the consequences that reward and maintain the problem behavior. This information is typically gathered through multiple methods, including interviews, rating scales, checklists, reviews of records and files, direct observations in natural settings, and the process of functional analysis. Not all methods are necessarily used within a single FBA. A major outcome of FBA is a hypothesis statement that identifies the function(s) (i.e., purpose) that the problem behavior serves for the person. FBA helps us understand why problem behavior occurs (i.e., variables that are associated with the problem behavior). Details on FBA procedures and outcomes are described in the following sections of this chapter.

An FBA of Maya's behavior was conducted through file reviews, interviews, and direct observations led by the behavior specialist on Maya's team. Situations were categorized where Maya was most likely and least likely to engage in hitting, spitting, yelling, and sticking her tongue out. Through functional assessment interviews with Maya's former and current teachers and her family and through systematic observations of her behavior during the school day, Maya's team identified two routines where her problem behaviors were most likely to occur: (a) hallway transition periods and (b) activities with minimal structure (i.e., lunch, recess, group activities). In both situations, Maya's team identified that Maya's problem behaviors were preceded by low levels of peer attention and were followed by and seemingly rewarded by immediate access to peer attention.

FBA is neither a process for producing a diagnosis nor a process for determining if a behavior problem is a manifestation of a disability (Carr et al., 1994; Durand, 1990; Sugai, Lewis-Palmer, & Hagan-Burke,

1999–2000). The focus of FBA is on understanding the relationship between environmental events and problem behavior, on how to change the environment, not the student. A medical approach would likely focus on identifying deficits in the *child*, but an approach based on FBA focuses on identifying deficits in the *environment* (i.e., the conditions that establish and maintain problem behavior). FBA and PBS emphasize the engineering of effective environments as the key to producing desired behavior change.

FBA is less concerned with the fundamental etiology of problem behavior (i.e., how it originated) and more concerned with the environmental conditions (i.e., consequences) that *currently* maintain the behavior. The conditions under which a problem behavior initially develops may be very different from the conditions that currently maintain it. For example, Guess and Carr (1991) have suggested that some forms of severe self-injury may have begun as simple forms of self-stimulation (or responses to short-term illness), only later to develop into complex and destructive behaviors maintained by their social consequences. O'Reilly (1997) found that a 26–month-old girl's self-injurious behavior was correlated with the presence of recurrent otitis media (an ear infection that produces ear pain, ear fullness, or hearing loss). Naturally, such behavior would draw the attention of any caring parent. Thus, although the behavior began as a reaction to ear pain, it was ultimately emitted in the absence of ear pain due to a parent's contingent attention. FBA and PBS (a) use a behavioral approach rather than a medical approach to focus on (b) environmental conditions that set up, trigger, and maintain problem behaviors rather than on diagnostic labels in order to (c) remediate deficient environments rather than "fix" or "cure" students with problem behaviors.

Why Conduct an FBA?

The 1997 amendments to the Individuals with Disabilities Education Act (IDEA) included the requirements that schools use FBA and PBS. Although many school personnel may have already considered the use of FBA and PBS to be "best practices" and begun to use them, the 1997 IDEA amendments provided a legal mandate. This mandate has triggered thoughtful reviews and questions about (a) the extent to which school personnel have the technical capability to implement effective FBA and PBS (e.g., Ervin et al., 2001); (b) the degree to which FBA and PBS demonstrate external validity across the full range of settings, students, and behaviors that constitute a school-based application (e.g., Nelson, Roberts, Mathur, & Rutherford, 1999); (c) the social validity of FBA (e.g., Reid & Nelson, 2002); and (d) the extent to which interventions based on FBA can be demonstrated to be more effective than interventions not derived from an FBA (e.g., Gresham et al., 2004). These are important questions that should trigger further research determining whether the federal confidence in FBA and PBS is warranted. Such research is beginning to emerge.

For example, two meta-analyses of behavior intervention and PBS research have found that the presence of pretreatment FBA was associated with increased effectiveness of an intervention (Didden, Duker, & Korzilius, 1997; Marquis et al., 2000). Marquis and colleagues found strong differences in the percentage of behavior reduction resulting from PBS interventions when FBA was conducted and used in planning the intervention. They concluded, "These results indicate that doing an assessment and using it to plan the PBS intervention probably results in a better outcome" (p. 161).

Further support for the beneficial effect of using FBA to plan interventions was provided in two recent studies involving students with problem behaviors in general education settings (Ingram, Lewis-Palmer, & Sugai, in press; Newcomer & Lewis, in press). These two studies compared interventions that were logically derived from a preceding FBA (i.e., were "FBA indicated") to interventions that were either "contraindicated" by FBA or not tied to a FBA hypothesis. In both studies, the interventions that were logically linked to an FBA produced substantial reductions in problem behavior in comparison to commonly used interventions that were not linked to FBA.

Finally, relevant to the question of whether FBA is doable by typical school personnel is a recent study by Bergstrom, Horner, and Crone (2004). This study found that, following training and limited technical assistance, school-based teams (a) independently developed FBA hypotheses that were later confirmed to be accurate by a researcher who independently conducted a functional analysis, (b) independently developed and implemented behavior support plans—based on the preceding FBA—that significantly reduced students' disruptive behavior and increased their on-task behavior, and (c) completed the FBA processes in a relatively short period of time, accurately implemented the interventions, and rated the interventions as being high in "acceptability."

In addition to informing decisions regarding the selection of effective behavior support procedures, FBA provides the conceptual logic needed to make multicomponent support plans work as intended. Many problem behaviors necessitate multicomponent support plans (e.g., modifying the curriculum, teaching new skills, reinforcing alternative behavior, and extinguishing problem behavior). However, the complexity of multicomponent interventions can increase the difficulty of implementation. Without the conceptual logic provided by an FBA, there is a danger that an individual intervention procedure that appears sound when examined in isolation may be revealed as illogical when considered as a component of an integrated intervention package. FBA helps ensure that the multiple elements of an intervention work together rather than at cross-purpose.

Recall Isha, who was at risk of being excluded from her school because she would scream, pull her hair, and scratch at staff when she was asked to shift from one activity to another. When Isha was requested to alter her typical routine in an unpredictable manner, she found the process highly aversive and engaged in these dangerous behaviors that often resulted in her predictable routine being reinstated. Based on this knowledge, her staff could have chosen to "extinguish" the problem behavior by disallowing her predictable routine to be reinstated, hoping to reduce the problem behavior by withholding the reinforcer. Although this might have worked and would have made some programmatic sense as an isolated support strategy, the staff instead chose to use a package of integrated procedures that combined (a) redesigning Isha's schedule to prevent problem situations, (b) teaching her new ways to request predictability, (c) introducing systematic consequences to prevent problem behaviors from being rewarded, and (d) providing clear rewards to Isha as she moved through her events.

The conceptual logic underlying FBA, as well as emerging research results demonstrating the effectiveness and utility of FBA, argues for continued research and application. Basing interventions on the function of problem behavior rather than attempting to overpower problem behavior through the application of interventions involving arbitrary contingencies of reinforcement appears to be a fruitful approach to helping students overcome problem behavior.

The Outcomes of FBA

Broadly considered, FBA produces information that results in six outcomes: (a) description of the student's problem behavior and daily routines; (b) identification of consequent conditions that maintain the problem behavior; (c) identification of antecedent conditions that set the occasion for (or "trigger") the problem behavior, as well as antecedent conditions that *do not* trigger the problem behavior; (d) identification of setting events that make the problem behavior more sensitive (or less sensitive) to the maintaining consequences and their associated antecedents; (e) production of a written hypothesis that synthesizes the foregoing information into a testable statement about the problem behavior; and (f) direct observations of the student during typical daily routines for the purpose of tentatively confirming (or disconfirming) the hypothesis (O'Neill et al., 1997).

Who Is Involved in FBA?

Depending on the school or district and its policies, the person (or persons) with the responsibility for conducting or leading an FBA may be a school psychologist, behavior specialist, counselor, special educator, teacher, or some other member of a behavior support team; however, FBA involves a team process with many team members sharing responsibilities. Typically, the process for achieving the six FBA outcomes begins with interviews of school personnel and others who are most knowledgeable about the student's problem behavior (e.g., people who have actually witnessed the student's problem behavior). The informants may include teachers, a bus driver, a school nurse, parents, and, if possible, the student him- or herself. A review of existing records and data also may be undertaken.

Various manuals and accompanying forms and questionnaires have been developed to aid in conducting interviews that identify problem behaviors, daily routines, and the problem behaviors triggering and maintaining consequences (e.g., O'Neill et al., 1997; see Dunlap & Kincaid, 2001, for a review of FBA manuals). As we note in a following section, there are also several instruments that can be used to facilitate direct observation of the student during his or her daily routines. However, even as we present such instruments in the following pages, we believe it is more important to understand the concepts that underlie the use of the instruments than to understand how to complete a specific questionnaire or form.

Regardless of the instruments used, it is useful to think of FBA as proceeding in three phases: defining the challenge, developing the hypothesis, and validating the hypothesis. Completing these phases is a necessary precursor to developing an effective and efficient BSP.

Defining the Challenge

This phase of FBA is concerned with achieving the first FBA outcome: a description of the student's problem behavior and daily routines. A successful behavior support effort cannot be initiated until those involved reach agreement about the nature of the problem behavior. This is best accomplished by first defining the problem behavior in operational terms. An operational definition specifically describes what the student is doing when he or she is said to be engaging in "problem behavior." A problem behavior that is described as "anger" or "frustration" lacks the clarity of a description such as "hitting," "refusing to follow the teacher's instructions," or "throwing textbooks." Operational definitions help ensure that those who are called on to implement the BSP are operating with a common understanding of the behavioral challenge. There are many tools that assist teams in identifying and defining problem behavior, identifying daily routines, and organizing problem behavior by daily routines. Two examples of tools we have used are the Teacher Assistance Team Request for Assistance form (presented in Figure 2-2) and the Functional Assessment Checklist for Teachers & Staff (FACTS—Part A) (presented in Figure 2-3). Maya's team used both of these tools in defining the challenge.

A sample Request for Assistance form was completed by Maya's homeroom teacher in collaboration with the school behavior specialist, Trudy Schwartz, on 09/18/03, to initiate a referral for assistance with Maya's problem behaviors. This request for assistance was the impetus to formalize convening a behavior support team in hopes that they could ultimately develop a BSP that would help Maya learn different ways to communicate rather than communicating by using problem behaviors. On the Request for Assistance form, Maya's problem behaviors initially were identified by her homeroom teacher as aggressiveness, poor attention, poor work completion, and disruptiveness.

Later, on 10/01/03, Trudy used "Part A" of a tool called the Functional Assessment Checklist for

FIGURE 2–2
Request for Assistance Form

Date _____**9/18/03**_____

Student Name _____**Maya**_____

Teacher/Team _____ **Trudy** _____
IEP: (Yes) No (Circle)
Grade ___**6th**___

Situations	Problem Behaviors	Most Common Result
Various situations including lunch, hallways, recess, and classrooms	Shows aggression, is disruptive and inattentive; is not completing academic work.	Peers respond to her–laugh or confront her

1. What have you tried/used? How has it worked?
Talked with parents, teacher, and planned positive reinforcer

What have you tried to date to change the situations in which the problem behavior(s) occur?

			Other?
____ Modified assignments to match the student's skills	____ Changed seating assignments	____ Changed schedule of activities	
✓ Arranged tutoring to improve the student's academic skills	____ Changed curriculum	____ Provided extra assistance	

What have you tried to date to teach expected behaviors?

			Other?
✓ Reminders about expected behavior when problem behavior is likely	____ Clarified rules and expected behavior for the whole class	____ Practiced the expected behaviors in class	
✓ Reward program for expected behavior	____ Oral agreement with the student	____ Self-management program	
✓ Systematic feedback about behavior	____ Individual written contract with the student	____ Contract with student/with parents	

What consequences have you tried to date for the problem behavior?

			Other?
____ Loss of privileges	____ Note or phone call to the student's parents	____ Office referral	
____ Time-out	____ Detention	____ Reprimand	
____ Referral to school counselor	✓ Meeting with the student's parents	____ Individual meeting with the students	

Source. Todd, A. W., Horner, R. H., Sugai, G., & Colvin, G. (1999). Individualizing school-wide discipline for students with chronic problem behaviors: A team approach. *Effective School Practices, 17*(4), 72–82.

FIGURE 2–3
Functional Assessment Checklist for Teachers and Staff (FACTS—Part A)

Step 1   Student/Grade:_____**Maya, Grade 6**_____   Date:_____**10/01/03**_____
          Interviewer:_____**Trudy**_____   Respondent(s):__**Homeroom and Study Hall Teachers**__

Step 2   **Student Profile:** Please identify at least three strengths or contributions the student brings to school.
          ____**Likes being around people, loves fish and aquariums, likes music**____

Step 3   **Problem Behavior(s): Identify problem behaviors**

✓ Tardy	✓ Fight/Physical Aggression	✓ Disruptive	___ Theft
___ Unresponsive	___ Inappropriate Language	___ Insubordination	___ Vandalism
___ Withdrawn	___ Verbal Harassment	___ Work not done	___ Other _____
	✓ Verbally Inappropriate	___ Self-injury	

Describe problem behavior: **hits peers, yells, spits, throws objects, sticks tongue out**

Step 4   **Identifying Routines: Where, when, and with whom problem behaviors are most likely**

Schedule (Times)	Activity	Likelihood of Problem Behavior						Specific Problem Behavior
		Low 1	2	3	4	5	High 6	
9:00	Bus to class	1	2	3	4	5	(6)	Tongue out, yell, spit
9:15	Language Arts	1	(2)	3	4	5	6	
10:15	Break	1	2	3	4	5	(6)	Tongue out, yell, hit, spit
10:30	Math	1	(2)	3	4	5	6	
11:30	Homeroom	1	2	3	(4)	5	6	Tongue out
12:00	Lunch	1	2	3	4	5	(6)	Yell, spit, hit
12:30	Teen Health	1	2	(3)	4	5	6	Tongue out
1:30	Current Events	1	(2)	3	4	5	6	
2:30	Choir	1	2	3	(4)	5	6	Tongue out, yell
3:30	Class to Bus	1	2	3	4	5	(6)	Tongue out, yell, hit, spit
All day	Hallway transitions	1	2	3	4	5	(6)	Tongue out, yell, hit, spit

Step 5   **Select one to three routines for further assessment. Select routines based on (a) similarity of activities (conditions) with ratings of 4, 5 or 6 and (b) similarity of problem behavior(s). Complete the FACTS–Part B for each routine identified.**
          Hallway transitions–arrival and dismissal, lunch

Teachers and Staff (FACTS) to begin an FBA interview with Maya's homeroom and study hall teachers. During these interviews, Maya's problem behaviors were more specifically defined as hitting peers, sticking out her tongue, spitting, yelling, and throwing objects.

In addition to identifying and operationally defining problem behavior(s), defining the challenge also involves identifying the student's typical daily routines and determining the occurrence of problem behavior(s) in those routines. Routines are sequences of behavior that are a usual part of daily life that result in socially important outcomes. For example, eating breakfast, traveling to school, participating in morning circle, engaging in recess activities, and transitioning from one school activity to the next are common routines for students. A routine involves a predictable sequence of events that results in predictable outcomes. A challenge of PBS is to ensure that a student is not excluded from typical routines because of problem behavior but rather is provided with behavioral support that results in the problem behavior being rendered irrelevant, ineffective, or inefficient during those routines.

We strongly recommend that an FBA describe the student's full daily routines and identify those routines where the student's problem behavior is most likely— and least likely—to occur. For students, a daily routine can be described in terms of the daily schedule of school activities. The FACTS—Part A (see Figure 2-3) incorporates this as step 4, providing a section to record the daily routines, to rate the likelihood of problem behavior within each routine, and to identify the specific problem behavior(s) that occurs within each routine.

During the course of leading the FBA interview for Maya, Trudy recorded Maya's school routines/schedule directly on Part A of the FACTS (see Figure 2-3). Organizing Maya's problem behaviors within the contexts of daily routines helped Maya's team understand that her problem behaviors were most likely to occur during (a) hallway transition periods (including transitions to and from the school bus area) and (b) activities with minimal structure (i.e., lunch, break, less structured group activities such as homeroom and choir). The specific problem behaviors identified were sticking out tongue, yelling, hitting, and spitting.

Developing the Hypothesis

Once the student's problem behavior has been operationally defined and organized within the contexts of his or her typical daily routines, we focus on gathering information that will lead to developing a hypothesis about when and why the problem behavior occurs. To gather the information required to arrive at a hypothesis, the person responsible for conducting the FBA will continue interviewing the school personnel and others who are most knowledgeable about the student's problem behavior. Depending on the time available, this may involve simply continuing with the same interview that produced the operational definition of the student's problem behavior and a description of his or her daily routine. Typically, it is useful to talk with at least two people who have daily contact with the student and have witnessed the problem behavior. As noted, it may also be appropriate to interview the student if he or she can participate in an interview effectively.

Interviews, Checklists, and Rating Scales Several interview instruments, checklists, and rating scales are available for gathering the information required to complete this phase of the FBA. Structured interviews (Crone & Horner, 2003; O'Neill et al., 1997; Willis, LaVigna, & Donnellan, 1987); checklists, such as the FACTS (Crone & Horner, 2003; March et al., 2000) and the Functional Analysis Checklist (Van Houten & Rolider, 1991); and rating scales, such as the Motivation Assessment Scale (MAS) (Durand, 1988), organize information about problem behaviors, antecedent stimuli (including setting events), and consequences to help determine behavioral function. Comprehensive interview forms (e.g., O'Neill et al., 1997; Willis et al., 1987) also solicit information about the student's repertoire of adaptive behavior, particularly behavior that may serve to replace the problem behavior, his or her communication skills, the quality of the support environment, and the success (or failure) of previous support plans. Interviews have the advantage of (a) being relatively low in cost, (b) allowing for the inclusion of multiple people who have important information about the student, and (c) providing a rich array of information that can be used to structure more detailed analyses of problem behavior.

An FBA interview concerning a complex, challenging pattern of behavior may take anywhere from 45 minutes to 2 hours. In our experience, the time required to complete an interview can vary considerably, depending not only on the complexity of the problem but also on the number of people participating in the interview and their knowledge of the student, talkativeness, and level of agreement. Using a structured interview or a checklist helps keep the process focused. Consistent with the outcomes of this phase of FBA, the interview should produce—at a minimum—the following: (a) identification of consequent conditions that maintain the problem behavior; (b) identification of antecedent conditions that set the occasion for (or "trigger") the problem behavior, as well as antecedent conditions that *do not* trigger the problem behavior; and (c) identification of setting events that make the problem behavior more sensitive (or less sensitive) to the maintaining consequences and their associated antecedents.

Identification of Consequent Conditions That Maintain the Problem Behavior An important aspect of behavior–environment relationships is the consequence(s) produced by a person's behavior, including problem behavior. Behavior is useful in that it serves a *function* for the person. We assume that any behavior that occurs repeatedly is serving some useful function (i.e., is producing an outcome that is reinforcing).

Behavior may serve two major functions (i.e., produce two major outcomes): (a) *obtaining* something desirable or (b) *avoiding or escaping* something undesirable. In more technical terms, obtaining desirable things is referred to as *positive reinforcement*, while escaping or avoiding undesirable things is referred to as *negative reinforcement* (if such consequences result in continued occurrences of the behaviors). Figure 2–4 provides a framework for organizing the possible functions of problem behaviors into six categories (three under "Obtain" and three others under "Escape/Avoid"). Events that may be obtained or escaped/avoided may require interactions that involve other persons or things (i.e., are socially mediated events) or may be internal to the person with problem behavior and not require the presence of others. Some problem behaviors may serve multiple functions (Day, Horner, & O'Neill, 1994).

FIGURE 2–4
Functions of Behaviors

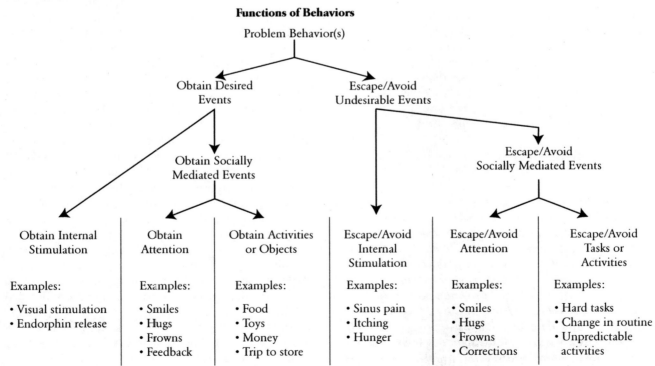

Source: From O'Neill, R. E., Horner, R. H., Albin, R. W., Sprague, J. R., Storey, K., & Newton, J. S. (1997). *Functional assessment for problem behavior: A practical handbook (2nd ed.).* Pacific Grove, CA: Brooks/Cole.

Developing a hypothesis about the function of problem behavior(s) based on the information collected in an interview(s) is a critical outcome of the FBA process and is essential for developing an effective and efficient BSP. Some FBA interview forms, such as the Functional Assessment Interview from O'Neill et al. (1997) and the FACTS—Part B (presented in Figure 2-5), provide a place on the form to record a hypothesis that identifies the function of problem behavior.

Using Part B of the FACTS Checklist, Trudy and Maya's team found that during the "hallway transitions" portions of Maya's routine (e.g., traveling from the school bus to her first class, during the break between her language arts and math classes), her problem behaviors were maintained by getting peer attention. This is noted in the Summary of Behavior section, step 6 on the form. (Note that Part B of the FACTS would be completed for each different type of routine associated with a high likelihood of problem behaviors.)

Identification of Antecedent Conditions That Do and Do Not Trigger the Problem Behavior

Interview questions will inquire about routines during which the problem behaviors occur, including *when, where,* and with *whom* they occur and the *specific activities* within the routine that may be triggering problem behavior. It is useful to identify any aspect of a routine that may serve as a trigger (e.g., particular academic demands, free time, transitioning to the next routine, types of prompts). Interview questions should also solicit information about routines that do not evoke problem behavior. Note, for example, that the FACTS—Part A (see Figure 2-3) provides a place to identify the likelihood of problem behavior across all routines, including those where problem behaviors do not occur or are unlikely.

The FBA interview concerning Maya produced findings about antecedent conditions that trigger—and do not trigger—her problem behaviors. Using Part A of the FACTS, Trudy inquired about the likelihood that Maya would engage in problem behaviors during specific time periods of her daily routine. The FACTS shows that the likelihood of Maya's engaging in problem behaviors was rated as very "high" in the context of the following routines: transitioning from the bus to class, break, lunch, transitioning from class to the bus, and throughout the day during hallway transitions.

Each of these routines involved a hallway transition for Maya (e.g., traveling from the school bus to her first class, going to lunch, going to break). In contrast, the likelihood of Maya's engaging in problem behavior was rated as relatively low during the following routines: language arts, math, and current events. These routines involved classroom activities that were highly structured. Step 4 of Part B of the FACTS indicates that during hallway transitions, relevant predictors (antecedent triggers) for Maya's problem behavior appear to be that she is (a) socially isolated, although (b) with peers, during (c) an unstructured time (transitions in the hallway).

Identification of Setting Events

Recognition of the role that setting events play in problem behavior is relatively new (Carr, Reeve, & Magito-McLaughlin, 1996; Horner, Day, & Day, 1997; Horner, Vaughn, Day, & Ard, 1996). Setting events are conditions that temporarily alter the value of reinforcers that maintain problem behaviors. For example, sleep deprivation is a setting event that may make some tasks more aversive than usual and decrease the value of the social praise obtained by doing these tasks. The result is that sleep deprivation may increase the value of escaping from boring tasks (e.g., via tantrums) (Durand, 1990). Time spent alone may be a setting event that increases the value of social attention and thereby increases the likelihood of problem behaviors that result in peer or teacher attention. Setting events help explain why on some days an instructional session goes well and on other days the same instruction occasions problem behavior.

Isha did not like shifting from her routine, and asking her to do so was a trigger for problem behavior. However, Isha did not always engage in problem behavior when she was asked to shift to another activity. On some days, Isha would shift without problem behavior. However, on days when pollen counts were very high and her allergy was acting up (and she had not taken her allergy medication), Isha was much more likely to engage in problem behavior when asked to shift to another activity. Isha's allergy was a setting event for her problem behavior. It did not trigger problem behavior by itself, but it did increase the likelihood of problem behavior when Isha was asked to shift to another activity.

The design of behavior support is improved when information about powerful setting events is available

FIGURE 2–5
Functional Assessment Checklist for Teachers and Staff (FACTS—Part B)

Step 1   Student/Grade: __**Maya, Grade 6**__   Date: __**10/01/03**__
          Interviewer: __**Trudy**__   Respondent(s): __**Homeroom and Study Hall Teachers**__

Step 2   **Routine/Activities/Context:** Which routine (only one) from the Facts–Part A is assessed?

Routine/Activities/Context	Problem Behavior(s)
Hallway Transitions	Sticking out tongue, yelling, spitting, hitting peers

Step 3   **Provide more detail about the problem behavior(s):**

What does the problem behavior(s) look like? **Tongue out, yelling, spitting, hitting peers during transitions**

How often does the problem behavior(s) occur? **Moderate to high frequency (lower in other routines)**

How long does the problem behavior(s) last when it does occur? **Until peer gives attention or teacher interrupts**

What is the intensity/level or danger of the problem behavior(s)?

Step 4   **What are the events that predict when the problem behavior(s) will occur? (Predictors)**

Related Issues (setting events)		Environmental Features	
___ illness	Other:	___ reprimand/correction	___ structured activity
___ drug use	__**long breaks from school**__	___ physical demands	✓ unstructured time
✓ negative social	__**social isolation**__	✓ socially isolated	___ tasks too boring
___ conflict at home	__**before school**__	✓ with peers	___ activity too long
___ academic failure		___ Other	___ tasks too difficult

Step 5   **What consequences appear most likely to maintain the problem behavior(s)?**

Things That Are Obtained		Things Avoided or Escaped from	
___ adult attention	Other: _____	___ hard tasks	Other: _____
✓ peer attention	_____	___ reprimands	_____
___ preferred activity	_____	___ peer negatives	_____
___ money/things	_____	___ physical effort	_____
		___ adult attention	_____

SUMMARY OF BEHAVIOR

Step 6   Identify the summary that will be used to build a plan of behavior support.

Setting Events and Predictors	Problem Behavior(s)	Maintaining Consequence(s)
"Mondays" and low peer attention Hallway transitions	Sticking tongue out, yelling, spitting, and hitting	Peer attention

Step 7   **How confident are you that the <u>Summary of Behavior</u> is accurate?**

Strategies for Preventing Problem Behavior	Consequences for Problem Behavior
Not very confident	Very Confident

1	2	3	4	⑤	6

Step 8   **What current efforts have been used to control the problem behavior?**

Strategies for Preventing Problem Behavior		Strategies for Responding to Problem Behavior	
___ schedule change	Other: __**peer mentor,**__	___ reprimand	Other: __**call home**__
___ seating change	__**precorrect behavior**__	___ office referral	__**teach to use conversation**__
___ curriculum change	__**before transitions**__	___ detention	__**book**__

and is used to design support procedures that address relevant setting events and their effects. Because setting events may be distant in time (i.e., they may have occurred earlier in the day or the night before) and may not have clearly visible effects or indicators, asking interview questions about potential setting events may be the best way to learn about them. Thus, using the FBA interview to gather information about general medical status, social interaction patterns, daily activities, and other possible setting events that may increase (or decrease) the person's sensitivity to the previously identified maintaining consequences and their associated triggering antecedent conditions is an important aspect of the FBA interview.

Maya's team identified that possible setting events for Maya's problem behaviors are long breaks from school (a weekend, a holiday) and social isolation before school. These have been recorded on Part B of the FACTS in step 4.

Other Information of Interest Depending on the time available for the interview, gathering additional information can ultimately prove useful when the time comes to develop the BSP. For example, it will be useful to inquire about appropriate behavior that is already part of the student's repertoire, particularly behavior with which the student may be able to secure the maintaining consequence currently gained via problem behavior. For example, a student may have demonstrated that she can ask for help or ask for a break from an activity by signing or signaling. If the student appears to be engaging in tantrums to escape difficult academic tasks, the BSP could include a prompt for the student to use the sign or signal to ask for a break (and then provide the break) as an alternative to escaping from the task via a tantrum. If the student does not already have a usable signal, the BSP could include a teaching component designed to help the student acquire this important skill.

In thinking about appropriate alternative behaviors, communication is the single most important skill to be considered for students with severe problem behaviors. Different theories have been proposed to explain why this is so, but the consistent conclusion is that effective support requires understanding the ways in which a person communicates important information to others in the environment. PBS plans often include teaching or enhancing communication skills. Therefore, it is essential to inquire about the communication skills a person currently uses (Donnellan, Mirenda, Mesaros, & Fassbender, 1984).

Isha had experience using a symbol system to communicate simple requests. Her support team recognized that this type of communication response could be used as an alternative behavior to replace Isha's problem behavior. Their hypothesis was that Isha's problem behavior was maintained by getting to stay in activities she was doing and getting activities reinstated when she was asked to shift to another activity. What Isha needed was a better way, an acceptable way, to communicate that she wanted to stay with her current activity. The team determined that they could teach Isha to request more time by pointing to a symbol in a communication book.

It may also prove wise to use the interview as an occasion to identify reinforcers that will be effective with the student (e.g., objects, events, activities). Prior to developing the BSP, one may want to assess the student's preferences with regard to reinforcing objects, activities, and events. Such assessments typically involve exposing the student to a variety of potential reinforcers, including edibles, toys/objects, entertainment (e.g., music, TV, movies), games, outings, domestic and personal care activities, and various forms of social attention and sensory stimulation (Green, Reid, Canipe, & Gardner, 1991; Pace, Ivancic, Edwards, Iwata, & Page, 1985).

Interviews with Maya's teachers and parents indicated that Maya thrived on peer attention and that many of her inappropriate behaviors are maintained by peer attention. Maya's desire to gain peer attention was incorporated into her support plan by arranging for Maya to have a peer mentor to be with during nonstructured routines on the bus and at school. Having a peer mentor during routines that were difficult for Maya meant that she had regular access to peer attention and did not need to engage in problem behavior to get peer attention (i.e., problem behavior was made irrelevant).

Finally, one may also want to ask about the history of the student's problem behavior (e.g., how long it has persisted), the various programs and interventions that have been used to manage the behaviors, and the degree of success achieved by implementing those programs. Learning about the types of supports that have been attempted and their effects can provide clues about the things that influence problem behaviors. For example, if a time-out program was tried in the past and had the effect of *increasing* the frequency of a behavior, this might indicate that the behavior is motivated by escaping or avoiding situations or demands. In many cases, it may be hard to obtain clear and reliable information about what has been tried and how well it worked or did not work; however, it is usually worthwhile to make the attempt.

Produce a Written Hypothesis as a Testable Statement At this point, one should be in a position to synthesize the previously gathered information into a testable hypothesis statement about the problem behavior. The hypothesis statement describes the relationship between setting events, triggering antecedents, the behaviors of concern, and maintaining consequences.

> *Trudy's hypothesis statement (Summary of Behavior) regarding Maya's problem behavior is recorded in step 6 on Part B of the FACTS. She has noted that Maya is likely to stick her tongue out at peers, yell, spit at them, or hit them during hallway transitions (particularly on Mondays after a weekend break from school) with the maintaining consequence (function) being to gain their attention. Trudy and her colleagues have indicated that they have a high degree of confidence in this hypothesis statement by giving it a rating of 5 on a 6-point scale in step 7.*

Table 2-1 provides samples of other hypothesis statements derived from hypothetical FBA interviews.

These statements are broken down into setting events, immediate antecedents, problem behaviors, and maintaining consequences.

Validating the Hypothesis

Once a testable hypothesis statement has been produced, the final stage of the FBA can occur: validating the hypothesis. Because the hypothesis statements will ultimately guide the development of a BSP and because it is often difficult to define hypothesis statements with a high degree of confidence, it is necessary to validate (test) the accuracy of the hypothesis. Two major strategies for validating hypothesis statements are (a) direct observation of the student in the context of the relevant routines and (b) formal functional analysis manipulations, where mini-experiments are conducted to demonstrate a functional relationship between the problem behavior and environmental events. Conducting a functional analysis requires a relatively great degree of skill. For this reason, we begin by discussing the direct observation option for verifying the hypothesis.

Direct Observation Direct observation of behavior has long been a cornerstone of applied behavior analysis (e.g., Baer, Wolf, & Risley, 1968). The antecedent, behavior, consequence (ABC) chart (Bijou et al., 1968) was an early method to supplement interview data with direct observation. ABC charting involves watching the focus person and recording, in narrative style, information about the problem behavior and its

TABLE 2–1
Sample Hypothesis Statements from Hypothetical FBA Interviews

1. When Sarah is getting little attention in morning circle, she is likely to shout profanities and throw things to get attention from her peers. The longer she has gone without direct attention, the more likely she is to engage in shouting profanities.
2. When Monica is asked to do independent seat work, she is likely to tear up materials and hit her teacher to escape from the task demands. This process is even more likely if she has had a negative interaction with the teacher earlier in the day.
3. When Jolene is prompted to stop using the computer, she is likely to fall to the floor and scream. The problem behaviors are maintained by keeping access to the computer, and the likelihood is greatest when Jolene has had limited time on the computer earlier in the day.
4. In situations with low levels of activity or attention at home, Dan will rock and begin to chew his fingers. These behaviors appear to be maintained by self-stimulation.
5. When Bishara is asked to dress himself or do other nonpreferred self-care routines, he will begin to slap his head. Head slaps appear to be maintained by escape from the self-care routines and are even more likely if he has been asked to stop a preferred activity to engage in the self-care routine.
6. When Anya begins to have difficulty with a reading or math assignment, she will put her head down, refuse to respond, and/or close her books. Anya's refusal is maintained by avoiding the assignment and is far more likely to occur if she has had less than 5 hours of sleep the previous night.

antecedent and consequent events. The narrative approach used in ABC charting is limited in that its narrative style does not lend itself to gathering measures of observational reliability. ABC charting can also be difficult to use when observing high-frequency behaviors. Finally, ABC charting may tell us little about conditions that are associated with the *absence* of problem behavior since ABC charting is event driven and occurs only when a problem behavior occurs.

An extension of the ABC chart, called scatter plot analysis, was developed by Touchette, MacDonald, and Langer (1985) and elaborated by Doss and Reichle (1991). The scatter plot is a grid that allows one to record the occurrence of problem behavior (via a shorthand behavior code) within designated time intervals (e.g., hour or half-hour periods) across multiple days. The scatter plot has the advantage of documenting both when problem behaviors occur and when they do not occur. Touchette et al. documented that by focusing on the features of those periods where problem behavior was observed, interventions that altered those periods resulted in reductions of problem behavior.

A more recent adaptation of the scatter plot observation form that also incorporates elements of ABC charting is the Functional Assessment Observation form (O'Neill et al., 1997). This system for conducting direct observations allows for the identification of events that reliably occur just prior to problem behaviors and events that occur just after problem behaviors. By identifying these relationships, one can infer antecedent events that trigger problem behaviors and consequence events that maintain the problem behaviors. When the contents of the form are structured in accordance with information previously gained via interviews (e.g., identified problem behavior, antecedents, consequences, routines), the form can be a useful tool. However, it should be noted that direct observation systems seldom focus on distant setting events.

While direct observation methods are more objective and precise than interviews, their results must also be viewed with caution. Given that simple direct observation does not involve manipulation or control of targeted variables, the data demonstrate correlations, not causal relationships, between environmental events and behavior. An example will illustrate the potential risk of relying solely on direct observation data to design a behavior support plan. Consider the case of a student who engages in severe head hitting.

A record of direct observations showed that when the student hit her head, the teacher usually went to her side, provided a reprimand, and attempted to redirect her to play with a toy. Multiple direct observations of this series of events suggested that the student's head hitting was maintained by the teacher's attention. However, a later, more extensive analysis indicated that the student had chronic sinus infections and that head hitting lessened the pain from the infections. In this case, attempts to replace head hitting with requests for attention would have been ineffective. However, medication to relieve the sinus pain was effective. Multiple factors can affect problem behavior, and care is needed when developing and confirming FBA hypotheses.

Some studies have documented that carefully conducted direct observations can be used as the basis for designing effective BSPs (Lewis-Palmer, 1998; Mace & Lalli, 1991; March & Horner, 1998; Repp, Felce, & Barton, 1988, Sasso et al., 1992), while others have demonstrated that less accurate findings also may work (Lerman & Iwata, 1993). The full range of appropriate applications of direct observation methods have not been documented across settings, subjects, and qualifications of personnel. Future investigations should delineate appropriate applications of direct observation versus experimental analysis methods (e.g., functional analysis).

At this time, it appears that interviews followed by direct observations designed to confirm (or disconfirm) hypotheses can lead to useful conclusions about the antecedents and consequent events controlling problem behavior. The relatively low cost, effort, and skill required to conduct interviews and direct observations offer a practical alternative to functional analysis for many practitioners.

It is important that direct observation procedures be structured to provide clear and useful information while not overburdening those responsible for collecting the data. The results of an FBA interview should be used to guide the direct observations. Observations and an observation data form should focus on the behaviors and environmental conditions identified during the interview process (O'Neill et al., 1997). Maya's team used the Functional Assessment Observation form (O'Neill et al., 1997) to collect data (see Figure 2-6).

On 10/06/03, 5 days after completing the FACTS, Trudy collected direct observation data to validate

FIGURE 2–6
Functional Assessment Observation Form

Functional Assessment Observation Form

Name: **Maya**

Starting Date: 10/06/04   Ending Date: 10/06/04   Perceived Functions

Time	\[Behaviors\] Tongue out	Yell	Hit peer	Spit	Throw objects	\[Predictors\] Demand/request	Difficult task	Transitions	Interruption	Alone (no attention)	Hall	Classroom	Lunchroom	Attention	\[Get/Obtain\] Desired item/Activity	Self-Stimulation	\[Escape/Avoid\] Demand/request	Activity (transitions)	Person	Other/don't know	\[Actual Consequence\] Sit alone	Comments: (if nothing happened in period write initials)
9:00 Hall	2	1 3	1 3	2				1 2 3		1 2 3				1 2 3						3		
9:15 Language Arts				4					4			4		4								
10:15 Hall/break	6	5 7	5 7	6				5 6 7		5 6 7				5 6 7						5 7		
10:30 Math																						E.G.
12:00 Lunch	8 10	9 10	9 10	8						8 9 10			8 9 10	8 9 10						10		
12:30 Teen Health																						S.P.
1:30 Current Events/Choir																						C.J.
3:30 Hall	11	11								11				11						11		
Totals																						

Events: ~~1~~ ~~2~~ ~~3~~ ~~4~~ ~~5~~ ~~6~~ ~~7~~ ~~8~~ ~~9~~ ~~10~~ ~~11~~ 12 13 14 15 16 17 18 19 20 21 22 23 24 25

Date: 10/06/04

Source: O'Neill, R., Horner, R. H., Albin, R. W., Sprague, J. R., Storey, K., & Newton, J. S. (1997). *Functional assessment for problem behavior: A practical handbook* (2nd ed.). Pacific Grove, CA: Brooks/Cole.

(or disconfirm) *the team's hypothesis that Maya is likely to stick her tongue out at peers, yell, spit at them, and/or hit them during hallway transitions (particularly on Mondays after a weekend break from school) for the function of gaining their attention. To collect the data, Trudy used the Functional* *Assessment Observation form. Data were collected for the entire school day across all of Maya's routines.*

A quick orientation to other aspects of the structure of the Functional Assessment Observation form may be helpful. The first group of columns on the form lists the problem behaviors.

For Maya, these are sticking out her tongue, yelling, hitting peers, spitting, and throwing objects.

The second group of columns lists the hypothesized predictors (antecedent triggers) for the problem behaviors.

In Maya's case, generic predictors, such as "Demand/ Request" and "Alone," have been supplemented with more specific predictors: hall, classroom, and lunchroom.

The next set of columns lists the perceived functions of the problem behavior, organized into two subgroups: (a) get/obtain and (b) escape/avoid. Within each of these subgroups are listed generic functions of problem behavior (e.g., get attention, desired activity/item, self-stimulation, and escape/avoid a demand/request, activity, or person). Finally, the last set of columns provides a place to record actual consequences of a problem behavior (i.e., specific consequent events that occurred when problem behavior occurred).

In Maya's case, being made to sit alone is an actual consequence that she experienced when she hit another student.

On the Functional Assessment Observation form, problem behaviors are recorded as events rather than frequency counts. A single event includes all instances of a problem behavior of a given type (e.g., spitting) that are separated by no more than a 3-minute time gap. Counting behavior events is easier than trying to count every instance of a behavior, particularly with problem behaviors that have hard-to-determine beginnings and endings. Each time a problem behavior event occurs, the data collector records the sequence number of the event (e.g., 1 for the first event that occurred, 2 for the second event that occurred) in each of the relevant columns of the form.

Maya's first problem behavior event (i.e., event 1) occurred between 9:00 a.m. and 9:15 a.m. while she was making a hallway transition and included her yelling at and then hitting a peer (note the 1 in each of those columns). The data collector has also recorded that the predictors for event 1 were transitions and hall (note the 1 in each of those columns) and that the perceived function of the event was

attention (note the 1 in that column). There was no consequence delivered for event 1. During this same time period, two other distinct problem behavior events occurred (i.e., events 2 and 3). Event 3 involved Maya's yelling and hitting a peer again, and the data collector has recorded the predictors as transitions and hall, the perceived function as attention, and the actual consequence as Maya's being made to sit alone.

Note also that when no problem behavior events occur during an observed portion of a student's routine, the observer simply writes his or her initials in the final column of the form. This makes it clear that although an observation did occur, no problem behavior occurred.

The data on Maya's direct observation form show that she experienced no problem behaviors during her math, teen health, or current events classes.

In all, Maya engaged in 11 problem behavior events on 10/06/03, the last of which occurred around 3:30 p.m., when she was making a hallway transition. At the bottom of the form, the data collector has drawn a slash mark through events 1 through 11, drawn a vertical line after the number 11, and written the date as 10/06/03. Thus, a quick check reveals that 11 behavioral events occurred on 10/06/03. If the same form were to be used to collect data on the following day, 10/07/03, the first behavioral event of that date would be recorded as event 12.

Validation (or disconfirming) of the hypothesis can be undertaken once sufficient data have been collected.

There is confirmation that the FBA interview correctly identified Maya's problem behaviors in that no problem behaviors other than those that were revealed in the interview have been recorded. Maya engaged in four behavioral events that included sticking her tongue out (events 2, 6, 8, and 10), seven events that included yelling (events 1, 3, 5, 7, 9, 10, and 11), seven events that included hitting a peer (events 1, 3, 5, 7, 9, 10, and 11), and so on. Except for event 4, all behavior events included multiple problem behaviors, which may be an indication that the cluster of behaviors serves the same function.

The FBA hypothesis was that Maya was more likely to engage in problem behaviors during hallway transitions (particularly on Mondays after a weekend break from school) than at other times in order to gain their attention. A review of the data for 10/06/03 (a Monday) indicates that of the 11 behavioral events, seven (64%) occurred during hallway transitions (i.e., events 1, 2, 3, 5, 6, 7, and 11). This provides support for the hypothesis, although the data also reveal that three other behavioral events occurred during lunch (i.e., events 8, 9, and 10). For all 11 events, the form shows that the perceived function was attention, thus providing confirmation for that portion of the original hypothesis.

In summary, Maya's direct observation data provide a confirmation of the original hypothesis, although her BSP may need to address not only the problem behaviors that occur during hallway transitions but also those that occur during lunch. In developing such a plan, it will be important to consider the prevailing environmental conditions during Maya's math, teen health, and current events classes, when the probability of her problem behaviors appears to be low.

There are many forms for collecting direct observation data. The key issue is that direct observation systems can be used to validate FBA hypotheses developed through interview procedures. In cases where the hypothesis is at least tentatively confirmed, development of a related BSP can be initiated. In cases where the hypothesis is at least temporarily disconfirmed, the direct observations will either provide enough information to revise the hypothesis statement accordingly or launch another round of focused information gathering from additional informants, followed by another round of direct observations. Ideally, successive rounds of information gathering will be sharpened until a final round of direct observations succeeds in at least tentatively confirming the final hypothesis statement.

Where problem behaviors and environmental conditions are so complex that a series of direct observations fail to result in a tentatively confirmed hypothesis or where behavior support plans that have been implemented with fidelity nevertheless fail to produce reductions in problem behavior, it may be necessary to conduct a functional analysis. Technically, functional analysis is a process that is separate and distinct from FBA. Functional analysis should not be undertaken lightly; it requires time and a high level of behavioral skills. However, some problem behavior may be so complex that its solution requires a functional analysis.

Functional Analysis Within applied behavior analysis, functional analysis refers to the explicit manipulation of variables in order to demonstrate a functional relationship between an environmental event and a behavior. As such, a functional analysis is a mini-experiment. The conceptual foundation for functional analysis has been described by Bijou et al. (1968), Carr (1977), and Skinner (1953), among others.

In a highly influential study, Iwata, Dorsey, Slifer, Bauman, and Richman (1982) demonstrated what has become the classic methodology for conducting a functional analysis: *the manipulation of consequent variables.* They examined—in an analog setting—the relationship between self-injury and various consequent events (i.e., contingent attention, contingent escape from academic demands, alone, and unstructured play/control). This study conclusively demonstrated the wisdom of deriving interventions based on the function (or purpose) of a problem behavior rather than merely imposing arbitrary contingencies of reinforcement or punishment on problem behavior in a "trial-and-error" approach designed to overpower the problem behavior regardless of its function. The functional analysis conducted by Iwata et al. revealed that some participants engaged in high rates of self-injury only when self-injury resulted in escape from difficult tasks; other participants engaged in self-injury only when the behavior resulted in adult attention, and still others engaged in self-injury in all conditions.

Despite the success and widespread use of functional analysis by researchers, its "ecological validity" has sometimes been questioned (Hanley & Iwata, 2003). Functional analysis is usually conducted under well-controlled conditions in settings that may not entirely duplicate the settings in which the problem behavior occurs (e.g., a functional analysis might be conducted in the corner of a classroom rather than in the midst of the typical classroom activities). Nevertheless, functional analysis is not limited to such analog settings. Variations of the basic analog protocol have been demonstrated in schools and communities (Durand & Carr, 1991; Lalli, Browder, Mace, & Brown, 1993; Northup et al., 1995; Sasso et al., 1992; Sprague & Horner, 1992; Umbreit, 1995), clinical outpatient settings (Wacker, Steege, Northup, Reimers, et al., 1990), and homes (Arndorfer, Miltenberger, Woster,

Rortvedt, & Gaffaney, 1994; Lucyshyn, Albin, & Nixon, 1997).

Regardless of the setting in which functional analysis is conducted, it is a complex procedure that is currently much more likely to be conducted by a trained behavior analyst than by a teacher. A particularly cautionary aspect of functional analysis is that, by its very nature, it evokes problem behavior. That is, in manipulating successive consequent variables, the behavior analyst is searching for the reinforcer for the problem behavior and the antecedent condition that reliably triggers the problem behavior by setting the occasion for delivery of the reinforcer (e.g., a difficult academic task that reliably evokes problem behavior because of a history of the problem behavior resulting in escape from the task). A functional analysis that targets, for example, aggression or self-injury is not to be undertaken lightly because the analysis will "cause" those problem behaviors to occur. Despite these cautions about functional analysis, there has been at least one demonstration of a methodology that effectively taught teachers to use functional analysis in actual elementary-level classroom settings (Moore et al., 2002) in which the target problem behavior was students' yelling out during class.

There are some variations in how functional analysis is conducted that could perhaps be adapted to increase the likelihood of its use by typical intervention agents, such as teachers. For example, Wacker and his colleagues (Northup et al., 1991; Wacker, Steege, Northup, Reimers, et al., 1990; Wacker, Steege, Northup, Sasso, et al., 1990) have developed a *"brief" functional analysis protocol* that involves an analog assessment phase followed by a "contingency reversal" phase. During the analogue assessment phase, functional analysis conditions (e.g., attention, escape) are alternated in rapid sessions (5 to 10 minutes per session, two or three consecutive sessions per condition) to identify the maintaining consequences (i.e., the function) of problem behavior. In the subsequent contingency reversal phase, the participant is taught an appropriate response that produces the maintaining consequence identified in the analog assessment phase (e.g., how to say "Come here, please" to gain attention). The effect on problem behavior of reinforcing or not reinforcing this new appropriate response is then tested in a series of contingency reversals. This brief functional analysis procedure can result in identification of maintaining consequences (functions) for problem behavior during the course of a 90-minute evaluation.

As an example of the brief functional analysis methodology, consider Figure 2-7. During the analog assessment phase, the hypothetical student's rate of aggression is high during the attention condition sessions (when the student is provided with attention contingent on engaging in aggression but otherwise ignored), and his rate of requesting attention or assistance is low. During the escape condition sessions (when the student is prompted/assisted through a difficult academic task and allowed to escape the task contingent on engaging in aggression), his rates of both problem behavior and requesting attention or assistance are low. The analog assessment phase suggests that aggression is maintained by getting attention. This hypothesis is further tested during the contingency reversal phase conditions. The first condition of the contingency reversal phase replicates the analog assessment condition that tested attention as the maintaining consequence. However, prior to the onset of this condition, the student is taught to sign "Come here, please," and attention is delivered to the student contingent on his signing. During this condition, the student's rate of aggression is low, and his rate of signing is high. This condition is then reversed to replicate the analog condition in which only aggression produces attention and then reversed one final time to assess the rate of aggression when attention is again delivered contingent on the participant's appropriate signing.

Another possibility for increasing the likelihood that functional analysis could be conducted in schools is the option of focusing on the *manipulation of antecedent variables* rather than consequent variables. This is sometimes referred to as a *structural analysis* (Axelrod, 1987). Structural analysis involves a focus on discovering a relationship between an antecedent condition and a behavior. This typically is done using a single-subject withdrawal (ABAB) design approach. Manipulating antecedent conditions while holding consequent conditions constant may be much easier—and even natural—for teachers (e.g., Vollmer & Van Camp, 1998; Wacker, Berg, Asmus, Harding, & Cooper, 1998). Many curricular, instructional, and other antecedent variables (e.g., type of task, task difficulty, level of attention, choice) can be, and have been, manipulated in school settings to identify relationships between antecedents and problem behavior (Carr & Durand, 1985a; Dunlap et al., 1991; Munk & Repp, 1994).

FIGURE 2–7
Brief Functional Analysis

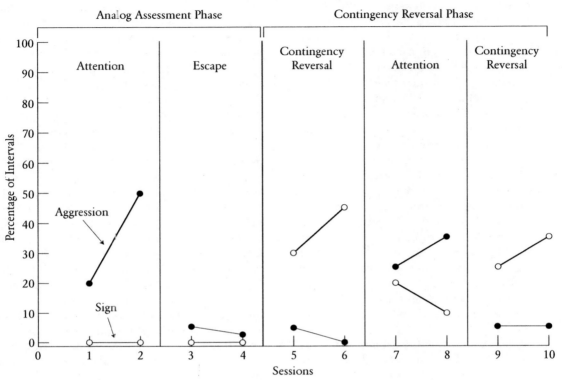

Although functional analysis is considered the "gold standard" for defining the maintaining function of problem behaviors, we recommend that functional analysis should be attempted (a) only with the support of a trained behavior analyst and (b) only when other sources of FBA do not provide a clear set of validated hypothesis statements.

Summary of Assessment for Behavior Support Planning

In completing the assessment processes that precede development of a BSP, you will have engaged in person-centered planning and will have conducted an FBA. The FBA will have produced six outcomes: (a) description of the student's problem behavior and daily routines, (b) identification of consequent conditions that maintain the problem behavior, (c) identification of antecedent conditions that set the occasion for (or

"trigger") the problem behavior as well as antecedent conditions that *do not* trigger the problem behavior, (d) identification of setting events that make the problem behavior more sensitive (or less sensitive) to the maintaining consequences and their associated antecedents, (e) production of a written hypothesis that synthesizes the foregoing information into a testable statement about the problem behavior, and (f) direct observations of the student during typical daily routines for the purpose of tentatively confirming (or disconfirming) the hypothesis (O'Neill et al., 1997). If necessary, you may also have requested the help of a trained behavior analyst in conducting a functional analysis.

The areas of assessment and their phases and outcomes are summarized in Table 2-2. After addressing the outcomes, you will be prepared to develop a BSP.

TABLE 2–2
Areas, Phases, and Outcomes of the Assessment Process

Area	Phase	Outcomes
Person-centered planning	Not applicable	A written plan, consistent with student's and family's vision of a desired lifestyle, and referenced to relevant aspirations; for example:
		Being present and participating in community life
		Gaining and maintaining satisfying relationships
		Expressing preferences and making choices in everyday life
		Having opportunities to fulfill respected roles and to live with dignity
		Continuing to develop personal competencies
Functional behavioral assessment	Defining the challenge	Description of student's problem behaviors and daily routines
	Developing the hypothesis	Identification of consequent conditions that maintain the problem behavior
		Identification of antecedent conditions that set the occasion for (or "trigger") the problem behavior as well as antecedent conditions that do not trigger the problem behavior
		Identification of setting events that make the problem behavior more sensitive (or less sensitive) to the maintaining consequences and their associated antecedents
		Production of a written hypothesis that synthesizes the foregoing information into a testable statement about the problem behavior
	Validating the hypothesis	Direct observations of that tentatively confirm (or disconfirming) the hypothesis
		Functional analysis, with aid of trained behavior analyst, that confirms the hypothesis

Using Assessment Information to Guide Behavior Support Plan Content

Once the assessment phase of the PBS process is completed, the next step is developing, implementing, and evaluating a comprehensive, positive behavior support plan (BSP). At this point in the support process, the six outcomes for a functional assessment should be completed, and a person-centered vision of broader lifestyle goals for the focus student should be agreed on by the support team. The information gathered in the functional assessment and person-centered planning processes provide the foundation for the BSP. However, as the development and implementation of the BSP progresses, it is important to remember that the functional assessment and person-centered planning processes are ongoing. Both assessment processes should be done on a recurring basis as the student's BSP impacts both appropriate and problem behaviors and as changes in lifestyle, routines, and living settings occur.

A BSP provides a guide for the behavior of those people providing support (e.g., teachers, parents, classroom assistants, specialists). We often think of a BSP as the plan for changing the behavior of a student with problem behaviors. In fact, although "designed" for a focus student, a BSP actually describes changes and behaviors that we as teachers, administrators, family members, friends, and peers will make happen and perform. A comprehensive BSP is a blueprint for designing and maintaining effective environments that render problem behaviors irrelevant, inefficient, and ineffective. The changes we make in the physical setting, the daily schedule, what we teach, the way we teach, and the way we respond to appropriate and problem behaviors are what will produce changes in the behaviors of the student. It is through changes in our behavior that we effect changes in the behavior of students with problem behaviors. As such, written BSPs should be clear in describing the exact changes expected in the behavior of those who will implement the plan and in the settings in which the plan will be implemented. In the following sections, we describe important features of a positive BSP.

A Positive BSP Should be Technically Sound

In designing comprehensive positive behavior support, it is essential that a BSP be *technically sound* (Crone & Horner, 2003; Horner, 1999; O'Neill et al., 1997). Technically sound means that the procedures in the support plan are logically linked to functional assessment hypotheses and also are grounded in the basic principles of human behavior and biomedical sciences (Alberto & Troutman, 2003; Carr et al., 2002). Interventions that are technically sound are also evidence based. Research or clinical application data should exist supporting the effectiveness and logic behind each procedure used in a plan (e.g., Carr & Carlson, 1993).

A Positive BSP Should be Contextually Appropriate

In addition to being technically sound, a BSP should be *contextually appropriate* (Albin et al., 1996; Horner, 1999; Lucyshyn, Kayser, Irvin, & Blumberg, 2002). Contextually appropriate refers to how well support plan procedures "fit" their implementers and settings. The term "contextual fit" (or "goodness of fit") has been used to describe the compatibility between a BSP and the values, skills, and resources of BSP implementers both at home and school (Albin et al., 1996). Contextual fit influences the selection of procedures within a BSP as well as whether the plan procedures are put into place at all, are implemented with fidelity, and are implemented for extended periods of time (Horner, Albin, Borgmeier, & Salantine, 2003; Moes & Frea, 2000; Sandler, 2001). To be effective, PBS plans must be implemented with fidelity by typical support providers, in natural school, home, and community settings, often for extended time periods. The contextual fit of the BSP is as important to its effectiveness as is the technical soundness of the plan.

A Positive BSP Should be a Collaborative Endeavor

We strongly recommend that a collaborative team process be used in the design, implementation, evaluation, and modification of the plan. The team should include all the key stakeholders involved in supporting a student with problem behaviors, including teachers and school staff who will implement the plan, family and friends, the student with problem behaviors (when appropriate), school and other administrators who must support the BSP implementation process, and any others (e.g., behavior or related-services specialists, respite providers) involved in supporting the student (Anderson, Albin, Mesaros, Dunlap, & Morelli-Robbins, 1993; Crone & Horner, 2003; Todd, Horner, Sugai, & Colvin, 1999). Collaboration among all stakeholders is likely to promote good contextual fit. A collaborative team process also provides the framework for a support approach that is dynamic and capable of responding to changing support needs. Behavior support needs of persons with severe problem behaviors are likely to be long term in nature. Support should be designed with longevity in mind and with the expectation that the nature of the support will change as the person's skills, needs, and preferences change. Sustained plan implementation, ongoing monitoring of effects, and timely adaptation and modification of plan procedures and features are essential elements of effective comprehensive behavior support. A collaborative team process involving all key stakeholders facilitates high-quality performance of these elements.

Todd et al. (1999) have described a team-based approach to PBS (i.e., "discipline") in schools that utilizes a two-tiered model. The first tier is a school-based "core behavior support team," consisting of a school administrator, someone with behavioral expertise, and a representative sample of school staff (i.e., teachers and others). The core team has responsibility for coordinating and managing all aspects of behavior support within a school, including both schoolwide and individual student systems of support. The core team serves as a resource for the school and staff in the area of behavior support. The second tier involves "action teams" that conduct the individualized behavior support process. Each student requiring a BSP would have his or her own action team. Each action team would consist of a member (or members) of the school's core team (e.g., a school behavior specialist), the student's teacher(s), the student's parents/family, and any other school or community members who are involved in the student's life or are interested in participating (e.g., a counselor, social worker, speech/language therapist, physical therapist, school bus driver, probation officer, respite care provider). In this two-tiered model, the core team is responsible for receiving and managing staff requests for assistance with students' behavioral problems, forming and supporting action teams, and assisting as needed in the design, implementation, and evaluation of BSPs. The action team is responsible for conducting person-centered planning and the FBA, developing and implementing a comprehensive positive BSP, supporting the student and teachers in support plan implementation, and collecting data to evaluate support plan effectiveness (Crone & Horner, 2003).

Maya's school had instituted a schoolwide PBS system that identified three expectations for all students: be respectful, be responsible, and be safe. School staff had translated these expectations into specific student behaviors that were expected in the various settings (e.g., hallways, cafeteria, classrooms, bus loading zone, playground) and activities (e.g., entering school, assemblies, fire drills, after-school functions) that make up a "school day." Importantly, staff had taught these expected behaviors to all students, so that students at Maya's school knew what behaviors were expected of them. In addition, Maya's school had strategies for monitoring students and rewarding them for doing expected behaviors (e.g., the school held a weekly raffle on Fridays and students received raffle tickets to acknowledge appropriate behaviors).

Although Maya participated in the schoolwide system, by itself, the schoolwide system was not sufficient to meet Maya's behavioral support needs. Maya required more individualized support. That is why Trudy Schwartz, the behavior specialist, initiated the individual student behavior support system in Maya's school by completing a Request for Assistance form. With this Request for Assistance, an action team was set up for Maya that included Trudy, Maya's homeroom teacher and another regular education teacher who had her in class for part of the day, Maya's educational assistant, and Maya's mother. This action team set about the task of further assessing Maya's behavior and designing, implementing, and monitoring a BSP.

A Positive BSP Should be Comprehensive

The goal of PBS is to have a broad positive impact on the life of a person with disabilities and challenging problem behaviors (Carr et al., 2002; Horner, 1999). Successful behavior support should translate into real differences in a person's life across all contexts in which behavior support needs are present (e.g., home, school, respite care, community). The following three features characterize a comprehensive BSP:

1. *All problem behaviors performed by the focus person are addressed:* The need for behavior support often is prompted by the occurrence of a few intense problem behaviors. Teachers and families have noted, however, that high-frequency occurrences of low-intensity behaviors (e.g., whining, refusal) may be as disruptive, problematic, and damaging to the student and those around him or her as higher-intensity aggression, self-injury, and property destruction (Horner, Diemer, & Brazeau, 1992; Turnbull & Ruef, 1996). Research also indicates the value of organizing support around all the problem behaviors that are maintained by the same function (e.g., all behaviors that produce attention, all behaviors that are maintained by escape from tasks) (Sprague & Horner, 1992, 1999). Both our current understanding of behavioral theory and the goal of producing change that is of broad impact argue for focusing behavior support on the full range of problem behaviors a person performs rather than on just one or two high-intensity behaviors.

2. *A comprehensive support plan is implemented across all relevant settings and times of day:* Just as addressing all problem behaviors is important, so too is implementation of behavior support procedures across the relevant scope of a person's entire day. In the past, it was not unusual for individual behavioral interventions to be implemented for limited periods of time, across limited settings or situations. The research literature shows clearly that single intervention procedures can have a dramatic effect in reducing severe problem behavior across brief periods in specific contexts. However, to achieve true lifestyle impact, behavior support must produce broad and lasting effects across the relevant range of contexts, conditions, activities, and routines that a person with severe problem behaviors experiences in the course of the day. A challenge for PBS is to develop comprehensive support strategies that can be implemented and sustained across the entire day and the full range of conditions encountered (Horner, 1999).

3. *A comprehensive support plan blends multiple procedures:* It would be unusual for a single intervention procedure to address the full spectrum of problem behaviors performed by an individual with severe problem behaviors and to cover the full range of settings where problems occur. Comprehensive support

will more likely involve the creative blending of multiple procedures. For example, strategies for curricular revision and schedule modification may be used to minimize contact with highly aversive events, instructional procedures will build new skills, and consequences throughout the day will be modified to increase the rewards associated with communication and learning and decrease the rewards that follow problem behaviors. Collectively, these multiple changes result in an environment that minimizes and redirects access to problem events, builds new skills, and provides constructive feedback that both promotes appropriate behavior and minimizes the rewards for problem behavior.

A Positive BSP Should be Sustainable

PBS has moved the delivery of behavioral intervention for persons with severe problem behaviors from specialized and restrictive settings into regular, integrated community settings. A challenge facing families, schools, and community support providers today is to deliver effective behavior support in typical homes, schools, and community settings for as long as such support is needed. PBS plans, in most instances, will be implemented by the "typical people" (e.g., family members, friends, teachers, and classroom assistants, paid caregivers) who live and work in those settings. To be effective over the long term, BSP implementation must be sustainable (i.e., capable of being implemented with reasonable fidelity by typical people for extended periods of time). We have two recommendations to facilitate sustained implementation of a BSP across all relevant settings and contexts in a student's life for extended periods. First, the BSP must continue to have good contextual fit over time. As the BSP changes over time, team members should continue to monitor for contextual fit. Second, it is important that the BSP procedures can be relatively easily embedded and implemented within the typical routines and activities that make up the student's daily life at school, at home, and in the community. If BSP procedures require teachers, families, or other support providers to make substantial changes in their daily or other regular routines and activities as part of plan implementation, then plan procedures are much less likely to be implemented across all contexts and times of day, and implementation is much less likely to be sustained over time.

Competing Behavior Analysis

Competing behavior analysis (CBA) provides a conceptual bridge for moving from functional assessment information to the design of a comprehensive BSP (Crone & Horner, 2003; Horner & Billingsley, 1988; O'Neill et al., 1997). Conducting a CBA provides a framework to logically link the multiple intervention procedures and support strategies of a comprehensive BSP to information collected in the FBA. Thus, CBA is a strategy for producing a BSP that is technically sound. A separate CBA should be completed for each response class of problem behaviors identified in a FBA. If a student performs one set of problem behaviors (throws and destroys materials) to escape difficult tasks and another set (calls out, pounds desk) to get attention, then two CBAs will be completed, one for each set of behaviors (i.e., each response class). If one set of behaviors serves multiple functions (Day et al., 1994), then separate CBA should be completed for each function.

The process for conducting a CBA involves four basic steps: (a) summarize the FBA information to construct a hypothesis statement for each response class of problem behaviors; (b) identify appropriate desired and alternative replacement behaviors and the contingencies associated with them; (c) identify potential intervention procedures, across four support strategy categories, that promote the occurrence of appropriate behaviors and make problem behaviors irrelevant, ineffective, and inefficient; and (d) select the set of strategies from the options proposed that are technically sound and likely to result in behavior change and are a good contextual fit (Crone & Horner, 2003; O'Neill et al., 1997).

The process of summarizing FBA information to construct a summary statement for a response class involves listing, from left to right, the setting event(s), immediate antecedents (predictors), problem behavior(s) in the response class, and maintaining consequence(s) that have been identified in the FBA. The maintaining consequence(s) for problem behavior indicates (or suggests) the function of the problem behavior (refer back to Figure 2–4 for a listing of potential functions). For example, the functional assessment summary statement for Isha (described at the beginning of the chapter) indicates that she screams, pulls her own hair, and scratches at staff (problem behavior) when she is asked to shift (transition) from one activity to another (antecedent). Isha's problem behaviors, at least sometimes, lead to a consequence of her getting to stay in her current activity (i.e., getting her predictable routine reinstated) (maintaining consequence). Screaming, pulling her hair, and scratching staff become more likely when Isha is in new or unpredictable situations or when she suffers from her pollen allergy (setting event). The consequence that occurs for Isha's problem behavior suggests that the function of her problem behaviors is escape from transitions, which are aversive to Isha. This information would be diagrammed as follows:

Setting Event	Antecedent	Problem Behavior	Consequence	Function
• New or unpredictable situations • Pollen allergy	Asked to shift to another activity	• Screams • Pulls own hair • Scratches	Gets to stay in current activity	Escapes aversive transition

The second step in completing a CBA is to identify a desired alternative behavior that will compete with the problem behavior. Two questions can be asked: (a) Given that the setting event(s) and predictor(s) have occurred, what is an appropriate behavior that would be the *desired behavior* for the person to perform in that situation? and (b) Given that the setting event(s) and predictor(s) have occurred, what would be an *alternative replacement* behavior that could produce exactly the same consequence as the problem behavior(s) (i.e., a functionally equivalent behavior) (O'Neill et al., 1997)?

For Isha, the desired behavior would be that she transition from activity to activity without incident when asked. The current (actual) maintaining consequence for shifting without incident for Isha is teacher praise and acknowledgment for "acting like an adult." A functionally equivalent alternative for Isha would be requesting predictability by asking to stay in the current activity using an appropriate communication response (e.g., a symbol requesting "more time"). Her team reasons that requesting to stay in the current activity is an appropriate functionally equivalent response (i.e., produces the same maintaining consequence as the problem behavior) that can compete as a replacement for Isha's problem behaviors (Carr, 1988). When she asks appropriately to stay in the current activity, Isha will receive additional time in the activity (e.g., 1 more minute). This is not what staff want Isha to do, but it is preferable to her problem behavior and is an acceptable option as staff work on other strategies in Isha's plan to address her problem behavior and transitions.

An important aspect of alternative replacement behaviors is that they may serve as short-term solutions while a support team also implements other strategies within a comprehensive support plan aimed at increasing desired behaviors and eliminating the need for alternative replacement behaviors. This CBA would be diagrammed as in Figure 2–8.

This depiction of the CBA provides support team members with a literal picture of the current contingencies for Isha in the context of transitions from activity to activity and sets the occasion for the team to define what to change in the context (e.g., contingencies, antecedents, skills, consequences) to make the problem behaviors irrelevant, ineffective, and inefficient.

The third step in the CBA process is to build a list of possible behavior support procedures. The goal here is not simply to look for a single intervention that would eliminate the problem behavior(s) but to identify a range of strategies and procedures that would reduce the likelihood of problem behavior(s) and increase the likelihood that either or both of the competing behaviors (i.e., desired or replacement) would occur. Such a multicomponent support plan might address setting events (e.g., for Isha, designing a schedule to reduce unpredictability of activities), the immediate antecedents (e.g., asking Isha to shift activities only after first presenting a preinstruction or reminder that a transition was coming), behaviors (e.g., teaching Isha to ask for more time on an activity), and consequences (e.g., increase reinforcers for the desired behavior of shifting to new activities throughout the day, ensure that problem behavior does not result in escaping the transition but that requesting more time does). A comprehensive BSP will have multiple components addressing the full range of variables that influence which behaviors occur from among the alternatives available. This third step often involves a brainstorming

FIGURE 2–8
Competing Behavior Analysis for Isha

Student Name: Isha

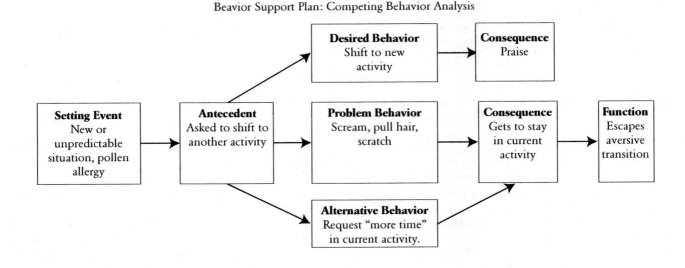

Beavior Support Plan: Competing Behavior Analysis

process to first create a menu of potential strategies from which support team members can then select the best options and strategies for their situation. In this way, the resulting plan is more likely to be both technically sound (i.e., based on the functional assessment) and have good contextual fit (i.e., strategies are identified that work best for the team members and context) (Albin et al., 1996; Crone & Horner, 2003; O'Neill et al., 1997).

The fourth step in building a plan of behavior support involves review of the proposed list of strategies and selection of specific procedures that the team identifies as effective, doable, and an appropriate fit with their skills, values, schedules, resources, and administrative support system. This fourth step is extremely important. The people who will be implementing the plan procedures (and, in many cases, the student with problem behaviors) decide on and define the final features (procedures) of the BSP. The first three steps have ensured that technically sound information is being considered. The features of effective behavior support are defined. The final step adds form to those features and addresses the issue of the plan being contextually appropriate and a good fit for the

student, plan implementers, and the context (settings) where the plan will be implemented. This fourth step is of particular importance when a behavioral consultant from "outside" the school is involved in the design of support. The behavioral consultant can be of tremendous assistance in the process of functional assessment and coordination of the competing behavior model. The final selection of the specific strategies that make up a behavior plan, however, must be done with very active participation of people who know the student best and who will be implementing the final plan. Support team consensus that a plan's procedures are doable, consistent with the team members' values and skills, in the best interest of the student, and likely to be effective is a key element in moving forward to implementation of the plan. Figure 2–9 presents a completed CBA for Maya illustrating the completion of these four steps.

The functional assessment hypothesis statement for Maya could be stated as follows: "During lunch, hallway transitions, and less structured activities, Maya engages in sticking her tongue out, yelling, hitting, and spitting at peers, with these behaviors maintained by

FIGURE 2–9
Competing Behavior Analysis for Maya

Student name: Maya

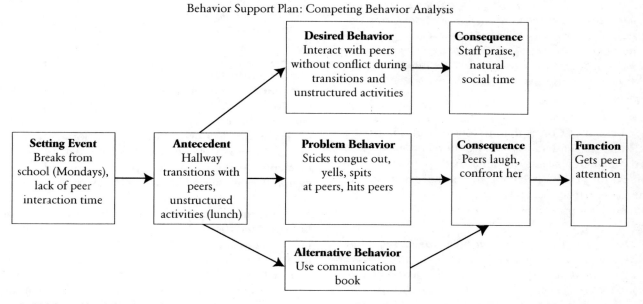

Behavior Support Plan: Competing Behavior Analysis

(Make problem behavior irrelevant)   *(Make problem behavior inefficient)*   *(Make problem behavior ineffective)*

Setting Event Strategies	Antecedent Strategies	Behavior Teaching Strategies	Consequence Strategies
• Call peer on phone on Sunday night • Provide peer mentor during unstructured times	• Provide pictorial schedule and review for social times • Staff and peers prompt use of communication book • Precorrect before all transitions • Increase hall monitoring by staff	• Teach how to use pictorial schedule as a communication book • Teach peers about communication book	• Ask peers to ignore inappropriate behavior • Peers ask Maya to use communication book (low-level problem) or notify staff (high-level problem) • Remove from setting if hitting occurs • Increase social times throughout day

Maya receiving attention from her peers, in the forms of laughter, yelling back, and confrontations when she does the behaviors. Maya's problem behaviors are even more likely when two setting events are present: breaks *from school ('Mondays') and lack of peer interaction time."*

This hypothesis statement is diagrammed as follows:

Setting events	Antecedents	Problem behaviors	Consequences	Function
● "Mondays" ● Lack of peer interaction time	● Hallway transitions ● Unstructured activities (lunch, break)	● Yelling ● Sticking out her tongue ● Hitting peers ● Spitting at peers	Peers laugh Peers yell back Peers confront	Obtains peer attention

The desired behavior for Maya in the problematic routines identified (hallway, lunch, unstructured activities) is that she talks and interacts with peers appropriately and without conflict. In assessing what consequences were currently present to maintain this desired behavior, Maya's team concluded that talking appropriately with peers would produce natural social time that would be reinforcing for Maya. They also tried to praise her for appropriate behavior.

A benefit of CBA is that it focuses attention on the existing consequences available to maintain desired behavior. Often, teams may find that the existing reinforcers for desired behavior are unimpressive and inadequate, particularly relative to the maintaining consequence for problem behavior.

The alternative replacement behavior identified by Maya's team was teaching Maya to use a communication book to initiate and conduct a conversation with peers. This behavior would produce the peer attention that Maya desired. Maya's peers also would be taught about the conversation book and how it worked with Maya.

The third step in the CBA for Maya had the support team identifying several potential intervention procedures and support strategies that could be used to make Maya's problem behavior irrelevant, inefficient, or ineffective. These procedures and strategies are organized as setting event, antecedent, teaching, and consequence manipulations.

After brainstorming a variety of potential support plan components, Maya's team carefully reviewed and discussed the procedures and identified which ones they would include in Maya's plan. In determining which procedures to actually implement, Maya's team considered how effective they thought each procedure would be with Maya; whether they had the skills, resources, and capacity to implement the procedure; how comfortable they were with implementing the procedure; and whether the procedure was reasonably doable within Maya's academic program and school routines. The strategies with an asterisk (*) next to them were selected by Maya's team for inclusion in her comprehensive BSP.

Contents of a Written BSP

Elements of Effective Behavior Support

Horner, Sugai, Todd, and Lewis-Palmer (1999–2000) presented a checklist for assessing the quality of behavior support that delineates 10 features of BSPs and the planning process that produces them. An adapted version of this checklist is presented in Figure 2–10. The 10 features include elements related to the completion of an FBA, the support planning process, the development and features of a written support plan, and the evaluation and assessment of the plan and its effects. In this section, we use the checklist as a guide in describing key elements of a written BSP as well as elements to address in the support planning process even if they do not need to be included in the written BSP.

The elements of a written positive BSP are organized around the goal of creating an effective environment that promotes and supports appropriate behavior and makes problem behavior irrelevant, inefficient, and ineffective. Accomplishing this goal typically necessitates development and implementation of a multicomponent support plan that focuses on proactive strategies for prevention and teaching as well as on reactive strategies for responding to both appropriate and problem behaviors. The actual format, length, and style of a written BSP may vary. Rather than focusing on a particular form or format to use, we shall focus on the information presented in a written plan and on the processes described. Following are recommendations for the elements of behavior support planning and a written BSP (for more information, see Crone & Horner, 2003; Horner, Albin, Sprague, & Todd, 2000; Horner et al., 1999–2000; O'Neill et al., 1997).

1. *Define academic and lifestyle context for behavior support*: Person-centered planning is a key element of the assessment process in PBS. A written BSP should begin with a brief summary of the person-centered goals and vision that guide the BSP and the support team's planning efforts and decisions. This summary may also describe the connection between the BSP and desired or projected personal outcomes for the student. Whenever a BSP is proposed and developed, there should be a rationale for the plan and objectives for the plan's components that are directly related to the health, safety, and lifestyle of the focus student (Carr et al., 2002; Horner et al., 1990; Meyer & Evans, 1989). This summary places the BSP within the broader context of the student's life.

FIGURE 2–10

Checklist for Assessing the Quality of Behavior Support Planning:
Does the Plan (or Planning Process) Have These Features?

1. _____ Define academic and lifestyle *context* for behavior support

2. _____ Operational description of problem behaviors

3. _____ Problem *routines* identified

4. _____ Functional assessment hypotheses stated

5. Intervention/*Foundations* (issues that cut across routines)
   a) _____ health and physiology
   b) _____ communication
   c) _____ mobility
   d) _____ predictability
   e) _____ control/choice
   f) _____ social relationships
   g) _____ activity patterns

6. Intervention/*Prevention Strategies* (make problem behavior irrelevant)
   a) _____ schedule
   b) _____ curriculum
   c) _____ instructional procedures

7. Intervention/*Teaching Strategies* (make problem behavior inefficient)
   a) _____ replacement skills
   b) _____ new adaptive skills

8. Intervention/*Consequence Strategies*

   Extinction (make problem behavior ineffective)
   a) _____ minimize positive reinforcement
   b) _____ minimize negative reinforcement

   Reinforcement (make appropriate behavior more effective)
   _____ maximize positive reinforcement

   Negative Consequences (if needed)
   _____ negative consequences contingent on problem behavior

   Safety/Emergency Intervention Plan (if needed)
   _____ clear plan for what to do if/when crisis behaviors occur

9. Evaluation and Assessment
   a) _____ define the information to be collected
   b) _____ define the measurement process
   c) _____ define decision-making process

10. Ensure Contextual Fit
   a) _____ values
   b) _____ skills
   c) _____ resources
   d) _____ administrative system
   e) _____ perceptions that program is in best interest of student

2. *Operational description of problem behaviors*: Clear definitions of problem behaviors, stated in observable and measurable terms, are an important initial step in designing a BSP. Clear definitions assist a support team to reach agreement on the nature and severity of the problems faced. Definitions or descriptions of problem behaviors should focus both on individual behaviors (e.g., screaming, hitting, talking out, throwing objects) and on response classes (i.e., groups of behaviors maintained by the same consequences). It is rare that a student engages in only one problem behavior. More likely, a student engages in several behaviors that "work together" and are members of a response class. In some cases, behaviors in a response class may occur in very predictable patterns, such as an escalating sequence (Albin, O'Brien, & Horner, 1995), that can and should be identified as part of operationally describing the problem behaviors.

3. *Problem routines are identified*: An important consideration in describing problem behaviors is to define the behaviors within the routines and contexts in which they occur (Lucyshyn et al., 2002; O'Neill et al., 1997). Too often, problem behaviors are described or defined as if they were characteristics or traits of the person (e.g., he's aggressive, he's a biter, she's noncompliant). Defining problem behaviors within the routines in which they occur (e.g., Maya's problem behaviors occur during transitions and activities with minimal structure but do not occur in predictable and highly structured activities) emphasizes that a student's behavior must be understood in relation to the context in which it occurs (i.e., antecedent stimuli, setting events, and consequences). Defining problem behavior within routines assists the support team in understanding the function of the behavior, the environmental variables affecting and controlling the behavior, and the scope of behavior problems (e.g., whether behavior problems are limited to a single routine or a small number of routines or are present across a large number and broad range of routines) as well as in identifying patterns of problem behavior (e.g., finding similar problem behaviors or the absence of problem behaviors across routines with similar features).

4. *Functional assessment hypotheses are stated*: For each response class of problem behaviors identified in the FBA, a hypothesis statement should be presented that identifies setting events, antecedents/predictors, the behaviors in the response class, and the maintaining consequences. The hypothesis

statement(s) provides the basis for a CBA and the subsequent generation of potential intervention procedures. For response classes that have multiple functions, a separate summary statement must be produced for each function, identifying the different setting events and predictors for each different maintaining consequence (i.e., function). Having the functional assessment hypothesis statements presented at the beginning of a written BSP serves as a reminder for plan developers and implementers of the underlying basis for the plan's procedures and goals. Hypothesis statements may be written in the BSP in sentence format or in a table format that presents the components of a hypothesis statement (setting events, antecedents, problem behaviors, consequences, and function). Examples of each format were presented for Maya in the CBA section earlier in this chapter.

5. *Intervention/Foundations (issues that cut across routines)*: One of the roots of PBS is the recognition that problem behaviors may result from and communicate, intentionally or unintentionally, the absence of or failure of living environments to provide basic foundational features in a person's life. These features cut across specific routines, activities, and settings. They include a person's health and physiological status, ability to communicate, mobility, predictability of environments, control and choice exercised by the person, social relationships, and activity patterns. These features must be addressed in the behavior support planning process. Some of them (e.g., mobility) may not be equally important or reflected within a written BSP for all people. However, for each of the features that are relevant for a focus person, the written BSP should describe the importance of the feature and the strategies and procedures of the plan that address the feature.

> *For Isha, predictability of the environment is a major factor in her problem behavior, and ensuring predictability is a guiding objective for her BSP.*
>
> *For Maya, the ability to communicate effectively and appropriately is a major issue and a guiding factor in her support plan.*

This should be communicated within the written plan.

6. *Intervention/Prevention strategies*: Prevention strategies help make problem behavior irrelevant. The guiding question in planning for prevention is, "How can we redesign environments (e.g., classroom, school,

home) proactively to eliminate or minimize as much as possible the occurrence of problem behaviors?" The overall goals of prevention strategies are making the environment as predictable as possible and providing opportunities for choices accommodating individual preferences. Three specific environmental manipulations include (a) *restructuring schedules* to modify or avoid antecedent stimuli that evoke problem behavior, to remove setting events that increase the likelihood of problem behaviors or to minimize their effects with neutralizing routines when they do occur (Horner et al., 1996, 1997), and to make positive reinforcers readily available for appropriate behavior so that positives far outweigh negatives (e.g., at least a 4:1 to 6:1 ratio of positives to negatives); (b) making sure *curricular content* is at an appropriate level for the learners and is relevant (e.g., age and context appropriate), useful (e.g., functional), interesting, and stimulating (Ferro, Foster-Johnson, & Dunlap, 1996); and (c) making sure *instruction* is appropriately designed, paced, and adapted for individual learners (Munk & Repp, 1994).

7. *Intervention/teaching strategies*: Teaching strategies help make problem behaviors inefficient by teaching students (a) appropriate replacement skills that are functionally equivalent to problem behaviors as identified within the CBA and (b) new adaptive skills that we want or expect them to perform as identified within the CBA. Academic and social skill deficits often are associated with increased levels of problem behavior or, at the least, put students at risk for problem behavior (Gresham, 2002). Adaptive skills to teach may include academic, social, community and independent living, leisure, recreational, self-management, and coping skills. Adaptive skills are often (or should be) the focus of long-term objectives on an IEP.

Appropriate replacement skills constitute an intermediary step toward performance of adaptive skills. A replacement skill within the CBA framework is an appropriate behavior that will produce the same maintaining consequence as problem behavior and thereby act as a replacement skill. The term "functional equivalence" is used in describing replacement skills because they produce the same maintaining consequence as problem behavior (Carr, 1988). Frequently, the alternative skill identified for teaching in a BSP is an appropriate communication response.

Isha engaged in problem behavior to avoid transitions to another activity. The alternative behavior identified for Isha in her CBA was an appropriate communication response: using a symbol to request more time in the current activity and thus avoiding the transition momentarily.

Teaching an alternative communication response is an intervention termed functional communication training (FCT) (Carr & Durand, 1985a; Carr et al., 1994; Durand, 1990). FCT is a well-researched and empirically documented procedure that builds on the idea that problem behavior frequently serves a communicative purpose, particularly for people with disabilities who may have limited communication skills and repertoires (Carr & Durand, 1985b, 1987; Donnellan et al., 1984). Teaching appropriate communication skills through FCT can have a rapid and long-lasting effect in reducing problem behavior to zero or near-zero levels (Berotti & Durand, 1999; Carr & Durand, 1985a; Durand & Carr, 1991, 1992). The basic steps for applying FCT include the following (see Carr et al., 1994, for a more complete description of FCT procedures):

1. Identify the function of the problem behavior through FBA. To use FCT, it is essential to know whether the function of problem behavior is to obtain desired reinforcers (e.g., attention, tangible materials or items, preferred activities, comfort) or to escape or avoid activities, items, or situations that the student finds aversive (e.g., things that are difficult, boring, painful, effortful, disliked).

2. Identify a request response to teach the student. This should be an appropriate response that will serve as a replacement behavior for problem behavior. The request response may be a verbal response; a manual sign; a gesture; the use of a card with a printed symbol, word, or picture; the use of an AAC device; or any other response that allows the student to communicate a message to others. The request response should be easy for the student to learn (perhaps a response already in his or her repertoire) and easy for others to perceive and interpret (or learn to interpret). The request response should match the function of problem behavior (e.g., getting attention: "I want to play"; getting more time on an activity: "More time please"; escaping a difficult task: "I want a break" or "Help me please").

3. Engage the student in an activity or context related to problem behavior and teach the student to use the alternative communication response. Do this by prompting the student to use the communication response before a problem behavior occurs and then immediately honoring the request. Fulfilling

the request immediately is very important, particularly in the beginning of teaching, so that the student learns that the appropriate response works to fulfill the request even more efficiently than problem behavior.

In addition to communication responses, functionally equivalent replacement skills may include self-management skills (e.g., self-scheduling to produce "predictability" or self-recruited feedback to produce teacher attention), self-control or coping responses (e.g., relaxation training to reduce stressful arousal), social skills (e.g., a social initiation response that produces peer attention), and appropriate responses to produce stimulation similar to that produced by problematic "self-stimulation" behavior.

   8. *Intervention/consequence strategies*: Consequence strategies help make problem behavior ineffective. They also are used to promote the performance of desired behaviors. Consequence strategies are reactive, with consequences delivered after a response (behavior) has occurred. Traditionally, consequence strategies have served as the mainstay for applied behavior analysis and behavior management. While PBS emphasizes proactive and teaching strategies in providing behavior support, consequence strategies still play an important role and are likely to be included in a comprehensive BSP. This is particularly true with students, as schools have a long history of relying on consequence strategies to change behavior. Many school discipline policies spell out specific consequences (usually negative consequences, such as punishment) for infractions of school rules. Students requiring a BSP are likely to have consequence procedures incorporated into their BSPs.

   The principles of human behavior identify three consequence procedures that are applied in the process of behavior support: extinction, reinforcement, and negative consequences (punishment). There has been much discussion and debate regarding whether any punishment procedure is acceptable within PBS (Horner et al., 1990; Repp & Singh, 1990). A goal of PBS is to minimize, if not eliminate, use of negative consequences to control people and their behavior. The use of severe punishers and heavy reliance on punishment procedures are not acceptable in providing behavior support. Procedures that cause or rely on pain, tissue damage, and humiliation should never be used, and those that seclude, restrict, or restrain students may also be unacceptable and require substantial

review and consideration. It is our experience and belief, however, that some negative consequences, including procedures that fit the technical definition of punishment, are a natural part of learning and life and, therefore, may be an appropriate part of a comprehensive positive BSP (Horner et al., 1990; Janney & Snell, 2000). The procedures that we believe are acceptable mirror procedures that would be typical of what is found in public schools and considered acceptable for nondisabled children. Such procedures should be age appropriate. Examples of punishment procedures that may be included in a BSP are mild reprimands and negative feedback (e.g., being told "no" or "that behavior is unacceptable"), redirection involving no or minimal physical contact, reasonable response cost or loss of activity (e.g., the blocks are put away when you throw them at classmates, computer time is lost when you push classmates to get to the computer first), and some mild forms of time-out (e.g., you have to sit on the bench for a minute because you were rough-housing in recess).

   School-based support teams need to carefully consider, plan, and regularly review the use of appropriate consequences, both positive and negative, in a BSP. Many state and local education agencies have policies that guide and that may prohibit or restrict the use of different punishment procedures as well as the use of sweets and snacks as positive reinforcers. Teams should be aware of state and district policies, and BSP procedures should be in compliance with those policies.

Extinction   Extinction is the withholding of reinforcement for a behavior that has been reinforced in the past. Extinction is used in a BSP to make problem behaviors ineffective. One objective for a BSP is to minimize the extent to which problem behaviors continue to "work" (i.e., produce desired reinforcers) for a student. Putting problem behavior "on extinction" is a procedure that will reduce the occurrence of problem behavior. However, implementers of extinction should anticipate the possibility of an increase in problem behavior—an extinction burst—when the procedure is first implemented. An extinction burst raises particular concerns if the problem behavior placed on extinction is dangerous. It is important to keep in mind that problem behavior may be maintained by either positive reinforcement (e.g., getting adult or peer attention, obtaining desired activities or objects) or negative reinforcement (e.g., escape or avoidance of aversive tasks or demands, having teachers or peers stay away or leave you alone). This will be identified in the FBA process, and an appropriate extinction procedure can be designed and implemented.

Extinction is a challenging intervention to implement logistically and can be problematic when implemented alone (Shukla & Albin, 1996). In a comprehensive BSP, an extinction contingency for problem behavior is typically used in combination with prompts and reinforcers for an alternative replacement behavior such as a functional communication response. The idea is to prompt and teach a replacement behavior that is effective and reinforced while making problem behavior ineffective by eliminating or reducing the reinforcement it receives.

Isha escapes transitions, which she finds aversive, by engaging in screaming, pulling her hair, and scratching at staff. These behaviors are negatively reinforced by Isha's avoiding transitions (i.e., staff let her stay with the activity she is doing). The team realizes that simply placing Isha's problem behavior on extinction would require staff to not allow her to avoid the transition. This strategy would probably be too difficult to carry out because staff would have to prompt and assist Isha through the transition, which could lead to dangerous situations (e.g., she might become highly agitated).

A better procedure is to combine extinction of problem behavior with prompting and teaching an alternative replacement behavior, a communication response.

Isha's team decided to teach her to ask for more time. When the problem behavior is placed on extinction, Isha also will be prompted and taught to ask for more time. When she asks appropriately, the communication response will be honored and reinforced with additional time on the current activity. The team reasoned that engaging in problem behavior should not lead to Isha's getting to stay in an activity longer but that asking appropriately for more time can be reinforced.

Reinforcement Procedures Positive reinforcement for desired and appropriate replacement behaviors is included in a BSP to help make those behaviors more effective and efficient, which also makes problem behavior relatively more inefficient. As noted in the CBA section of this chapter, the presumed maintaining consequences for desired behaviors are too often inadequate to compete successfully with the maintaining

consequences for problem behavior. The CBA helps show support teams when existing reinforcers are not strong enough and do not provide sufficient incentive to support performance of desired behaviors. An essential component in a BSP is the regular delivery of strong positive reinforcement in terms of both the quality and the schedule of reinforcers, contingent on the occurrence of desired appropriate behaviors. Reinforcers for desired behavior must be strong enough and delivered with sufficient frequency to compete successfully with the consequences that maintain problem behaviors. For some students, it may be necessary to identify effective reinforcers through systematic reinforcer or preference assessments (Durand, Crimmins, Caulfield, & Taylor, 1989; Green et al., 1991; Roane, Vollmer, Ringdahl, & Marcus, 1998).

A commonly heard comment regarding the frequency of positive reinforcement is that a student needs or demands too much positive reinforcement. The issue is often that teachers and other support providers have difficulty delivering reinforcers frequently enough to meet students' needs. Self-management strategies offer one solution for this problem. Students may be taught to self-monitor their behavior and then to self-recruit reinforcement or feedback from staff (Mank & Horner, 1987; Smith & Sugai, 2000; Todd, Horner, & Sugai, 1999). A self-management approach to delivering positive reinforcement reduces the demand on staff to constantly monitor student performance and remember to deliver frequent reinforcers while at the same time increasing the independence and self-determination of the student. The student self-monitors and then cues staff that a reinforcer or feedback of some type should now be delivered.

Punishment Procedures As noted previously, punishment procedures may be included in a BSP when they are useful in making a support plan effective and beneficial for a student with problem behavior, appropriate to the contexts in which they are used, and implemented ethically and reasonably. In some cases, school or district policies may delineate some punishment procedures that will be included and implemented for all students in a school regardless of whether they have an individual BSP or IEP. Mild punishment procedures may sometimes be used in a manner similar to extinction, that is, as a procedure that helps make problem behavior ineffective or inefficient. In these cases, mild punishment of problem behavior is used in combination with prompting and reinforcing or teaching an appropriate alternative behavior, such as a functional communication response.

If punishment procedures are included in a BSP, clear guidelines for the use of punishers must be included in the written BSP. Behavior(s) that result in delivery of punishment should be clearly defined. Students and staff should be informed regarding school disciplinary policies and how, when, and what punishments will be used. A significant problem with the use of punishment procedures in schools is inconsistent and confusing implementation (Mayer & Sulzer-Azaroff, 2002). Support teams should use the least intrusive punishment that they expect to be effective and should carefully monitor the implementation and effects, including side effects, of the punishment procedure. The level of intrusiveness of punishment should be logically balanced by the value of the anticipated behavior change for the student with problem behaviors (Horner et al., 1990).

Safety or Emergency Intervention Plan An emergency/crisis plan should be included in the comprehensive BSP for any student with severe problem behaviors who engages in (or has some likelihood of engaging in) high-intensity self-injurious, aggressive, or destructive behaviors that threaten his or her safety and health or the safety and health of others. The purpose of an emergency/crisis plan is to protect people from harm, not to teach or change behavior. An emergency/crisis plan should (a) precisely define what constitutes an emergency/crisis; (b) describe in detail the specific intervention procedures to be implemented, including procedures designed to defuse and deescalate crisis behavior as well as procedures to deal with crisis behaviors directly once they occur; (c) define specific criteria for ending implementation of any intrusive or restrictive emergency procedures (e.g., criteria for ending an emergency restraint procedure); (d) describe in detail specific procedures for data collection related to the emergency/crisis; (e) detail reporting procedures to be followed and identify who should be informed; (f) describe training and caregiver support procedures designed to maintain capacity to respond effectively to emergency/crisis behaviors; and (g) describe debriefing, feedback, and other follow-up procedures to be implemented after implementation of emergency/crisis intervention. Readers interested in learning more about behavioral crisis prevention and management are referred to Carr et al. (1994) and Colvin et al. (1993).

9. *Evaluation and assessment*: The written BSP should include descriptions of data collection procedures, including forms and directions for using them, and procedures for ongoing monitoring and evaluation of plan effects. The evaluation plan will specify the behaviors to be tracked, the form(s) to be used, procedures for summarizing and sharing the information collected, and the person(s) responsible for each of the evaluation activities. A process for regular review and analysis of evaluation information should be identified so that timely decisions can be made regarding ongoing implementation and modification of plan procedures. An effective strategy is to set a regular meeting schedule for the support team to review plan effects and any issues arising related to plan implementation.

10. *Ensure contextual fit*: A BSP will be effective only if it is implemented with consistency and fidelity. Ensuring contextual fit is an element of the support planning process that may not show up in the written BSP but is important to ensuring fidelity and sustainability of implementation of the plan (Albin et al., 1996). Factors to consider in assessing the contextual fit of a BSP are the values of the implementers, skills of the implementers, resources available for BSP implementation, and administrative support provided for BSP implementation. In addition, the extent to which the BSP is perceived by implementers as being in the best interests of the focus student and its perceived effectiveness are considerations for contextual fit and the fidelity and sustainability of BSP implementation.

BSP Implementation Plan
Another feature of effective behavior support planning and BSP implementation that promotes effective implementation of support plans, although it is not included on the Horner et al. (1999–2000) checklist, is a written implementation plan. An implementation plan that provides a guide for getting the procedures and features of a comprehensive BSP into place and operational is an often-overlooked element of effective behavior support. Unfortunately, we have experienced many cases in which excellent behavior support plans have been developed but never fully implemented. Developing an implementation plan as part of the overall process of providing comprehensive support facilitates both initial and sustained implementation of planned procedures. The implementation plan identifies responsibilities and time lines for activities required to make plan

procedures happen. For example, it would identify who will obtain or develop needed materials and forms and when. The implementation plan also might describe procedures for implementing each of the various plan components, identify the sequence in which plan procedures will be implemented, and set target dates and time lines for implementation. The implementation plan can be used to identify any resources needed for plan implementation, training needs of those who will implement plan procedures, and strategies for meeting those training needs. Just as the comprehensive support plan itself is the product of a collaborative team

FIGURE 2–11
Sample Written Behavior Support Plan for Maya

Student:	Maya Reimeriz	Adoption Date:	10/20/03
DOB:	06/14/91		
Contacts:	Mrs. J. Reimeriz (555-6789)–mother		
Action team:	Ms. Craig (homeroom teacher), Ms. Schwartz (behavior specialist), Mr. Martinez (teacher), Ms. Durham (educational assistant), Mrs. Reimeriz (mother)		

Vision and Rationale for Support

Maya is 12 years old and lives at home with her parents and two older brothers. She has Down syndrome and moderate to severe intellectual disabilities (see student file for test scores). Her parents are very committed to Maya's inclusion in regular education classes and school settings. Maya enjoys fish, has a fish aquarium, and hopes to work at a fish or pet store in the future. A personal futures plan for Maya was done in September and produced the following goals: (a) high school graduation; (b) apartment living with a friend; (c) employment in a fish or pet store; (d) skill development in cooking, clothing care, basic household chores, money management, personal care, and time management; (e) joining a community group; and (f) maintenance of good physical health through diet and exercise. Currently, Maya reads at a first-grade level; follows step-by-step directions by reading words, icons, and photos; adds and subtracts single-digit numbers; identifies numbers 1 to 10; and copies two- to three-word phrases. She takes care of most of her dressing and personal care needs. Maya enjoys talking and listening to music with peers. Her mother notes that she likes to cook at home.

Maya engages in problem behaviors that are becoming increasingly intense. Her behaviors currently threaten her continued participation in regular school settings. The major concern is that in situations where Maya is not receiving social attention from peers, she will yell at the peers and then sometimes hit them. The hitting is becoming more frequent, and conflicts with peers are becoming more intense. She also sticks her tongue out at people and spits at people (although she rarely hits them with spit). She also has a history of throwing objects. Maya's parents and school staff are concerned for her future. Her team agrees that her life at school and home will be greatly improved by learning new social and communication skills to replace her problem behaviors.

Team Agreements

✓ Maya will receive her education in the neighborhood middle school.
✓ Maya's behavior support plan will be based on functional assessment outcomes.
✓ Maya's support plan will be implemented and evaluated on a consistent and regular basis for a specified period of time (i.e., the school year).
✓ Behavior support for Maya is a high priority since, with age, aggressive and inappropriate behaviors may become more frequent, disruptive, and problematic and may put her and those around her at even more risk.

FIGURE 2–11 (*Continued*)
Sample Written Behavior Support Plan for Maya

Description of Problem Behaviors

1. *Sticking tongue out*: Maya sticks her tongue out of her mouth as she orients her face to peers. Tongue protrudes clearly as she faces peer. Licking her lips and having her mouth relax open (no visibility of tongue) are not examples of sticking tongue out.

1. *Yelling*: Maya screams words (e.g., hey, hi-hi-hi, student names) or vocalizes (e.g., ahh) in a very loud tone. Intensity is clearly above hallway (or ambient) noise level. Speaking to peers and saying hi in a normal voice intensity are not examples of yelling.

3. *Spitting*: Maya spits in the direction of her peers. Spitting includes actual fluid being spit out or the imitation and intent to look as if fluid will be spit out. Spit does not need to hit someone to count as spitting.

4. *Hitting peers*: Hitting peers is defined as Maya striking (i.e., making contact with any degree of force) or attempting to strike (i.e., swinging at or punching at someone with no contact) peers with an open hand or fist. Accidentally bumping someone or tapping someone's shoulder to get their attention are not examples of hitting peers.

Maya's behaviors often happen in a sequence. When she sticks her tongue out, her peers usually laugh and imitate her. When peers walk away from Maya or don't respond to her sticking out her tongue, she often yells or spits at the closest peer(s). If peers challenge her or yell back at her, she may hit them. If Maya is particularly agitated about peer attention, she may yell and hit from the very beginning.

Summary of FBA and Hypothesis Statement

The functional behavioral assessment included the completion of a Request for Student Support Team Assistance; the FACTS, Parts A and B; and a full day of direct observation on a Monday using the Functional Assessment Observation form (O'Neill et al., 1997). From this process, the team identified two routines where Maya's problem behaviors were most likely to occur: (a) hallway transition periods and (b) activities with minimal structure (e.g., lunch, recess, large-group activities). In each case, Maya's team identified that Maya's problem behaviors were preceded by low levels of peer interaction and attention and rewarded by immediate access to peer attention (peers laugh, make comments, and yell back at her). The team agrees that Maya's problem behaviors are maintained primarily by getting peer attention. A diagram of the summary hypothesis statement for Maya is included on her competing behavior analysis form (see attached form). [Note that this form, which is included as Figure 6-9 in this chapter, would be attached as part of the written behavior support plan.]

General Intervention Plan for Maya

Overview: The main goals of Maya's behavior support plan will be to (a) reduce the unpredictability of when Maya will have opportunities to have access to and interactions with peers by providing her with a picture schedule, (b) teach Maya to use her picture schedule as a conversation book so that she can approach peers and initiate a conversation in an appropriate and respectful manner, and (c) provide Maya with a peer mentor during less structured activities so that she will get peer attention naturally and not have to engage in her problem behavior routine to get it. To help make the conversation book work for Maya, the team has agreed to spend 15 to 20 minutes explaining it to the other students and explaining how they should respond when she approaches them with it.

FIGURE 2-11 (*Continued*)

Sample Written Behavior Support Plan for Maya

Because hitting is not acceptable for any student, if Maya hits other students, the team and her parents have agreed to follow the school discipline policy on fighting. Maya will be removed from the situation to the vice principal's office, and her parents will be contacted.

Specific Procedures for Maya

Specific elements of Maya's behavior support plan are identified with an asterisk on the attached competing behavior analysis form.

Behavior Support Plan: Action Plan

Tasks	Person responsible	By when	Review date	Evaluation decision • Monitor • Modify discontinue
Prevention: Make problem behavior irrelevant (environmental redesign)				
Identify and schedule peer mentors	Ms. Craig	10/20	10/24	
Teaching: Make problem behavior inefficient (teach new skills)				
Teach use of picture schedule	Ms. Durham	10/30	10/31	
Teach use of communication book	Ms. Schwartz	10/30	10/31	
Extinction: Make problem behavior ineffective (minimize reward for problem behavior)				
Explain Maya's communication book and how to respond to it to students	Ms. Schwartz	10/30	10/31	
Reinforcement: Make desired behavior more rewarding.				
Ensure that Maya has opportunities for social interaction with peers	Ms. Craig and Ms. Durham	10/30	10/31	
Safety: Ensure safety of all (what to do in dangerous situations) (if needed)				
Use school discipline policy for hitting–give office discipline referral and send to vice principal	Ms. Craig informs staff	10/24	10/31	

FIGURE 2–11 (*Continued*)
Sample Written Behavior Support Plan for Maya

Behavior Support Plan: Evaluation Plan for Maya

Behavioral goal (use specific, observable, measurable descriptions of goal)

What is the short-term behavioral goal?

Teach Maya to use the communication book to approach peers in the hallway. Maya will approach peers
in the hallway with her communication book at least once per transition for 5 consecutive days.

Expected date: 10/30/03

What is the long-term behavioral goal?

Maya will interact appropriately with her peers in all school settings (classrooms, hallways, and so on)
for 4 weeks with no incidences of yelling, spitting or hitting.

Expected date: 05/31/04

Evaluation Procedures

Data to be collected	Procedures for data collection	Person responsible	Time line
Is plan being implemented?			
Peer mentor	Check in with teachers	Rachel	Daily for 2 weeks
Use of the communication book	Observations in the hallway	Trudy and Latisha	Daily for 2 weeks
Use of the picture schedule	Observations at bus and in classrooms	Latisha and teachers	Daily for 2 weeks
Is plan making a difference?			
Number of conversations with peers	Observations in hallway	Trudy and Latisha	Daily for 2 weeks
Number of incidents	Reports from staff	Trudy compiles	Weekly for first month
Office discipline referrals for hitting	SWIS^{TM} system	Trudy checks	Check weekly to start

Plan review date: weekly review for first month

Note: If emergency behavior management procedures are necessary, attach safety plan as separate sheet.

process, an implementation plan also should reflect consensus from the support team.

The implementation plan can also provide aids (e.g., checklists, one-page summaries) to promote implementation fidelity and long-term maintenance (Lucyshyn & Albin, 1993). Team and caregiver support strategies and procedures for sustaining long-term implementation of a support plan can be incorporated into the implementation plan. Procedures for sustaining a collaborative team process over time and for maintaining the team's focus on their vision and goals for a focus person's lifestyle are essential for the long-term delivery of effective comprehensive behavior support.

Examples of a written behavior support plan and an implementation plan for Maya are presented in Figure 2-11.

Summary

PBS is among the most exciting developments in the support technology available to children and adults with severe disabilities. Problem behaviors have long been a major obstacle to important living, educational, and employment opportunities. For too long we have assumed that to be part of typical environments, a person first needed to acquire appropriate behaviors. We now have learned that appropriate behaviors are best learned when appropriate supports are delivered *in* typical contexts. The procedures associated with PBS provide the means for assessing and designing support that will both reduce problem behaviors and develop the constellation of skills needed to have a real impact on how a person lives.

This chapter provides (a) a structure for understanding problem behaviors; (b) a set of procedures for conducting assessments that can transform chaotic, painful, confusing situations into understandable, logical patterns that can be addressed; and (c) a process for building support plans that will be both effective and doable.

The science of behavior analysis has defined an important set of mechanisms that describe how human beings learn from their environment. This science has been transformed into teaching and support procedures that have the potential to produce important changes in the behavior of children and adults with disabilities. PBS is the marriage of this science with fundamental values about the way people with disabilities should be part of our society. The challenge is to use the science with precision and the values with distinction. Those implementing PBS need the self-discipline to learn the science before they venture to change someone else's behavior, the wisdom to learn the values so they apply the technology with discretion, and the humility to work collaboratively and to continually assess the impact of interventions on the lives of those who receive support.

References

Alberto, P. A., & Troutman, A. C. (2003). *Applied behavior analysis for teachers* (6th ed.). Englewood Cliffs, NJ: Merrill/Prentice Hall.

Albin, R. W., Lucyshyn, J. M., Horner, R. H., & Flannery, K. B. (1996). Contextual fit for behavior support plans: A model for "goodness-of-fit." In L. K. Koegel, R. L. Koegel, & G. Dunlap (Eds.), *Positive behavioral support: Including people with difficult behavior in the community* (pp. 81-98). Baltimore: Paul H. Brookes.

Albin, R. W., O'Brien, M., & Horner, R. H. (1995). Analysis of an escalating sequence of problem behaviors: A case study. *Research in Developmental Disabilities, 16*, 133-147.

Anderson, J. L., Albin, R. W., Mesaros, R. A., Dunlap, G., & Morelli-Robbins, M. (1993). Issues in providing training to achieve comprehensive behavioral support. In J. Reichle & D. P. Wacker (Eds.), *Communicative alternatives to challenging behavior: Integrating functional assessment and intervention strategies* (pp. 363-406). Baltimore: Paul H. Brookes.

Arndorfer, R. E., Miltenberger, R. G., Woster, S. H., Rortvedt, A. K., & Gaffaney, T. (1994). Home-based descriptive and experimental analysis of problem behaviors in children. *Topics in Early Childhood Special Education, 14*(1), 64-87.

Axelrod, S. (1987). Functional and structural analysis of behavior: Approaches leading to reduced use of punishment procedures. *Research in Developmental Disabilities, 8*, 165-178.

Baer, D. M., Wolf, M. M., & Risley, T. G. (1968). Some current dimensions of applied behavior analysis. *Journal of Applied Behavior Analysis, 1*, 91-97.

Bergstrom, M. K., Horner, R. H., & Crone, D. A. (2004). *School-based team members conducting functional behavioral assessments in the general education environment. Manuscript under review.*

Berotti, D., & Durand, V. M. (1999). Communication-based interventions for students with sensory impairments and challenging behavior. In J. R. Scotti & L. H. Meyer (Eds.), *Behavioral intervention: Principles, models, and practices* (pp. 237-250). Baltimore: Paul H. Brookes.

Bijou, S., & Baer, D. M. (1961). *Child development: Vol. 1. A systematic and empirical theory*. New York: Appleton-Century-Crofts.

Bijou, S. W., Peterson, R. F., & Ault, M. H. (1968). A method to integrate descriptive and experimental field studies at the level of data and empirical concepts. *Journal of Applied Behavior Analysis, 1*, 175-191.

Carr, E. G. (1977). The motivation of self-injurious behavior: A review of some hypotheses. *Psychological Bulletin, 84*, 800-816.

Carr, E. G. (1988). Functional equivalence as a mechanism of response generalization. In R. H. Horner, R. L. Koegel, & G. Dunlap (Eds.), *Generalization and maintenance: Lifestyle changes in applied settings* (pp. 194–219). Baltimore: Paul H. Brookes.

Carr, E. G. (1994). Emerging themes in the functional analysis of problem behavior. *Journal of Applied Behavior Analysis, 27*, 393–399.

Carr, E. G. (2000). Reconceptualizing functional assessment failures: Comments on Kennedy. *Journal of Positive Behavior Interventions, 4*, 205–207.

Carr, E. G., & Carlson, J. I. (1993). Reduction of severe behavior problems in the community using a multicomponent treatment approach. *Journal of Applied Behavior Analysis, 26*, 157–172.

Carr, E. G., Dunlap, G., Horner, R. H., Koegel, R. L., Turnbull, A. P., Sailor, W., et al. (2002). Positive behavior support: Evolution of an applied science. *Journal of Positive Behavior Interventions, 4*, 4–16, 20.

Carr, E. G., & Durand, V. M. (1985a). Reducing behavior problems through functional communication training. *Journal of Applied Behavior Analysis, 18*, 111–126.

Carr, E. G., & Durand, V. M. (1985b). The social-communicative basis of severe behavior problems in children. In S. Reiss & R. Bootzin (Eds.), *Theoretical issues in behavior therapy* (pp. 219–254). New York: Academic Press.

Carr, E. G., & Durand, V. M. (1987, November). See me, help me. *Psychology Today*, 62–64.

Carr, E. G., Horner, R. H., Turnbull, A. P., Marquis, J. G., McLaughlin, D. M., McAtee, M. L., et al. (1999). *Positive behavior support for people with developmental disabilities: A research synthesis*. Washington, DC: American Association on Mental Retardation.

Carr, E. G., Levin, L., McConnachie, G., Carlson, J. I., Kemp, D. C., & Smith, C. E. (1994). *Communication-based intervention for problem behavior: A user's guide for producing positive change*. Baltimore: Paul H. Brookes.

Carr, E. G., Reeve, C. E., & Magito-McLaughlin, D. (1996). Contextual influences on problem behavior in people with developmental disabilities. In L. K. Koegel, R. L. Koegel, & G. Dunlap (Eds.), *Positive behavior support: Including people with difficult behavior in the community* (pp. 403–423). Baltimore: Paul H. Brookes.

Catania, A. (1992). B.F. Skinner, organism. *American Psychologist 47*(11), 1521–1530.

Colvin, G. (1993). *Managing acting-out behavior*. Eugene, OR: Behavior Associates.

Colvin, G., Sugai, G., & Patching, B. (1993). Precorrection: An instructional approach for managing predictable problem behaviors. *Intervention in School and Clinic, 28*, 143–150.

Crone, D. A., & Horner, R. H. (2003). *Building positive behavior support in schools: Functional behavioral assessment*. New York: Guilford.

Day, H. M., Horner, R. H., & O'Neill, R. E. (1994). Multiple functions of problem behaviors: Assessment and intervention. *Journal of Applied Behavior Analysis, 27*, 279–289.

Didden, R., Duker, P. C., & Korzilius, H. (1997). Meta-analytic study on treatment effectiveness for problem behaviors with individuals who have mental retardation. *American Journal on Mental Retardation, 101*, 387–399.

Donnellan, A. M., Mirenda, P. L., Mesaros, R. A., & Fassbender, L. L. (1984). Analyzing the communicative functions of aberrant behavior. *Journal of the Association for Persons with Severe Handicaps, 3*, 201–212.

Doss, S., & Reichle, J. (1991). Replacing excess behavior with an initial communicative repertoire. In J. Reichle, J. York, & J. Sigafoos (Eds.), *Implementing augmentative and alternative communication* (pp. 215–237). Baltimore: Paul H. Brookes.

Dunlap, G., Foster-Johnson, L., Clarke, S., Kern, L., & Childs, K. E. (1995). Modifying activities to produce functional outcomes: Effects on the disruptive behaviors of students with disabilities. *Journal of the Association for Persons with Severe Handicaps, 20*, 248–258.

Dunlap, G., Kern-Dunlap, L., Clarke, S., & Robbins, F. R. (1991). Functional assessment, curriculum revision, and severe behavior problems. *Journal of Applied Behavior Analysis, 24*, 387–397.

Dunlap, G., & Kincaid, D. (2001). The widening world of functional assessment: Comments on four manuals and beyond. *Journal of Applied Behavior Analysis, 34*, 365–377.

Durand, V. M. (1988). The Motivation Assessment Scale. In M. Hersen & A. Bellack (Eds.), *Dictionary of behavioral assessment techniques* (pp. 309–310). Elmsford, NY: Pergamon.

Durand, V. M. (1990). *Severe behavior problems: A functional communication approach*. New York: Guilford.

Durand, V. M., & Carr, E. G. (1991). Functional communication training to reduce challenging behavior: Maintenance and application in new settings. *Journal of Applied Behavior Analysis, 24*, 251–264.

Durand, V. M., & Carr, E. G. (1992). An analysis of maintenance following functional communication training. *Journal of Applied Behavior Analysis, 25*, 777–794.

Durand, V. M., Crimmins, D. B., Caulfield, M., & Taylor, J. (1989). Reinforcer assessment I: Using problem behavior to select reinforcers. *Journal of the Association for Persons with Severe Handicaps, 14*, 113–126.

Ervin, R. A., Radford, P. M., Bertsch, K., Piper, A. L., Ehrhardt, K. E., & Poling, A. (2001). A descriptive analysis and critique of the empirical literature on school-based functional assessment. *School Psychology Review, 30*, 193–209.

Ferro, J., Foster-Johnson, L., & Dunlap, G. (1996). The relationship between curricular activities and the problem behavior of students with mental retardation. *American Journal on Mental Retardation, 101*, 184–194.

Flannery, K. B., & Horner, R. H. (1994). The relationship between predictability and problem behavior for students with severe disabilities. *Journal of Behavioral Education, 4*, 157–176.

Fox, L., & Dunlap, G. (Winter 2002). Family-centered practices in behavior support. *Beyond Behavior 11*, 24–27.

Green, C. W., Reid, D. H., Canipe, V. S., & Gardner, S. M. (1991). A comprehensive evaluation of reinforcer identification processes for persons with profound multiple handicaps. *Journal of Applied Behavior Analysis, 24*, 537–552.

Gresham, F. M. (2002). Teaching social skills to high-risk children and youth: Preventive and remedial strategies. In M. A. Shinn, H. M. Walker, & G. Stoner (Eds.), *Interventions for academic and behavior problems II: Preventive and remedial approaches* (pp. 403–432). Bethesda, MD: National Association of School Psychologists.

Gresham, F. M., McIntyre, L. L., Olson-Tinker, H., Dolstra, L., McLaughlin, V., & Van, M. (2004). Relevance of functional behavioral assessment research for school-based interventions and positive behavioral support. *Research in Developmental Disabilities, 25,* 19-37.

Guess, D., & Carr, E. G. (1991). Emergence and maintenance of stereotypy and self-injury. *American Journal on Mental Retardation, 96,* 299-319.

Hanley, G. P., & Iwata, B. A. (2003). Functional analysis of problem behavior: A review. *Journal of Applied Behavior Analysis, 36,* 147-185.

Holburn. S., Jacobson, J. W., Vietze, P. M., Schwartz, A. A., & Sersen, E. (2000). Quantifying the process and outcomes of person-centered planning. *American Journal on Mental Retardation, 105,* 402-416.

Holburn, S., & Vietze, P. M. (2002). *Person-centered planning: Research, practice, and future directions.* Baltimore: Paul H. Brookes.

Horner, R. H. (1999). Positive behavior supports. In M. L. Wehmeyer & J. R. Patton, (Eds.), *Mental Retardation in the 21st Century* (pp. 181-196). Austin, TX: PRO-ED.

Horner, R. H., Albin, R. W., Borgmeier, C., & Salantine, S. P. (2003, May). *Moving from functional assessment to the design of behavior support.* Symposium presented at the Association for Behavior Analysis Annual Convention, San Francisco.

Horner, R. H., Albin, R. W., Sprague, J. R., & Todd, A. W. (2000). Positive behavior support. In M. E. Snell & F. Brown (Eds.), *Instruction of students with severe disabilities* (5th ed., pp. 207-243). Upper Saddle River, NJ: Merrill/Prentice Hall.

Horner, R. H., & Billingsley, F. F. (1988). The effect of competing behavior on the generalization and maintenance of adaptive behavior in applied settings. In R. H. Horner, G. Dunlap, & R. L. Koegel (Eds.), *Generalization and maintenance: Lifestyle changes in applied settings* (pp. 197-220). Baltimore: Paul H. Brookes.

Horner, R. H., Day, H. M., & Day, J. (1997). Using neutralizing routines to reduce problem behaviors. *Journal of Applied Behavior Analysis, 39,* 601-614.

Horner, R. H., Diemer, S. M., & Brazeau, K. C. (1992). Educational support for students with severe problem behaviors in Oregon: A descriptive analysis from the 1987-1988 school year. *Journal of the Association for Persons with Severe Handicaps, 17,* 154-169.

Horner, R. H., Dunlap, G., Koegel, R. L., Carr, E. G., Sailor, W., Anderson, J., et al. (1990). Toward a technology of "nonaversive" behavioral support. *Journal of the Association for Persons with Severe Handicaps, 15,* 125-132.

Horner, R. H., Sugai, G., Todd, A. W., & Lewis-Palmer, T. (1999-2000). Elements of behavior support plans: A technical brief. *Exceptionality, 8,* 205-216.

Horner, R. H., Vaughn, B., Day, H. M., & Ard, B. (1996). The relationship between setting events and problem behavior. In L. K. Koegel, R. L. Koegel, & G. Dunlap (Eds.), *Positive behavioral support: Including people with difficult behavior in the community* (pp. 381-402). Baltimore: Paul H. Brookes.

Individuals with Disabilities Education Act, Amendments of 1997. (1997). H.R. 5, 105th Congress, 1st Sess.

Ingram, K.. Lewis-Palmer, T., & Sugai, G. (in press). Function-based intervention planning: Comparing the effectiveness of FBA indicated and contra-indicated interventions plans. *Journal of Positive Behavior Interventions.*

Iwata, B. A., Dorsey, M. F., Slifer, K. J., Bauman, K. E., & Richman, G. S. (1982). Toward a functional analysis of self-injury. *Analysis and Intervention in Developmental Disabilities, 2,* 3-20.

Janney, R., & Snell, M. (2000). *Behavioral support.* Baltimore: Paul H. Brookes.

Kincaid, D. (1996). Person-centered planning. In L. K. Koegel, R. L. Koegel, & G. Dunlap (Eds.), *Positive behavior support: Including people with difficult behavior in the community* (pp. 439-465). Baltimore: Paul H. Brookes.

Koegel, L. K., Koegel, R. L., & Dunlap, G. (1996). *Positive behavioral support: Including people with difficult behavior in the community.* Baltimore: Paul H. Brookes.

Lalli, J. S., Browder, D. M., Mace, F. C., & Brown, D. K. (1993). Teacher use of descriptive analysis data to implement interventions to decrease students' problem behavior. *Journal of Applied Behavior Analysis, 26,* 227-238.

Lerman, D. C., & Iwata, B. A. (1993). Descriptive and experimental analysis of variables maintaining self-injurious behavior. *Journal of Applied Behavior Analysis, 26,* 293-319.

Lewis-Palmer, T. (1998). *Using functional assessment strategies in regular school classroom settings with students at-risk for school failure.* Unpublished doctoral dissertation, University of Oregon, Eugene.

Lucyshyn, J., & Albin, R. W. (1993). Comprehensive support to families of children with disabilities and behavior problems: Keeping it "friendly." In G. H. S. Singer & L. E. Powers (Eds.), *Families, disability, and empowerment* (pp. 365-407). Baltimore: Paul H. Brookes.

Lucyshyn, J. M., Albin, R. W., & Nixon, C. D. (1997). Embedding comprehensive behavioral support in family ecology: An experimental, single-case analysis. *Journal of Consulting and Clinical Psychology, 65,* 241-251.

Lucyshyn, J. M., Kayser, A. T., Irvin, L. K., & Blumberg, E. R. (2002). Functional assessment and positive behavior support at home with families: Designing effective and contextually appropriate behavior support plans. In J. M. Lucyshyn, G. Dunlap, & R. W. Albin (Eds.), *Families and positive behavior support: Addressing problem behavior in family contexts* (pp. 97-132). Baltimore: Paul H. Brookes.

Mace, F. C., & Lalli, J. S. (1991). Linking descriptive and experimental analysis in the treatment of bizarre speech. *Journal of Applied Behavior Analysis, 24,* 553-562.

Mank, D. M., & Horner, R. H. (1987). Self-recruited feedback: A cost-effective procedure for maintaining behavior. *Research in Developmental Disabilities, 8,* 91-112.

March, R., & Horner, R. (1998, May). *School-wide behavioral support: Extending the impact of ABA by expanding the unit of analysis.* Presentation at the Association for Behavior Analysis Annual Convention, Orlando, FL.

March, R., Horner, R. H., Lewis-Palmer, T., Brown, D., Crone, D., Todd, A. W., et al. (2000). *Functional Assessment Checklist for Teachers and Staff (FACTS).* Eugene: University of Oregon, Department of Educational and Community Supports.

Marquis, J. G., Horner, R. H., Carr, E. G., Turnbull, A. P., Thompson, M., Behrens, G. A., et al. (2000). A meta-analysis of positive behavior support. In R. M. Gerston & E. P. Schiller (Eds.), *Contemporary special education research: Syntheses of the knowledge base on critical instructional issues* (pp.137-178). Mahwah, NJ: Lawrence Erlbaum Associates.

Mayer, G. R., & Sulzer-Azaroff, B. (2002). Interventions for vandalism and aggression. In M. R. Shinn, H. M. Walker, & G. Stoner (Eds.), *Interventions for academic and behavior problems II: Preventive and remedial approaches.* Silver Spring, MD: National Association of School Psychologists.

Meyer, L. H., & Evans, I. M. (1989). *Nonaversive interventions for behavior problems: A manual for home and community.* Baltimore: Paul H. Brookes.

Moes, D. R., & Frea, W. D. (2000). Using family context to inform intervention planning for the treatment of a child with autism. *Journal of Positive Behavior Interventions, 2,* 40-46.

Moore, J. W., Edwards, R. P., Sterling-Turner, H. E., Riley, J., DuBard, M., & McGeorge, A. (2002). Teacher acquisition of functional analysis methodology. *Journal of Applied Behavior Analysis, 35,* 73-77.

Mount, B. (1994). Benefits and limitations or personal futures planning. In V. J. Bradley, J. W. Ashbaugh, & B. C. Blaney (Eds.), *Creating individual supports for people with developmental disabilities* (pp. 97-108). Baltimore: Paul H. Brookes.

Munk, D. D., & Repp, A. C. (1994). The relationship between instructional variables and problem behavior: A review. *Exceptional Children, 60,* 390-401.

Nelson, J. R., Roberts, M. L., Mathur, S. R., & Rutherford, R. B., Jr. (1999). Has public policy exceeded our knowledge base? A review of the functional behavioral assessment literature. *Behavioral Disorders, 24,* 169-179.

New York State ARC v. Carey, 393 F. Supp. 715, 718-19 (E.D.N.Y. 1975) and *New York State ARC v. Carey,* No. 72-C356/357 (E.D.N.Y., 1975).

Newcomer, L. L., & Lewis, T. J. (in press). Functional behavioral assessment: An investigation of assessment reliability and effectiveness of function-based interventions. *Journal of Emotional and Behavioral Disorders.*

Newton, J. S., & Horner, R. H. (2004). Emerging trends in methods for research and evaluation of behavioral interventions. Pp. 495-515. In E. Emerson, T. Thompson, T. Parmenter, & C. Hatton (Eds.), *International handbook of methods for research and evaluation in intellectual disabilities.* New York: Wiley.

Nirje, B. (1969). The normalization principle and its human management implications. In R. Kugel & W. Wolfensberger (Eds.), *Changing patterns in residential services for the mentally retarded* (pp. 179-195). Washington, DC: President's Committee on Mental Retardation.

Northup, J., Broussard, C., Jones, K., George, T., Vollmer, T. R., & Herring, M. (1995). The differential effects of teacher and peer attention on the disruptive classroom behavior of three children with a diagnosis of attention deficit hyperactivity disorder. *Journal of Applied Behavior Analysis, 28,* 227-228.

Northup, J., Wacker, D., Sasso, G., Steege, M., Cigrand, K., Cook, J., et al. (1991). A brief functional analysis of aggressive and alternative behavior in an outclinic setting. *Journal of Applied Behavior Analysis, 24,* 509-522.

O'Brien, C. J., O'Brien, J., & Mount, B. (1997). Person-centered planning has arrived or has it? *Mental Retardation, 35,* 480-484.

O'Neill, R. E., Horner, R. H., Albin, R. W., Sprague, J. R., Storey, K., & Newton, J. S. (1997). *Functional assessment for problem behavior: A practical handbook* (2nd ed.). Pacific Grove, CA: Brooks/Cole.

O'Reilly, M. (1997). Functional analysis of episodic self-injury correlated with recurrent otitis media. *Journal of Applied Behavior Analysis, 30,* 165-167.

Pace, G. M., Ivancic, M. R., Edwards, G. L., Iwata, B. A., & Page, T. J. (1985). Assessment of stimulus preference and reinforcer values with profoundly retarded individuals. *Journal of Applied Behavior, 18,* 249-256.

Reid, R., & Nelson, J. R. (2002). The utility, acceptability, and practicality of functional behavioral assessment for students with high-incidence problem behaviors. *Remedial Special Education, 23,* 15-23.

Reiss, S., & Aman, M. (Eds.). (1998). *Psychotropic medication and developmental disabilities: The international consensus handbook.* Columbus: Ohio State University, Nisanger Center.

Repp, A. C., Felce, D., & Barton, L. E. (1988). Basing the treatment of stereotypic and self-injurious behaviors on hypotheses of their causes. *Journal of Applied Behavior Analysis, 21,* 281-289.

Repp, A. C., & Singh, N. N. (1990). *Perspectives on the use of nonaversive and aversive interventions for persons with developmental disabilities.* Pacific Grove, CA: Brooks/Cole.

Roane, H. S., Vollmer, T. R., Ringdahl, J. E., & Marcus, B. A. (1998). Evaluation of a brief stimulus preference assessment. *Journal of Applied Behavior Analysis, 31,* 605-620.

Sandler, L. (2001). *Goodness-of-fit and the viability of behavioral support plans: A survey of direct care adult residential staff.* Unpublished doctoral dissertation, University of Oregon, Eugene.

Sasso, G. M., Reimers, R. M., Cooper, L. J., Wacker, D., Berg, W., Steege, M., et al. (1992). Use of descriptive and experimental analyses to identify the functional properties of aberrant behavior in school settings. *Journal of Applied Behavior Analysis, 25,* 809-821.

Schalock, R., & Alonso, M. A. V. (2002). *Handbook on quality of life for human service practitioners.* Washington, DC: American Association on Mental Retardation.

Shavelson, R. J., & Towne, L. (Eds.). (2002). *Scientific research in education.* Washington, DC: National Academy Press.

Shukla, S., & Albin, R. W. (1996). Effects of extinction alone and extinction plus functional communication training on covariation of problem behaviors. *Journal of Applied Behavior Analysis, 29,* 565-568.

Skinner, B. F. (1953). *Science and human behavior.* New York: Macmillan.

Smith, B. W., & Sugai, G. (2000). A self-management functional assessment-based behavior support plan for a middle school student with EBD. *Journal of Positive Behavior Interventions, 2,* 208-217.

Sprague, J. R., & Horner, R. H. (1992). Covariation within functional response classes: Implications for treatment of severe problem behavior. *Journal of Applied Behavior Analysis, 25,* 735-745.

Sprague, J. R., & Horner, R. H. (1999). Low frequency, high intensity problem behavior: Toward an applied technology of functional analysis and intervention. In A. C. Repp & R. H. Horner (Eds.), *Functional analysis of problem behavior: From effective assessment to effective support* (pp. 98-116). Belmont, CA: Wadsworth.

Sugai, G., Horner, R. H., Dunlap, G., Hieneman, M., Lewis, T. J., Nelson, C. M., et al. (2000). Applying positive behavior support and functional behavioral assessment in schools. *Journal of Positive Behavior Interventions, 2*, 131-143.

Sugai, G., Horner, R. H., & Gresham, F. (2002). Behaviorally effective school environments. In M. R. Shinn, G. Stoner, & H. M. Walker (Eds.), *Interventions for academic and behavior problems: Preventive and remedial approaches* (pp. 315-350). Silver Spring, MD: National Association for School Psychologists.

Sugai, G., Lewis-Palmer, T., & Hagan-Burke, S. (1999-2000). Overview of the functional behavioral assessment process. *Exceptionality, 8*, 149-160.

Todd, A. W., Horner, R. H., & Sugai, G. (1999). Self-monitoring and self-recruited praise: Effects on problem behavior, academic engagement, and work completion in a typical classroom. *Journal of Positive Behavior Interventions, 1*, 66-76, 122.

Todd, A. W., Horner, R. H., Sugai, G., & Colvin, G. (1999). Individualizing school-wide discipline for students with chronic problem behaviors: A team approach. *Effective School Practices, 17*, 72-82.

Touchette, P. E., MacDonald, R. F., & Langer, S. N. (1985). A scatter plot for identifying stimulus control of problem behavior. *Journal of Applied Behavior Analysis, 18*, 343-351.

Turnbull, A. P., & Ruef, M. (1996). Family perspectives on problem behavior. *Mental Retardation, 34*, 280-293.

Umbreit, J. (1995). Functional analysis of disruptive behavior in an inclusive classroom. *Journal of Early Interventions, 20*, 18-29.

U.S. Department of Education. (1997). *To assume the free and appropriate education of all children with disabilities: Nineteenth annual report to congress on the implementation of the Individuals with Disabilities Education Act.* Washington, DC: Author.

Van Houten, R., & Rolider, A. (1991). Applied behavior analysis. In J. L. Matson & J. A. Mulick (Eds.), *Handbook of mental retardation* (pp. 569-585). New York: Pergamon.

Vollmer, T. R., & Van Camp, C. M. (1998). Experimental designs to evaluate antecedent control. In J. K. Luiselli & M. J. Cameron (Eds.), *Antecedent control: Innovation approaches to behavioral support* (pp. 87-111). Baltimore: Paul H. Brookes.

Wacker, D. P., Berg, W. K., Asmus, J. M., Harding, J. W., & Cooper, L. J. (1998). Experimental analysis of antecedent influences on challenging behavior. In J. K. Luiselli & M. J. Cameron (Eds.), *Antecedent control: Innovation approaches to behavioral support* (pp. 67-86). Baltimore: Paul H. Brookes.

Wacker, D. P., Steege, M., Northup, J., Reimers, T., Berg, W., & Sasso, G. (1990). Use of functional analysis and acceptability measures to assess and treat severe behavior problems: An outpatient clinic model. In A. C. Repp & N. Singh (Eds.), *Perspectives on the use of aversive and nonaversive interventions for persons with developmental disabilities* (pp. 349-359). Pacific Grove, CA: Brooks/Cole.

Wacker, D. P., Steege, M. W., Northup, J., Sasso, G., Berg, W., Reimers, T., et al. (1990). A component analysis of functional communication training across three topographies of severe behavior problems. *Journal of Applied Behavior Analysis, 23*, 417-429.

Wehmeyer, M., & Schwartz, M. (1997). Self-determination and positive adult outcomes: A follow-up study of youth with mental retardation and learning disabilities. *Exceptional Children, 63*, 256.

Willis, T. J., LaVigna, G. W., & Donnellan, A. M. (1987). *Behavior assessment guide.* Los Angeles: Institute for Applied Behavior Analysis.

Wolfensberger, W. (1983). Social role valorization: A proposed new term for the principle of normalization. *Mental Retardation, 21*, 234-239.

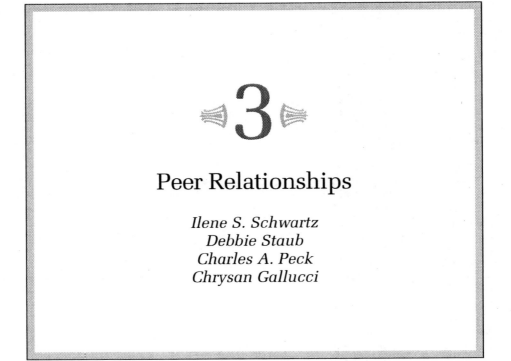

3

Peer Relationships

Ilene S. Schwartz
Debbie Staub
Charles A. Peck
Chrysan Gallucci

- Waving hello to your teacher when you enter the classroom
- Sharing materials with your classmates during an art project
- Arguing with a friend about who gets to use the swing first
- Helping a classmate clean up materials at the end of a science project

These are all examples of social behaviors that students with and without disabilities could practice at school. The development of these simple, as well as more complex, social behaviors are among the most important developmental outcomes of childhood (Shonkoff & Phillips, 2000). Human beings are the most profoundly social of all creatures. Our development, well-being, and happiness are utterly dependent on the quality of our relationships with others. From the earliest establishment of regularity and predictability of social exchanges between infants and caregivers (Kaye, 1982) to our uniquely human construction of "webs of significance" and meaning as adults (Geertz,

1973), the social relationships of our lives form the crucible within which we come to know the world, each other, and ourselves (Bruner, 1990). With this viewpoint in mind, we attempt in this chapter to highlight the role that social relationships play in the development of children and youth with disabilities and to describe some of the strategies teachers and other caregivers can use to support this process.

The study of social behavior has always been intricately woven into the study of educating people with disabilities. Although some early work in this area put the emphasis on skills (while ignoring the context in which the skills needed to be performed), current work in developmental psychology, special education, and applied behavior analysis emphasizes relationships and the context of those relationships. For example, Vygotsky (1978) and other social-cultural theorists place issues of relationships at the fulcrum of their claims about how children become competent members of human communities (e.g., Bruner, 1996;

Cole, 1996; Lave & Wenger, 1991). Behavior analysts emphasize the need to look at behavior in context, encouraging educators, families, and researchers to attend to the social and ecological validity of their interventions (Baer, Wolf, & Risley, 1987; Schwartz & Baer, 1991; Wolf, 1977). The purpose of this chapter is to focus the discussion of the social lives of children with disabilities on relationships rather than skills. We want readers to consider the context and function of social behavior and think about how the presence or absence of meaningful social relationships can impact the quality of life of students with severe disabilities.

To help bring these concepts to life, we want to introduce you to three students with severe disabilities. All these students attend inclusive schools and have friends. We could not have made that statement when we first met these students. They made friends as a result of participating in inclusive educational placements that valued social relationships, developed and maintained the contexts to support peer relationships, and provided systematic instruction for students, with and without disabilities, focused on facilitating those relationships. These students have different diagnoses, strengths, interests, and challenges, but all have been enriched by social relationships with their typically developing peers.

Three Case Examples

Sean

Sean is a first grader with autism. We first met Sean when he was attending an inclusive preschool. He was referred to the preschool after "being expelled" from three different child care programs. All the child care providers described Sean as a "sweet little boy, as long as you let him do his own thing." When Sean was asked by teachers or other children to participate in activities, he refused. Sometimes these refusals included screaming, hitting children, or throwing objects. Sean's parents were surprised when they observed him at the various child care programs and noticed that he was almost always "shunned" by the other children. But it was different in the inclusive preschool—Sean flourished. He learned to be more flexible, interact successfully with other children, and even manage his anger and disappointment. He also developed a love of baseball (shared by his parents) and learned how to trade baseball cards. In kindergarten, he learned to read, and by the beginning of first grade, he would often arrive at school after he had read the sports page for the latest update on his favorite teams.

Carrie

Carrie, who has Down syndrome, is in fourth grade and has attended inclusive classrooms since she was in second grade. Her teachers and peers characterize her as a playful, occasionally stubborn or shy, and always interesting child. Carrie has always been small for her age, and her carrot-top hair, perhaps a symbol of her fiery personality, hangs close to her shoulders. She loves to draw and is quite verbal but is often difficult to understand. She works with a communication specialist on her articulation and voice volume regularly. She is learning how to use pictures, symbols, and nonverbal communication to make herself better understood. Interestingly, often her peers

understand her communicative attempts better than adults. Her reading level is close to that of a typical first grader's. Carrie takes great pride in being a member of her school. In the past couple of years, she has shown significant growth in her ability to do things independently.

Cole

Cole is a 17-year-old young man with severe disabilities who attends high school as a junior. Cole started attending an inclusive school in third grade. His parents were active advocates for inclusion and believe that the presence of typically developing peers improved the quality of Cole's education and his life. Cole contracted spinal meningitis at age 1, resulting in early paralysis and severe seizures. Cole's serious health problems and challenging behaviors (e.g., tantrums, aggression toward adults and objects) have often been frustrating for both his family and teachers.

Described by his neurologist as having one of the most severe cases of seizure disorders in the state, Cole's "good" days and "bad" days are often determined by his rate of seizure activity and the effects of the medication he takes to control them. Cole uses an augmentative system as his primary mode for communication and is quite fluent with it. He has strong social initiation skills, and his expressive vocabulary has increased greatly in the past few years. With close friends and family, he is easily understood. Because of an increase in violent behaviors the summer of his seventh-grade year, Cole's parents enrolled him in a behavioral treatment group home for 18 months, where he lived full time as a resident. During that time, Cole was able to continue his education at the junior high school he had been attending. Currently, Cole lives with a foster family in close proximity to his parents, whom he sees regularly.

Peer Relationships and Developmental Outcomes

Social relationships are important both as developmental outcomes and as the context for learning. Researchers, educators, and parents all agree that developing friendships and positive relationships with peers is one of the important tasks of childhood (e.g., Hart & Risley, 1996; Hartup, 1983; Wolfberg, 1999). There is also increasing evidence that the lack of positive peer relationships (i.e., children who are ignored or rejected by their peers) is a risk factor for a number of troubling developmental outcomes, such as mental health problems and poor adjustment. Schools provide multiple opportunities for social interaction, and many classrooms actually require students to work together to achieve classroom and curricular goals. For example, in early childhood classrooms, using activity-based or embedded learning opportunities is considered a best practice (Sandall, Hemmeter, Smith, & McLean, 2004). In elementary schools, much of the curriculum is based on cooperative or experiential learning (Greenwood, Maheady, & Delquadri, 2002). Throughout school, the informal social curriculum is taught and learned on playgrounds, in clubs, and in the school hallways.

In addition to the personal satisfaction and support that people gain from personal relationships, students have the opportunity to learn important social, communicative, academic, and cognitive skills in the context of peer relationships. For example, during group activities in classrooms, students are participating in a social context in which they may learn to attend to group instructions, to observe what the group is doing as a cue for what is expected ("mass modeling"), and to make choices and regulate behavior without direct adult intervention. During free choice activities, students learn how to make choices, negotiate sharing materials with others, and are often highly motivated to learn the communicative, motor, or cognitive skills necessary to complete their preferred activities. All these may be recognized as critical skills for competent participation in a tremendous variety of highly valued activities, roles, and settings within our culture.

In the following section, we describe a conceptual framework we and our colleagues have developed that helps make sense of the complex connections between social experiences, skill acquisition, and participation in valued roles, activities, and settings (Billingsley,

FIGURE 3–1
Lunchtime is often hurried but filled with social exchanges between peers

Gallucci, Peck, Schwartz, & Staub, 1996; Peck et al., 1994; Schwartz 2000). We then offer a set of recommendations for interventions based on this framework. We conclude our chapter with some suggestions regarding assessment and evaluation strategies that we believe are useful in documenting outcomes related to peer relationships and with comments related to the effect of experiences with the inclusion of students with severe disabilities on the lives of children and adolescents who are typically developing.

In this chapter and elsewhere (Billingsley et al., 1996; Peck et al., 1994; Schwartz, 2000), we make the claim that *participation in socially valued roles, activities, and settings is both the most fundamental outcome of the developmental process and the primary means by which development is achieved.* This view is at odds with views of development as acquisition of skills, which has dominated the field of special education, including special education for individuals with severe disabilities, for many years. We do not consider skills to be unimportant. Rather, we broaden our analysis of how students with severe disabilities come to be more competent members of human communities to include more detailed consideration of the relationships between skill acquisition and a variety of social context factors.

Our changing views of development have emerged in part from talking to the parents of children with severe disabilities who participated in inclusive educational placements and hearing their stories about the profound effects these placements had on all aspects of their children's development. Cole's mother shares a typical story.

> Her son attended a segregated preschool and early elementary program. Although she was pleased with some of the academic skills he was learning, he was not making friends, he was not connected to the school or community, and as his parent she felt it was difficult to be connected to the school since the location of his program changed almost every year. After attending an inclusive school for 1 year, Cole had friends, had been invited to a birthday party, and was recognized by classmates in the supermarket who came over to say hello. Cole's mother became a member of the Parent–Teacher Association at the school.

Although being invited to a birthday party is not a developmental outcome measured by any state test of educational achievement, it is an important indicator of belonging, friendships, and membership. After hearing many stories from parents about the changes inclusive education made in the quality of life for their children with severe disabilities, we designed a research project to help us describe the effects of inclusive education on the academic and social development of students with severe disabilities. We implemented a 4-year program of research in which we followed 43 children with moderate or severe disabilities who have been enrolled full time in regular classrooms (Consortium for Research on Social Relationships, Cooperative Agreement #H086A20003, awarded to Syracuse University from the U.S. Department of Education). We collected and analyzed data from multiple sources, including classroom observations; interviews with teachers, parents, nondisabled peers, and paraeducators; video recordings and documents such as individualized education programs (IEPs); and examples of children's work, in an effort to describe outcomes that occur for students in inclusive school programs.

An important feature of this work has been our efforts to construct an understanding of outcomes for students with disabilities in active dialogue with parents, teachers, and students. In these conversations and in the more "objective" data we collected, we were confronted again and again by compelling evidence of change in children's lives that was not adequately

described in terms of the simple acquisition of skills. Analyzing hundreds of excerpts from our observational and interview data, we developed a conceptual framework that describes the types of outcomes we observed for students with severe disabilities in inclusive school settings. Because the framework was developed out of our observations of fairly typical school settings, including regular classrooms, playgrounds, cafeterias, and other activity contexts, it offers considerable guidance for teachers and specialists who wish to use these settings as a context for supporting the development of learners with severe disabilities.

The Outcome Framework

The outcome patterns that have emerged in our project are conceptualized in terms of three broad domains. First, our findings suggest that many of the children we studied in inclusive classrooms were in fact learning many of the same types of *skills* that have been the traditional focus of special education outcome assessment. These include social and communication skills, academics, and functional skills. A second domain of outcomes we observed was the extent to which children with severe disabilities achieve *membership* or a sense of belonging in the formal and informal groups that make up the social fabric of the classroom and school (Schnorr, 1990). Finally, we observed that children in inclusive classrooms may develop a wide variety of personal *relationships* with other children. Each of these broad outcome domains (i.e., skills, membership, and relationships) has strong effects on each other. Moreover, each of the domains may be viewed in terms of its relationship with a higher-order outcome, which we conceptualized as increased participation in valued roles, activities, and settings of the community and culture (Bronfenbrenner, 1979; Lave & Wenger, 1991). Figure 3–2 depicts the relationship between each of the three outcome domains and the higher-order goal of increased participation.

Ultimately, peer relationships are both an end in themselves (and an important one) and an important means of support that enable a child to participate in a variety of valued roles, activities, and settings. Relationships between children with severe disabilities and their nondisabled peers are strongly related to other types of outcomes, including the child's individual skills (e.g., social and communication skills) and status as a "member" of the class or social group. We describe each of these outcome domains in more detail.

FIGURE 3–2
Inclusive Education Research Group Outcome Framework

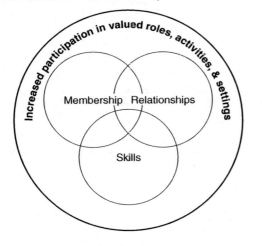

Membership

We use the term "membership" to refer to the phenomenological sense of belonging to a social group, such as a classroom, cooperative work group, or friendship clique. Membership is not something we can observe directly. However, we can make inferences about the extent to which a child is treated as a member of a group by observing things such as accommodations group members make to include a child, shared symbols used by the group (e.g., special T-shirts, team names, uniforms), and rituals that occur in the group context (e.g., special greetings, activities or roles performed only by group members).

Membership is an important outcome in and of itself in the lives of children, including those with severe disabilities (Ferguson, 1994). In fact, membership outcomes have received very high "importance" ratings from parents and teachers in social validation studies of the outcome framework (Peck et al., 1994). The extent to which students with severe disabilities are viewed as "members" of the classroom affects the kinds of opportunities they are likely to have for participating in social relationships and other classroom activities (Schnorr, 1990). Examples of membership include children with severe disabilities being included on the job chart alongside their nondisabled peers, providing a nonspeaking role (or a role using a voice output augmentative communication device) for a student with severe disabilities in a school play, and making sure that the names of the children with disabilities

are included on the monthly birthday list that is read by the principal at the school assembly (Copeland, Hughes, Agran, Wehmeyer & Fowler, 2002; Williams & Downing, 1998).

Relationships

This domain of outcomes refers to the characteristics and extent of personal (dyadic) relationships between children with disabilities and their peers. We characterized relationships between students with disabilities and other individuals (both with and without disabilities) on the basis of consistencies in their social interactions over time, interviews with teachers and parents, and (when possible) informal interviews with children themselves. As in most relationships, the qualitative features of the social relationships we observed between individual children are not static but often vary in specific contexts (Fiske, 1992).

Clearly, a high-priority outcome for children with severe disabilities, as for any child, is the development of friendships. Friendships have been the focus of most analyses of social relationships in the professional literature to date (Downing, Spencer, & Cavallaro, 2004; Fisher, 2001; Haring, 1991; Meyer, Park, Grenot-Scheyer, Schwartz, & Harry, 1998). However, other types of relationships also play an important role as sources of learning and support for students with severe disabilities. Our observations of the variety of relationships that emerge between children with disabilities and their nondisabled peers led us to identify four "types" of relationships—play/companion, helper (giver), helpee (receiver), and conflictual—each of which offers important learning opportunities for children. It is this range of relationships that adds richness and depth to the human interactions that factor into our quality of life. Examples of these relationships include the companionship of the person sitting next to you on the school bus, the helper who points out what page to turn to in the reading book, helping other students by handing out journals, and the conflict you may have with a peer when both of you want to use the last swing on the playground.

Skills

The third domain of outcomes we observed in inclusive classrooms is comprised of the academic and behavioral competencies children develop over time; these have been the predominant focus of traditional outcomes assessment in special education. Skills, particularly social and communicative skills, strongly affect (but do not exclusively determine) the extent to which students with severe disabilities are able to participate in a variety of social roles, activities, and settings. Our analysis of what children learn in inclusive settings and how they learn suggests that many critical skills are acquired in the contexts of social activities in which personal relationships and membership play an important part.

During one of our observations, Carrie and her classmates were going for a nature walk in the fields surrounding their school. Students were instructed to get their science notebooks so that they could write down the types of plants they identified during the walk. As the students gathered their notebooks and pencils, Carrie watched her peers, then went to her desk, picked up her science spiral notebook and her pencil, and got in line behind her friend Sophie. She watched as many children slipped their pencils down the spiral of their notebooks, and then after a little struggle and persistence she was able to store her pencil in the same manner.

Carrie's imitation of peers, independent task management, and use of fine motor skills occurred without direct adult intervention (Apolloni & Cooke, 1975; Garfinkle & Schwartz, 2002).

We have observed children learning new skills in the context of signing in every morning as they entered the classroom, counting out materials for distribution to classmates, checking off the names of children for a lunch count, listening to a book on tape and then participating in literature group, and many other social activities. The essence of this domain is to acknowledge all the teaching (often by peers) and learning that takes place outside of explicit, teacher-led instruction. We do not discount the importance of explicit instruction, which is the cornerstone of specialized instruction; rather, we are urging the consideration of strategies to make the informal instruction that takes place even more effective.

Linkages Among Outcome Domains

The relationships among the outcomes described previously are transactional (Bronfenbrenner, 1979; Sameroff & Chandler, 1975). The quality of a child's social relationships with peers is affected by (and affects) the child's status as a member of the group and is also affected by (and affects) the skills the child develops. All these factors contribute to the student's

access and participation in valued roles, activities, and settings in the school and community. The richest examples of inclusive educational practice we have observed suggest that multiple outcomes were likely to accrue for students involved.

In one classroom, we observed a child with severe behavior problems and a significant reading disability who read every night for 30 minutes into a tape recorder so that his friend with severe disabilities could listen to the story the next night for homework. Multiple positive outcomes resulted. The boys developed a nice friendship, both participated more fully in literature groups, and the child with the reading disability improved his reading fluency and comprehension (Pernat, 1995).

The intersection of membership, relationships, and skill development yielded instructional practices that benefited all students.

The framework we have described has some important implications for understanding issues of curriculum and instruction for learners with severe disabilities and others. First, the framework rejects the separation of social and academic outcomes that has been so prevalent in the field of special education. In fact, our observations suggest that the social aspects of a child's life in school (which we have defined in terms of membership and relationships) constitute the motivational contexts in which many fundamental life skills are learned. The false dichotomization of social and academic skill outcomes may in fact lead teachers away from creating functional and meaningful instructional contexts for learners with severe disabilities.

Recognizing the important linkages among membership, relationships, and the development of critical skills suggests that removing students from rich social contexts to emphasize one type of outcome (e.g., pulling a student out of the regular classroom for one-to-one skill instruction) is likely to affect the student's opportunities related to other outcome domains (Schnorr, 1990). Our model suggests many ways in which interventions can be designed that take advantage of the natural learning processes that are embedded in typical classroom life and other rich social contexts.

In the following section, we illustrate how the outcome framework can be used to describe and evaluate the peer relationships in the lives of Sean, Carrie, and Cole, the three children introduced earlier in this chapter. In particular, we draw the reader's attention to the critical functions that each child's social relationships play in providing opportunities to learn new

skills, to achieve a sense of membership or "belonging" to valued social groups, and to support participation in valued roles, activities, and settings.

 Three Case Illustrations

Sean

Membership

Since Sean entered the inclusive kindergarten, there has been a major shift in his membership. At first he was aloof, he ignored his peers, and after a little while they began to ignore him. In teacher-directed small groups, his teacher had to directly facilitate interactions between Sean and his peers. For example, she taught Sean how to trade baseball cards, an activity that the boys in the kindergarten class enjoy very much. After a few months, it was clear that Sean was becoming a member of the class. He was easily included in friendship groups and in schoolwide and classwide activities. One of the nicest changes has been his membership in outside-of-school activities, such as his T-ball team and church youth group. His mother reported that the last time she took him to buy shoes, he and the salesperson talked about the local baseball team the entire time. She said, "Sean seemed to actually enjoy talking to the salesman—I could have gone out for coffee."

Relationships

Sean and I are friends because we liked most of the things that the other one liked to do—like, I like to kick a ball, and he likes to kick a ball. I like to be with him, and he likes to be with me. I like to see him, and he likes to see me. He likes baseball, and so do I. He likes computer games, and I like computer games. He likes to look at pictures, and I like to look at pictures. He likes Harry Potter, and I like Harry Potter. (Typically developing classmate of Sean's)

Sean seems to have relationships across three of the four subdomains: play/companionship, helper, and helpee. We have never observed him engage in a conflictual interaction, and most often if conflict seems imminent, Sean leaves the area. In terms of play, he has found friends who share similar interests. He is an excellent reader and is often asked by other children to either read them stories during free choice or help them with their assignments during independent work. He has trouble with math and often asks other for help during this time and is also hesitant in crowded situations (e.g., lunch) and receives assistance from his peers to negotiate those situations.

Skills

Sean demonstrates close-to-grade-level academic work but still has severe deficits in social and communication

skills. He works with a speech-language pathologist and a peer during choice time on storytelling and conversational skills. He receives social skills instruction during recess on the playground, and teachers have been taught how to use discrete-trial teaching techniques during ongoing classroom activities to help Sean receive instruction where and when he needs it (McBride & Schwartz, 2003). He attends a school that has implemented a schoolwide positive behavior support plan (Sugai, Horner, & Gresham, 2002) and benefits from the emphasis on social codes that pervade the curriculum as well as from small-group instruction that is available to all students who need it.

Carrie

Membership

Yeah, she's a member of our class, I mean she does everything that everyone else does. She helps in the class garden, even though she might not do it as well as other kids can. I mean it's fine. It turns out in the end. She can say that she helped in the garden and she helped do stuff in our class because she does a lot of things. (Carrie's classmate)

The extent to which Carrie was viewed as a full member of her class varied over the course of the 4 years we followed her. Several factors contributed to this variation, but most notable was the type of classroom context in which Carrie participated. For example, the first year we observed Carrie, she was in class with a general education teacher who strongly supported cooperative learning. Carrie was included in all the class activities and assignments. However, with a more traditional general education teacher the next year, Carrie spent a considerable amount of her school day being pulled out of her classroom for specialized instruction. During her fourth-grade year, she was perceived by both the general education teacher and her peers as an important, contributing member of the class. She participated in small academic groups who were studying literature, social studies, and math. She was assigned roles in these groups, and accommodations were made so she could actively participate and contribute in a meaningful way.

Relationships

I think one of the things I see right now is Carrie's ability to have true friends. I'm talking about kids who call her on the phone and invite her to their house. That has happened more and more this year. (Carrie's teacher)

For Carrie, interactions with her typically developing classmates have been her greatest source of support and joy. Her peers helped her with academic work, made accommodations to include her in activities, and gave her feedback about her social behaviors. Carrie developed several lasting friendships over the 4 years of our research. In fourth grade, she was a peer tutor ("helper") for a first-grade class and helped another child with disabilities at the school on an informal basis.

Conflictual interactions with peers have been an ongoing issue for Carrie (e.g., grabbing at others, trashing others' personal property), but in this area Carrie made perhaps her greatest improvement. After conducting a functional behavior assessment (FBA) to better understand what was motivating and maintaining this challenging behavior (see chapter 2 for a complete discussion of FBA and positive behavior support), we provided systematic instruction to Carrie to teach her how to gain attention from her peers in a more appropriate manner. In addition, her peers learned to communicate with her about their feelings regarding these behaviors, and Carrie, who very much wants to be liked by her peers, has responded to their feedback.

Skills

I think that so much of her actual academic and functional development is because she has had lots of peers to model from, lots of peers to support her, to reinforce her. She sees meaning for what she is doing rather than being in some isolated situation. (Carrie's mother)

Carrie showed growth and improvement in all skill outcome areas. In fourth grade, Carrie's teacher reported that she exhibited more appropriate social skills with her peers and that she was making verbal requests to adults more frequently. Every year, Carrie showed academic improvement in math, reading, writing, and computer use. Carrie became more responsible and independent, both at home and at school. Carrie's mother and teacher also reported that Carrie made remarkable growth in her communication skills. Her articulation was greatly improved, and she was talking louder and more frequently to peers and adults. She also became more fluent in using symbols and gestures as repair strategies to help herself be more easily understood by peers and adults.

Cole

Membership

Cole sat down between Paul and another of his classmates and started eating his lunch. He talked to Paul and sat listening to peers as they talked. He occasionally repeated things they said, and they all laughed. (Observation notes, sixth grade)

As a sixth grader, Cole was very much a member of his class. He attended sixth-grade graduation as well as an overnight camping trip with the entire sixth grade at his elementary school. During his first year at junior high, Cole followed a class schedule similar to that of his typically developing classmates. However, during the last 2 years, Cole began to spend more time helping with school jobs and engaging in schoolwide recreation activities. A favorite activity during his sophomore year was to attend the varsity football games.

Relationships

Cole saw Chris (one of his student aides) walk in the room. As Chris walked toward Cole, Cole got very excited and said in a real distinct voice, "There's Chris! Look, he's back!" Chris smiled and said, "Hi, Cole." Cole said, "He's back, he's back!" (Observation notes during Cole's ninth-grade year)

Many of the interactions that Cole had with his peers in sixth grade were typical of "helpee" relationships. His peers helped Cole behave appropriately in class, and they found ways to ensure his participation. Outside of class, other boys often met him at the bus and invited him to play basketball during recess. His teacher commented, "You just get so much more out of Cole when he's with his peers." When Cole moved on to junior high, he was observed engaging in many friendly interactions with peers. He became particularly fond of older, typically developing male students at the junior high school and was often found "hanging out" with them. He continued to receive help from several student aides who accompanied him to his classes throughout the school day. While Cole's friendships with typically developing peers have not extended beyond the school campus, his peers seem very genuine in their affection for him.

Skills

Cole used to be real shy. He'd duck his head and not say a word and close his eyes if someone came close. Now he can talk about anything! (Typically developing friend in eighth grade)

Cole's most significant growth has been in social communication. For example, he learned how to interact much more appropriately with his peers, how to share, and how to wait for his turn patiently. He also displayed better receptive communication skills, which were reflected in his increased ability to follow directions. We observed Cole initiating many more social interactions with his typically developing peers, and we noticed an increased use of complete sentences to express his feelings or describe his day. He has learned a limited number of traditional academic skills, such as number and word recognition and counting, as well as independently moving through functional routines in his school and community, such as packing his lunch, taking the bus, and moving between classes at the junior high.

Relationships and Learning

These vignettes about Sean, Carrie, and Cole show how central the social relationships of each of these students' lives are to their learning. Their opportunity to interact with their classmates is one of the strongest motivations to participate in classroom activities. Teachers for each of these students comment on how other children understand their communicative attempts, make accommodations to enable their participation in activities, and give them helpful prompts and feedback about their behavior. One day, we observed an interaction between Cole and two of his friends that brings many of these issues into focus.

Cole, Chris, and Justin are sitting together as one of several small groups in the class. Cole whispers to Chris and laughs. Chris laughs and then asks Cole to pay attention to the teacher. Cole watches the teacher for a few minutes then turns to Justin and burps. Justin laughs. Chris tells Cole to knock it off. Chris then scratches the top of Cole's head. Cole does the same thing back to Chris. When their group is called up to perform their report, Chris tells Cole, "Just watch me and do what I do."

While some might see this interaction as a bit unruly and perhaps interfering with the lesson, we see it as a rich example of how typical classroom life is planted with opportunities for learning for students like Cole. It is clear that Cole is highly motivated to interact with his buddies. His communication attempts are, in fact, richly rewarded with their attention and laughter. In addition, one student takes an active role in teaching Cole to pay attention to what the teacher is saying and to what is happening in the group activity. Chris's final admonition to Cole, "Just watch me and do what I do," is perhaps one of the most important social skills Cole must learn if he is to get along without the direct assistance of others in complex social settings: observing the behavior of people around him as a source of guidance about how to "fit in" to a social situation.

In the following section, we use our conceptual framework to suggest a variety of curriculum goals related to social relationships as well as intervention strategies for addressing them. In making these recommendations, we promote a holistic view of student learning and development in which outcomes are conceptualized in terms of increased student participation in valued roles, activities, and settings. This approach recalls early insights about the value of "partial participation" proposed by Baumgart and her colleagues (Baumgart et al., 1982; Ferguson & Baumgart, 1991). That is, students should be encouraged to participate independently as much as possible and supported to complete the activity with assistance. Partial participation can also be facilitated by modifying or accommodating the activity (Sandall & Schwartz, 2002). For example, during a class meeting, students who are nonverbal can have the appropriate symbols in their communication book to participate in all activities of the meeting. We further develop the notion of participation here by placing it in the context of contemporary theories of *situated learning* (e.g., Lave & Wenger, 1991) as well as our own observations of student development in the context of inclusive schools. Situated learning means that instruction is provided in the context of meaningful and motivating activities and routines. Our assumption, supported by the theories of situated learning, is that students acquire specific skills (including important cognitive, communicative, and academic skills) in the context of engaging in meaningful activities in which their participation is supported by other children, teachers, and other adults.

Strategies for Intervention

Our suggestions for intervention strategies related to social relationships are based on three sources. First, recommendations are based on our own research and practice in working with students with severe disabilities in inclusive classrooms over the past years (Grenot-Scheyer, Staub, & Fisher, 2001; Meyer et al., 1998; Peck et al., 1992). Second, our observations are based on sociocultural theories of human development that we found of enormous value in making sense of what we observed (Cole, 1996; Lave & Wenger, 1991; Vygotsky, 1978). These views place the process of joint activity, or participation, at the center of the developmental process. Development is thus seen as a process of mutual change and adaptation rather than as a process that takes place exclusively within the learner (Lave & Wenger, 1991). The third source of influence consists of feedback from teachers, special educators, and parents about what is really workable in the context of typical practice (Meyer et al., 1998; Staub, 1998).

Designing "Usable" Interventions

The concept of *social validity* has been a key concept in behavioral interventions for over 25 years (Schwartz & Baer, 1991; Wolf, 1977). Socially valid interventions are those that are both effective and judged to be acceptable by consumers. Usable interventions are ultimately socially valid interventions. In an attempt to develop guidelines to help describe usable interventions, Meyer et al. (1998) held series of meetings with constituent groups, school-based teacher teams, and groups of adolescents attending inclusive schools. They suggest that usable interventions designed to affect the social lives of children with disabilities should be characterized as follows:

1. *Doable in context:* Interventions must be based on an understanding of the "average" classroom and what are practical and reasonable expectations.
2. *Feasible with available resources:* A careful analysis of long-term available resources should precede the implementation of an intervention.
3. *Sustainable over time:* Interventions are effective only if they are implemented correctly and consistently. For interventions to be usable, teachers and educational teams must be able to implement them for the long run, whether that is the school year or the entire time the student is in school. Time for sharing ideas and expertise is essential for sustaining the life and quality of an intervention.
4. *Constituency owned and operated:* Interventions that are created, facilitated, and supported by the ones carrying them make a large difference in how and for how long they are carried out.
5. *Culturally inclusive:* Interventions must be consistent with and respectful of the values, behaviors, and beliefs of the ones implementing and receiving them.
6. *Intuitively appealing:* Does the intervention make good, common sense? Is it appealing to the recipients and the ones carrying it out?

In the context of our research, we have had the opportunity to observe and record a variety of classroom practices that were associated with positive outcomes for children with and without disabilities. Although we organize our observations about classroom practice here in terms of specific domains and subdomains within our conceptual framework, many of the most promising things we have observed teachers doing are likely to have an effect on all three of the outcome domains (social relationships, membership, and skills).

Recognizing and Supporting Membership

Outcomes related to the domain we have termed "membership" are essentially phenomenological in nature, referring to the sense of "belonging," which students with disabilities may experience in a variety of formal and informal group contexts in inclusive schools. An important issue to consider in planning supports for students with disabilities in the membership domain is that the perceptions of adults regarding who is and is not a member of the group may not be consistent with those of students (Schnorr, 1990). In this context, teachers should listen carefully to what students have to say about their social experiences in the classroom and school (Grenot-Scheyer, Staub, Peck, & Schwartz, 1998).

We observed five contexts in which teachers, parents, and students viewed membership as an important outcome for students with disabilities. These include (a) small groups that were developed by teachers or peers, (b) the class, (c) the school, (d) friendship cliques, and (e) outside groups.

Small-Group Membership (Teacher Developed)

Carrie participates in a discussion with four typically developing classmates about the "Faithful Elephants," an award-winning short story. Carrie looks at sketches Anna has made from the story and points out different things she sees. Anna asks her, "Carrie, who do you think the person with the stick is?" Carrie smiles and says, "He feeds the elephant." Children around the group smile with appreciation at her response. Sharon, another group member, shares her "sketch to stretch" with the other students, and they respond to what they see in her sketch.

Description In our observations, we found that students with disabilities were often members of small groups at stations or centers, of reading or literature groups, in theme-related project groups, in art project groups, or in teacher-led games. We also found that the students with disabilities took a variety of roles in these groups, including listening, reading, sharing turn taking, and contributing to group work.

Strategies for Supporting Membership in Small Groups Perhaps the most critical strategy for supporting the membership of students with severe disabilities in small groups has to do with the general quality of the group work itself. There is a well-developed literature describing design and implementation of group work within regular classrooms that include a diverse array of student backgrounds and abilities (Cohen, 1986; Putnam, 1993). An important feature of cooperative learning methods within these small-group contexts is provision for each student to make a substantial contribution to the group without having to make the same contribution (Cohen, 1986).

> *Carrie's teacher often used reader's theater (Routman, 1994) as a means of demonstrating student's knowledge and comprehension at the completion of a novel or chapter of a book. As each reading group finished a novel, they wrote a script that represented the novel. All group members were expected to participate in the skit about the book, including Carrie, who was a beginning reader. However, the lines of the script that Carrie was expected to read, while they gave her a meaningful and sometimes central role in the skit, were tailored to her reading abilities. Carrie's general education teacher wrote about these experiences: "The students with disabilities have shined during these skits. They take pride in their performance and become totally engaged in the learning experience. At times they need prompts or reminders, but their group members take ownership and help each other as needed."*

In order for some students with disabilities to participate as members of small groups, teachers may need to make accommodations in the activities. The special education consulting teacher can assist the classroom teacher to plan roles and accommodations for individual student participation in groups. However, we have observed some of the best accommodations to be those invented by other students. Theresa found various ways to communicate with her classmate Cathy, who is nonverbal. Based on her experiences, Theresa played an active role in developing a communication book for Cathy and showing others how to use it. Nondisabled students are able to invent these and other accommodations for peers with disabilities only when they are in classrooms in which teachers respect their ideas and actively solicit their input.

Small-Group Membership (Peer Developed)
Description This outcome theme refers to formal and informal groups organized by students themselves, such as teams for basketball at recess or groups of children playing a game during free time in the classroom. Cole, a student with severe developmental delays, participated in a daily basketball game at recess.

> *Cole is waiting his turn to shoot the ball during the basketball game. He takes two steps forward and shoots underhand, his preferred method of shooting. He misses the first shot but makes the second. (You're allowed only one shot, but nobody says anything about him making a second shot.) After he makes it, he looks around, and all four of the kids in line say, "Good job," or "All right Cole!"* (Observation notes from Cole's sixth-grade year)

Many of the same qualities of the small groups that are developed by teachers were evident in small groups that are peer developed. For instance, students with disabilities in these small groups were given a role, specific accommodations were made by typically developing students to support their participation, and rituals (such as "high fives" and exclamations of "nice shot") were performed by group members.

Strategies for Supporting Small-Group Membership (Peer Developed) Teachers can support membership in small groups developed by students by creating unstructured situations for play and exploration (e.g., setting up free choice centers, not excluding students with disabilities from important "breaks" such as recess, providing games and other interactive materials for use during free time). Teachers can also plan ahead for peer support by conducting ability awareness training, setting up buddy systems, and having class discussions about ways in which peers with disabilities can be included in peer-directed activities (Gallucci, Staub, Peck, Schwartz, & Billingsley, 1996).

Class Membership
Description This outcome theme refers to the student's belonging to the class as a social group. We observed many examples of students with disabilities receiving the same roles, symbols, and rituals of the class as their typically developing peers, suggesting that they were "members" of these communities.

> *Ninth-grade band: Cole walks to the band room with his "student aide" for that period. About 30 kids are hanging out in front of the classroom. Cole is greeted by several students as they wait for the teacher. "Are*

you going to the game this afternoon?" one student asks. Cole nods. The teacher arrives, and the kids file into the room and start to take their instruments out and practice. The band teacher hands Cole a couple of percussion sticks and reminds him what to do. Cole hits his sticks together in time with the rest of the band members. (Observation notes, Cole's ninth-grade year)

The examples of class membership we found included students having roles in special events such as class plays, assembly presentations, parades, games, or celebrations. Students with disabilities were also often assigned roles within the class, such as taking attendance or passing out materials. Symbols of class membership we observed included certificates, portfolios, class hats worn for special occasions, being the "kid of the week," or being included on a classroom reading chart. Students with disabilities followed class schedules similar to those of their classmates and were included in the activities of their classes with adult and peer support.

Strategies for Supporting Class Membership

The overall social climate and sense of community that prevails in a classroom has a great impact on the likelihood that students with disabilities will be included as full members. One of the processes through we which we observed classroom teachers develop a stronger sense of community is the class meeting (Nelson, Lott, & Glenn, 1993). Class meetings are conducted in the general tradition of the "town meeting"; they may take a variety of forms but have as a common goal the creation of opportunities for children to have a voice in decisions about how the class is conducted and in setting norms and expectations for behavior in the classroom community. Schneider (1996) suggests that the first meeting begin with the inquiry, "What kind of classroom community do we want to have?" The meetings, once established, become a regular event.

In one fifth-sixth, multigrade class we observed, the topic of class membership came up during a class meeting. The group of students were concerned that one of their classmates, a student with autism, was being excluded from literature groups to work individually with a special education assistant. The group of students felt this was an important time for their classmate to be included "in the work we do." The students talked about the issues and agreed that everyone should par-

ticipate in literature groups in whatever way they could. Adjustments were made in the schedule of the student with disabilities, and accommodations were made to the curriculum. The student with autism soon became an active and valued member of a literature group. Equally important, all the students in this class experienced themselves as having some influence over how their class was run. Indeed, it actually became more of "their" class through this process of figuring out how to include their classmate with autism.

School Membership

Description Membership outcomes at the school level were indicated by (a) the student's participation in school rituals and activities, (b) by accommodations made by adults and other students to support such participation, (c) by the display of symbols of membership (such as school sweatshirts, logos, or other artifacts), and (d) by their presence in special settings, such as schoolwide assemblies and sporting events. Many times, the participation of students with disabilities in these events took on a personal and social significance that reflected the importance of membership to the student and others.

It is Friday morning assembly time. The principal of Austen Elementary School reads a list of names of all the students who have completed school service projects. The principal calls out Carrie's name. Carrie stands up with the rest of the students whose names the principal has called. She has a big smile on her face. Everyone clearly knows her, and the students clap for her and others as she beams with pride.

Strategies for Supporting School Membership

Opportunities for students to participate in school events that both reflect and contribute to a sense of membership are plentiful in most schools. In many schools we have observed, however, the importance of these opportunities is not recognized for children with disabilities. Teachers, administrators, and parents who appreciate the value of children's experience of belonging at school can include students with disabilities in active roles at school, such as taking turns announcing the daily bulletin over the school public address systems or taking tickets at a school basketball game. In addition, membership can be promoted by planning necessary supports and accommodations to ensure that students participate in schoolwide rituals and celebrations, including, of course, graduation. We found symbols of membership more evident at the upper elementary and middle school years, when these issues become more salient for *all* students. For example, symbols of membership at the middle school level included students having a class schedule, receiving a report card, carrying a school bag, or wearing a school sweatshirt. While many of these symbols of membership are taken for granted by many students, the absence of such symbols for students with severe disabilities may serve as subtle indicators to other students and adults of the marginalized social position of students with disabilities.

Friendship Groups/Cliques

Description Membership within a friendship group/ clique refers to a student belonging to a group of mutual friends whether or not there is a close relationship with any individual in the group. Carrie played each day with the same group of girls from her fourth-grade class during recess for more than 2 months.

> *Carrie leaves the cafeteria with Lindsay, Chelsea, and Jackie, heading to the playground, all holding hands. They run to the tire swing. Carrie, Lindsay, and Chelsea climb on the tire, and Jackie pushes them. Chelsea climbs off and sits on a log watching. Carrie and Lindsay swing for a while. Both are laughing really hard and trying to make the swing go faster.*

Strategies for Supporting Membership in Friendship Cliques As any parent knows, a child's membership in a friendship clique is one of the most valued experiences in a child's life, and if it doesn't occur naturally, it is one of the most difficult outcomes for adults to create. In our observations, this outcome was a relatively rare occurrence. The heart of friendship is voluntary association. Adults can create environments in which it is relatively safe for children to befriend vulnerable peers (Haring & Breen, 1992; Staub, 1998), and they can create social contexts in which it is attractive for nondisabled students to "hang out" (Gaylord-Ross, Haring, Breen, & Pitts-Conway, 1984; Gibbs, 1995; Snell & Janney, 2000), but friendship is ultimately a matter of choice among peers. The few examples we found of this included children playing with the same group of peers every day at recess or walking home regularly with the same group of friends.

While it may be difficult for teachers to "program" membership in friendship cliques for their students with severe disabilities, there are things that can be

done that might facilitate the development of groups from which these cliques may spring. For example, in several schools, we worked with teachers to create a regular meeting time for peers to discuss issues of inclusion, which resulted in the continued development of support systems for peers with disabilities. We did not include the students with disabilities in these discussions because the typically developing students expressed that they would be uncomfortable talking about their classmates in their presence. One of the effects of these groups was that some typically developing students began to feel more skillful at including students with disabilities in a variety of regular peer activities, some of which extended beyond school contexts (Gallucci et al., 1996).

Outside Groups

Description This final membership theme reflected a student's membership in community-based groups such as church choir, soccer team, Cub Scout troop, and an after-school folk dancing club. These groups may not be formally affiliated with the school but nevertheless may be composed of children who meet each other at school or who develop relationships that extend across both settings. In our research, parents reported a variety of these kinds of experiences. Karly was a member of her Brownie troop, which met once a week for an hour. Jonathan, a nonverbal student with autism, participated in his Sunday school classes at his community church. Carrie received her first communion with her typically developing peers from school.

Strategies to Support Inclusion in Outside Groups Interventions to support a student's membership in groups outside of school need not be highly technical. Parents need to identify groups that they would like their children to join. These may be sports, dance, scout or religious groups. Parents and teachers may advocate for the student's participation in these groups and provide an array of peer supports and accommodations in much the same way as in classroom settings. Intervention begins, of course, with recognition of the value of membership in these groups as both an experience in itself and a context for the development of skills and the enhancement of personal relationships. Often interventions to facilitate participation in these groups are quite simple, such as helping group leaders prepare visual supports and schedules for the student or brainstorming with group members about how a student can participate in the activity.

Recognizing and Supporting a Range of Relationships

Social relationships between students with severe disabilities and their peers take a wide variety of forms. We identified four major types of peer relationships that were evident in the lives of the students we studied: (a) play/companionship, (b) helpee, (c) helper, and (d) conflictual. Each of these types of relationships offers somewhat different developmental opportunities; participation in such a "range of relationships" is an important advantage to students (Gaylord-Ross & Peck, 1985). In the next section, we present examples of each of these types of relationships and describe some strategies we have observed teachers use to support students' learning in each.

Play/Companion Relationships

The play/companionship theme refers to relationships that revolve around the mutual enjoyment of an activity or interaction. The importance of play/companionship relationships and friendship as a dimension of a satisfying human life is widely acknowledged (Haring; 1991; Strully & Strully, 1985). We also believe that these kinds of relationships are extremely important for children as contexts for the development of social and communication skills and as avenues for achieving membership in larger social groups. When children repeatedly choose to spend time playing together or "hanging out," showing a preference for each other's company, they begin to achieve some of the richer outcomes of "friendship" (Copeland et al., 2002; Staub, 1998). The following excerpt from our observations illustrates the kind of play/companion relationship we often saw in inclusive classrooms.

> *It is free time. Marcy, a second-grade student with Down syndrome and moderate developmental delays, goes to the house area in the loft. Mellanie, a typically developing classmate, is there. Marcy smiles happily on seeing Mellanie, and the girls begin to chase each other up and down the loft. Both girls are laughing and smiling. Mellanie stays in the loft, and Marcy runs up the loft. Mellanie then chases Marcy to the stairs. Marcy runs back up the stairs. They do this over and over—maybe 20 times—before the teacher calls an end to free time.*

In spite of the instructional technology that has been made available to educators today, teachers cannot "program" their student's friendships. But they can build connections that may help foster and support friendships between and among their students. Teachers can use practices that encourage student participation, they can provide situations like the free-time activity described previously that encourage playful interactions to occur, and they can model caring, respectful, and interested attitudes toward each of their students. The following are some strategies for supporting play/companion relationships.

Time and Opportunity Students with moderate and severe disabilities and their classmates need varied, frequent, and regular opportunities to interact with each other. No matter how supportive the classroom may be for building and sustaining friendly relationships, if the student with disabilities is seldom present, it will be difficult for them to develop relationships in that setting (Schnorr, 1990; Snell & Janney, 2000; Staub, 1998). Furthermore, students with disabilities who do spend the majority of their school day in their general education classroom need to be engaged in activities that encourage frequent peer interaction and general social skills development. Our observations suggest that classrooms in which positive social relationships are more likely to develop are those in which children are given lots of opportunities to work together in a variety of small and large groups, to talk with each other about the work in which they are engaged, and to assist one another with academic and other classroom activities (Salisbury, Gallucci, Palombaro, & Peck, 1995; Salisbury & Palombaro, 1998). The richness of Carrie's relationships with her peers during her sixth-grade year was directly related to her teacher's design of a classroom environment with these very characteristics. In contrast, classrooms that are dominated by teacher talk, individual seat work, and activities in which helping one another is viewed negatively (and sometimes even defined as "cheating") are less suited for peer interactions of any kind, much less those we advocate here.

Classroom Climate The impact of the general emotional tone or climate of a classroom on children's feelings and performance has been well documented (Janney & Snell, 1996, 1997). While many benefits for children with and without disabilities derive from establishment of a warm and caring classroom environment (Hedeen, Ayres, & Tate, 2001), the emergence of play/companion relationships between children with severe disabilities and their typically developing classmates is likely to be particularly affected. In a climate in which children feel themselves vulnerable to judgment, rejection, and exclusion, they are not likely to take social risks inherent in affiliating themselves with peers who are obviously "different" in ways that are devalued in our culture. In order to make the classroom a place where typically developing children could develop positive personal relationships with their most vulnerable peers, it must be made a safe place for all kinds of differences to be acknowledged and accepted. The establishment of such a climate may not be an easy task in schools and communities in which some students experience judgment and exclusion related to race, social class. gender, or ethnicity. Thus, the task of making the climate of classrooms and other social settings safe and supportive for children with disabilities is fundamentally and inextricably linked with making these settings safe and supportive for all children (Meyer et al., 1998).

Paradoxically, the obvious vulnerability of students with severe disabilities may function as an opportunity for teachers to create a more caring and accepting classroom climate by demonstrating that even its most vulnerable members are respected and included (Peck, Gallucci, Staub, & Schwartz, 1998). For example, in Sean's kindergarten class, the "talking stick" activity honored a different student each day for their unique contributions to the class.

The "talking stick," a short totem pole such as a piece of wood, is passed around the circle of students. Each day the talking stick is given to a selected "honored student," and the other classmates go around the circle and make compliments to him or her. (Observer comment about the "talking stick" activity)

Sean was never shortchanged on compliments by his classmates on the day he was the "honored" student for the talking stick activity. Sean's classmates were able to identify his unique strengths and thus celebrate his differences. Moreover, the participation of Sean and others we observed in regular classrooms served as a context for students to clarify and affirm important values and practices related to individual rights, inclusion, and participation in the classroom.

Cooperative Goal Structures Bryant (1998), Putnam (1993), Sapon-Shevin (1992), and others have noted that classrooms using cooperative goal structures may

help generate friendships and foster the development of a variety of social and communicative skills that are important for all students. However, setting up cooperative group activities does not in itself ensure that positive interactions, relationships, and academic outcomes will occur (Ohtake, 2003). The success of such arrangements is dependent on thoughtful planning, guidance, and support from the teacher (Cohen, 1986). In cooperative activities that include students with severe disabilities, considerable creativity is often required to ensure their meaningful participation. While teachers must be careful not to delegate too much responsibility to their typically developing students for creating accommodations for students with disabilities, peers can be a valuable source of creative ideas (Salisbury et al., 1995), as the following excerpt reveals.

A group of students are planning a skit as part of their Winter Holiday pageant. One member of the group is Cathy, a student with moderate developmental disabilities and limited verbal skills. Her classmates are anxious that she not be left out of the dialogue of the skit and decide to record her parts on a tape player, which she activates when cued. (Observation notes)

The planning and preparation of Cathy's role in the skit turned out to be one of the highlights of the work the students did on the skit and one of the most meaningful aspects of the pageant.

Classroom Structures: Physical Considerations
The physical arrangements of a classroom may set the occasion for student interactions and the development of social relationships. Flexibility of seating arrangements, the amount of space available to carry out activities, and the placement of the teacher's desk are all factors that influence interactions in the classroom setting (Epstein & Karweit, 1983).

In Carrie's classroom, her teacher had salvaged an old couch that he covered with an attractive blanket and placed by the only window in the classroom. This spot has become an important setting for Carrie to engage in many playful interactions with her nondisabled classmates. (Observer comment)

Teachers as Models Studies suggest that children are more likely to acquire positive attitudes and behaviors when they experience warm and affectionate relationships with their teachers (Grenot-Scheyer, Fisher, & Staub, 2001; Lipsky & Gartner, 1998; McGregor & Vogelsberg, 1998). Many of the teachers we observed successfully serving children with disabilities in their regular classrooms were also notable for the respect, warmth, and compassion they demonstrated for every one of their students. They designed their classroom environments to promote student interaction, but they also showed students the kinds of behavior they expected by taking time to listen to students, by treating their feelings with respect, and by avoiding critical and judgmental behavior toward students. We believe that nondisabled students are extremely sensitive to the ways in which the classroom teacher and other adults respond to children with disabilities. The extent to which they see acceptance and caring modeled by the teacher impacts their own interpretation of being "different" in the classroom not only for their peer with disabilities but also for themselves.

Helpee Relationships

We observed numerous social relationships in which the student with disabilities was the recipient of assistance or support from another child. We termed these "helpee" relationships. Clearly, these kinds of relationships evolve naturally in the context of many social settings in which students often need special support for participation.

In eighth-grade home economics class, the teacher asks the students to go to their cooking stations and complete the steps of making lasagna. Jackie, a "student aide" for Gina, a 13-year-old girl with cerebral palsy who uses a wheelchair, pushes Gina to an adapted kitchen counter. The teacher hands Gina an egg. Jackie physically guides Gina, cracking open the egg and putting it in a bowl. While Jackie guides Gina through this process, she quietly encourages her and tells Gina, "You're doing a good job."

We found many examples of students with moderate and severe disabilities being helped by their typically developing peers in a variety of ways. There were many instances of typically developing students naturally helping out by picking up dropped items, cuing a student with disabilities to participate, or showing them where they should be. We observed peers helping classmates with disabilities with their school work, making transitions, and prompting appropriate behavior.

In these instances, it was often seat mates, buddies, or small-group members who offered the most help. While we observed help being provided in natural ways, we also found many examples of help being provided that was purposefully planned by teachers. At Gina's junior high school, for example, typically developing students were taught to be student aides to provide assistance to students with disabilities in each of their inclusive general education classes. We also noticed adults requesting help or support from nondisabled peers in the context of recess buddies, transition partners, or academic tutors.

There is a large body of literature on typically developing peers providing support to students with disabilities. Increases in social skills (e.g., Copeland et al., 2002; Hughes et al., 1999; Staub & Hunt, 1993), conversational turn taking (Hunt, Alwell, & Goetz, 1988), and improvements in academic skill development (Grenot-Scheyer et al., 1998) for students with moderate and severe disabilities at the elementary and secondary levels have all been associated with peer support programs.

Helping and Friendship Many researchers have noted the potential for relationships in which students were predominantly receiving help from others (what we have termed "helpee" relationships) to have adverse affects on the emergence of other kinds of peer relationships, including friendships (Copeland et al. 2002; Hughes et al., 1999; Meyer et al., 1998, Staub, Spaulding, Peck, Gallucci, & Schwartz, 1996; Voeltz, 1982). In our own research, Theresa and Cathy's story provides an illustration of how too much "help" may sometimes interfere with friendship.

Theresa and Cathy's friendship began in the third grade when they first made a connection on the school playground. Theresa, a very shy typically developing child, saw that Cathy, who has severe disabilities, was in need of a friend. Perhaps identifying with this need, Theresa initiated an interaction with Cathy that led to a 2-year friendship between the girls. However, by the time the two girls were attending their inclusive fifth-grade class together, Theresa's friendship with Cathy had changed, and its primary function had become helping. Theresa's ability to understand Cathy's communication attempts may have been one important reason as to why their relationship had shifted, as teachers began to routinely assign Theresa to help Cathy in a variety of classroom activities. Before the end of their fifth-grade year, Theresa had become Cathy's designated caretaker. Their classroom teacher and the special education assistant, challenged by supporting a classroom of 30 students, two of whom had moderate or severe developmental delays, began to rely on students who were most "connected" to the child with disabilities as a primary source of support. Sadly, Theresa became more and more overwhelmed as this responsibility grew, finally expressing relief when she and Cathy were not assigned to the same classroom the following year. What had begun as a true expression of interest, caring, and support had become an overwhelming responsibility for this fifth-grade girl, leading her to withdraw from the relationship.   (Staub, Schwartz, Gallucci, & Peck, 1994)

Cathy and Theresa's relationship raises some important issues for consideration when assigning typically developing students to help classmates or peers with disabilities. First, if typically developing students are asked to take on the role of tutor or caretaker for a classmate with disabilities, are they given the opportunity to communicate their dissatisfaction, discomfort, or unpreparedness for this role? Second, how does the role of helper affect the relationships among teacher, students without disabilities, and the student with disabilities? Third, considering respect and value for individual diversity and ability levels, how much "help" should adults be expecting typically developing students to provide their peers with disabilities, and how should this help be structured so that there is a balance between giving and taking (Staub et al., 1994)? Finally, how can students with severe disabilities be provided with the opportunity to "choose" the student they would like to receive help from (Janney & Snell, 1996)?

Strategies for Supporting Helpee Relationships

Relationships in which students with severe disabilities receive help from peers are perhaps the most frequent and naturally occurring of those we observed. However, we have noted a tremendous difference between classrooms in which these relationships are planfully supported by adults and those in which students are left to themselves to figure out when and how to help. We have also noted several limitations of these types of relationships, especially when they become the predominant mode of relationship. Following are some

strategies for structuring and supporting helpee relationships:

1. *Classwide helping procedures.* Teachers can support *all* students to have a voice in how the classroom is conducted, addressing issues of providing "help" to each other in ways that do not take over the activity. Teachers can also discuss with their students the kinds of help peers with disabilities may require. If these discussions take place within the context of all students helping each other, more naturalized systems of support may develop. We observed several classrooms where students and teachers had incorporated "helping" rules (Janney & Snell, 1996). For example, in Karly's and Deanne's multigrade, K–2 classroom, the "ask three before me" rule required students to ask at least three other classmates before they went to the teacher for assistance. The "elbow partner" rule was used when students were in need of help. For this rule, they were to first ask a classmate to their right elbow for help and, if that didn't work, ask a classmate to their left elbow for help.

2. *Peer tutoring programs.* Teachers can also set up structured systems, such as peer tutoring or peer buddy programs. We have described one such program, operated at the junior high school level, in some detail (Staub et al., 1996). Several components of the program were believed to contribute to its success. First, the open and frank ability awareness discussions that took place during the first week of the school year gave students an opportunity to learn about differences among people, and in the discussions they could express any fears and misconceptions they may have regarding disability issues. Second, the student aide role at Kennedy Junior High was highly valued by teachers, staff, and fellow classmates. Students who participated in the program received a good deal of recognition for their work. Finally, the special education teacher who carried out the student aide program was planful about balancing "helping" with opportunities for friendly interactions to occur. The student aides and the students with moderate and severe disabilities went on outings in the community, played games during "downtime," and occasionally attended plays or sporting events after school hours.

Unhelpful Help Giangreco and his colleagues (Giangreco, Edelman, Luiselli, & MacFarland, 1997) have described some of the problems that may develop when adult aides are in one-to-one tutoring roles with students with disabilities in inclusive classrooms. We have noticed similar problems in some peer-helping relationships. Peers are sometimes unaware of the needs of students with disabilities to do things for themselves and may rush in to help in ways that interfere with learning. Students who are in helping relationships with peers who have disabilities should receive direct guidance and support from teachers in making judgments about when help is needed and when it is not. Furthermore, students need to learn to ask students with disabilities if they want or need help before assuming they do and providing the help anyway (Janney & Snell, 1996).

Helper Relationships

This outcome theme refers to relationships and interactions in which the student with disabilities provides support or assistance to another child. This type of relationship is relatively unusual for children with disabilities—an observation we find distressing. Examples we observed of children with disabilities participating in relationships as helpers rather than as "helpees" were rich with opportunities for learning and self-concept enhancement. These relationships may also serve an important function in educating others about the many ways in which individuals with disabilities can make meaningful contributions to the welfare of others.

> *The students in Mr. Hathaway's sixth-grade class are working on their journals. Jonathan, a student with autism, is typing his journal onto the computer. As he slowly types the words into the computer, he is interrupted as Amy sits down beside him, her notebook in hand: "Hey, Jon, how do you spell 'conscience'?" asks Amy. A few minutes later, as Jonathan returns to his seat, another student stops him as he walks by, "Jon, how do you spell 'mechanical'?" (Jonathan is acknowledged to be the best speller in Mr. Hathaway's class.)*

In another situation we observed, Carrie served as a "peer tutor" for a first-grade class during the year she was in fourth grade.

> *Once a week, Carrie would visit the first-grade class to listen to the typically developing students read. This relationship gave Carrie a chance to experience herself in a role in which she was giving rather than receiving help, and she consistently responded with*

some of her most independent and mature behavior. Likewise, she was providing an "ear" to the first graders who were in need of practicing their reading skills. The effects of such an experience on Carrie's self-esteem were certainly important. The first graders benefited from having an eager listener attend to their reading, and, perhaps more important, they had the opportunity to see an older child with Down syndrome as a competent and mature role model.

Strategies for Supporting Helper Relationships

Teachers and other adults must plan opportunities for students with disabilities to help others. These opportunities may be focused on helping individuals, such as Carrie's work with first graders, or they may be group focused, such as having a student regularly pass out materials to their classmates. When students have special skills, such as Jon's, teachers may create a role for the student in which those skills can be used to assist others.

With support from teachers, many older students with moderate or severe disabilities may be able to develop meaningful helper relationships with younger children. In schools with preschool programs, child care programs for younger children, and (in high schools) teen parent programs, there may be many useful contexts in which students with disabilities can develop relationships in which they are the "helper." In our experience, the possibility and value of such relationships is seldom recognized by adults.

Conflictual Relationships

Students with severe disabilities, like other students, have occasional conflict with peers (Lieber, 1994). In a few instances, we observed relationships in which there was repeated verbal or physical conflict between the same two students. We termed such relationships conflictual or adversarial. The following vignette is an example of two students, one with a disability and one without, who experienced conflict with one another for almost an entire school year over the attention of a girl in their fifth-grade class.

> *Jake, a child with moderate developmental delays, walks over to Connor, a typically developing student, who is standing alone watching the other kids play at recess. Jake starts pushing Connor against the wall. He does this for several minutes. Connor walks away from Jake, but Jake follows him, still pushing at him. In between pushes, Jake gets right in Connor's face*

and looks at him with an angry expression. (Observer comment: Earlier in the day, Connor pushed Jake out of the way so he could stand next to Erika in line [the girl they both like].)

Other instances of conflict we observed included students who were fighting, teasing, or arguing with each other. In younger children, we found conflict over toys or games, especially within unstructured situations such as free time or recess. In the intermediate grades, we sometimes observed instances of students with disabilities exhibiting aggressive or inappropriate behaviors toward other students, particularly on the playground. Although most conflictual or adversarial interactions we observed were fleeting and episodic, if these behaviors occur frequently or are chronic in nature, a functional behavior assessment should be conducted to help the educational team understand what is motivating and maintaining the challenging behavior and interfering with the development of more appropriate peer relationships (see chapter 2).

Strategies for Supporting Learning in Conflictual Relationships Conflictual relationships, although unpleasant, can serve as important learning opportunities. Teachers can be planful in problem-solving and conflict resolution skills in the hope that students will learn from their conflicts with their peers. In some cases, students may learn to use structured strategies, such as the "conflict wheel" (Jones & Jones, 2000), to solve problems with each other. In other cases, group discussion and collective brainstorming and planning in class meetings may be used to address problems with individuals, small groups, or the entire classroom community (Nelson et al., 1993).

A particularly problematic issue we have observed has to do with the reluctance of many typically developing students to provide direct and honest feedback to peers with disabilities about undesirable or inappropriate behavior.

Carrie is sitting with her friends Terry and Yolanda at lunch. The girls are chatting and eating. Carrie has gotten some mayonnaise from her sandwich on her hands. Suddenly she leans over and wipes her hand on Terry's sleeve. "Oh . . . gross," exclaims Yolanda quietly to Terry. Neither of the girls say anything directly to Carrie. They move down the table so Carrie cannot reach them. (Observation notes, Carrie's fourth-grade year)

This vignette illustrates the problem of "double standards," which both children and adults often use in responding to the behavior of students with moderate or severe disabilities. While there are many situations in which tolerance, understanding, and accommodation are called for in supporting students with disabilities, there are also many in which tolerance may be viewed as disabling. In this situation, Carrie needed clear and direct feedback from her peers about her inappropriate behavior. Equally important, her peers needed to know how to set boundaries for what they would tolerate in ways that allowed them to remain comfortable in their relationship with Carrie. Simply moving away from Carrie was not a productive solution to this conflict for any of the students involved. Teachers have an important role to play in teaching nondisabled children how to be honest and direct with their peers with disabilities. In many cases, this involves helping nondisabled students appreciate the importance of their feedback to the learning of their peers with severe disabilities.

The intervention strategies that have been presented here, although focused on supporting outcomes in membership and relationships, do not preclude the importance of traditional skill development for individuals with severe disabilities. Indeed, the very skills educators work so hard on "teaching" students with severe disabilities (e.g., social communication skills, functional routines) were often acquired as an embedded outcome, along with the outcomes of membership and relationships. The reader is referred to other chapters in this text for more information on skill development in specific areas for students with severe disabilities. Although our emphasis is on supporting membership and relationships, we must acknowledge the important of effective use of evidence-based instructional strategies with students with severe disabilities. We know that instruction works. When you refer to the diagram of our conceptual framework (Figure 3–2), it is the point at the center, when skill development, membership, and relationships all intersect, that the best outcomes for all children are achieved.

Recognizing and Supporting Skill and Knowledge

This domain is where most of the effort of traditional special education has focused. When special educators discuss specially designed instruction and identify objects for children's IEPs, they mostly identify discrete, objective, and measurable behaviors. It is important that special education not lose its focus on discrete skills. One purpose of the outcome framework is to help educators consider how and when the skills being taught are being used. By considering how skills facilitate group membership and individual relationships, educational teams can better identify target skills that will yield true meaningful outcomes for students.

Strategies

There are a number of highly effective strategies for teaching discrete social skills to students with severe disabilities (for interesting reviews, see Joseph & Strain, 2003; McConnell, Missall, Silberglitt, & McEvoy, 2002; and Rogers, 2000). The skill areas of communication, motor, and academics are covered elsewhere in this volume, so our discussion will focus on discrete social skills. Brown and his colleagues (Brown, Odom, & Conroy, 2001) present a model for social skills interventions that include interventions that range in intensity and focus. That is, the model begins with interventions that address all the children in a classroom and are less intensive and increases in intensity to interventions that are developed for a specific child. The less intensive interventions, such as environmental design and affective interventions to influence attitudes, help establish the classroom climate and set the stage for social interaction. These interventions are directed to *all* the children in the classroom. The next level of intervention targets children who may be at risk for social problems and increases the intensity of the intervention. This level of intervention includes strategies such as incidental teaching of social skills and group instruction. These interventions require more planning and intervention on the part of the teacher and include fewer children directly. Finally, the most intensive interventions are developed in response to the needs of individual students and are presented to single students or small groups of students.

All levels of intervention as proposed by Brown and his colleagues can help facilitate the skills that result in improved peer relationships. When Sean was in kindergarten, his teacher used many strategies to create an environment where he was actively participating, was assigned valued roles and responsibilities, and where he was supported to contribute to the conversations that occurred in the classroom.

In Sean's kindergarten class, they had "Buddy Day" once a week. Although peer interaction was encouraged at all times, once a week special attention was given to children working in dyads. Children were dismissed to recess in pairs, worked in pairs on art projects, and ate lunch with their buddies.

These simple interventions helped set the stage for increasing relationships and membership and provided valuable opportunities for Sean to work on social-communicative skills.

Sean's teachers also used incidental teaching to address social skill development in the classroom. Incidental teaching involves identifying a child's initiation as a teachable moment and requiring the child to expand or elaborate his response. (See chapter 5 for more information.)

Sean often watched children play T-ball on the playground during recess. His motor skills had improved to the point that he was quite adept at hitting the ball off the tee, but he was hesitant about joining the other children playing. His teacher observed Sean watching the children play and saw him point to the ball as a child hit it. The teacher took advantage of this teachable moment to help Sean pick up the ball and join the game.

Sean also benefited greatly from explicit social skills instruction. This instruction was sometimes teacher directed and sometimes peer mediated (Odom et al., 1999). For example, after discovering Sean's love of baseball, the teachers decided to use explicit instructional techniques to teach him how to trade baseball cards. This skill was an extension of his turn-taking and conversation programs and was a wonderful vehicle for developing meaningful social relationships. The field of special education has a rich history of using evidence-based instructional strategies to teach many functional skills. It is important for educators to apply these strategies to teach social skills and to conduct those interventions in inclusive contexts.

Assessment and Evaluation of Peer Relationships

Although assessment and evaluation have always been cornerstones of special education, the systematic assessment of social behavior of individuals with disabilities has lagged behind measurement in other developmental domains. One reason for this may be the nondiscrete and complex nature of social behavior, while another may be that while the most authentic assessment of social behavior should probably occur within the classroom, those who have traditionally conducted such assessments are not comfortable or familiar with doing so in the classroom setting.

Since the publication of Strain, Cooke, and Apolloni's (1976) seminal book on the measurement and analysis of social behavior of students with developmental, learning, and behavioral disabilities, assessment approaches have relied primarily on the methodological strategies of applied behavior analysis. These approaches to measurement have been extremely valuable in identifying functional relationships between a variety of instructional variables and student social behavior. Recently, behavior-analytic methods have been extended conceptually and methodologically to the analysis of contextual factors affecting the quality and quantity of social relationships between students with disabilities and their peers (Breen & Haring, 1991; Haring, 1992; Meyer et al., 1998). In addition, Kennedy and his colleagues (e.g., Kennedy, Horner, & Newton, 1989; Kennedy & Itkonen, 1994) have demonstrated the value of methods drawn from social and community psychology in analyzing the networks of social relationships in which individuals with disabilities participate. These measurement approaches share a common focus on dimensions of social behavior that may be reliably quantified, such as the number of interactions a student with disabilities has with his or her peers or the duration of engaged time spent participating in an activity. With adaptation, such techniques can be highly useful to classroom teachers. However, our own work has been inspired in good part by our experience that social relationships between children with disabilities and their nondisabled peers, as well as other outcomes of their participation in regular class settings, are often not described adequately by quantitative measures.

There are several issues that constrain the effectiveness of quantitative measures as a means of documenting and evaluating change in social relationships, particularly when they are used in isolation. These include (a) the relative inflexibility of such measures in capturing unanticipated dimensions of change, (b) their relative insensitivity to issues of meaning embedded in social situations, and (c) the fact that teachers often

find these data of limited value in their daily work (Ferguson, 1987; Grigg, Snell, & Lloyd, 1989; Meyer & Evans, 1993). We do not suggest that quantitative measures be abandoned; in fact, they may be the most appropriate type of measure for most data collection in schools. However, in our own efforts to document outcomes for students with severe disabilities that their parents and teachers affirm as meaningful and important, we have found narrative data to be extremely valuable (for an elaboration on these arguments, see Schwartz, Staub, Gallucci, & Peck, 1995) and an effective complement to more quantitative measures. We have used a variety of simple data collection techniques drawn from the qualitative research tradition to enrich our description, analysis, and understanding of what is happening in students' social lives at school and elsewhere. Next, we briefly describe some of these techniques, including narrative observational records and interviews, and how we have used them. More complete accounts of how qualitative research strategies may be used to describe and evaluate change in educational settings are offered by Bogdan and Biklen (1992), Hubbard and Powers (1991), and others. Then we describe some more traditional strategies for collecting data and suggest how they may blended to meet the unique measurement needs that social behaviors present (Schwartz & Olswang, 1996).

Narrative Observational Records

Observational data recorded as narrative offer a highly flexible means of documenting the rich and dynamic flow of classroom events. Rich narrative descriptions of behavior in situational contexts may be a valuable source of insight about what is going on in a social setting. These descriptions are time consuming, and if not completed carefully, they may not provide the type of information necessary to evaluate a student's current level on goals and objectives or provide information that is useful in program planning. Figure 3-3 presents a form that can be used to gather short notes about social behaviors that can turn the outcome framework presented previously into a planning tool for writing an IEP. For example, narrative descriptions of interactions might help identify issues related to the quality of "helping" relationships emerging for children across the school year. Five examples of issues that we have observed to be of concern in some classrooms

FIGURE 3–3
IEP Planning Form

Membership

Membership Subdomain	Present Level of Performance/Participation	Supports and Instructional Needs, Possible Goals
School membership		
Class membership		
Teacher-created small groups		
Student-created small groups ("friendship cliques")		
Outside-of-school groups		

Relationships

Relationships Subdomain	Present Level of Performance	Supports and Instructional Needs, Possible Goals
Play/companionship		
Helper		
Helpee		
Conflict (Note: It is important to conduct a functional behavior assessment if these relationships are problematic or result in challenging behaviors.)		

Skills

Skills Subdomain	Present Level of Performance	Supports and Instructional Needs, Possible Goals
Communication		
Academic		
Motor		
Independence		

and that might be evaluated using narrative data include the following:

1. To what extent is assistance from peers and adults really helpful (or unneeded, intrusive, stigmatizing)?
2. Are nondisabled children becoming de facto aides to children with disabilities?
3. What are the attitudes, interpretations, and responses of nondisabled children who are not directly involved in inclusive classrooms (e.g., children on the playground or in the cafeteria)?
4. How do nondisabled peers respond to "inappropriate" behaviors of peers with disabilities? (e.g., Are they direct in giving feedback to the child? Do they respond pejoratively?)
5. In what ways are issues of inclusiveness part of regular class meetings and discussions, and to what extent are these issues considered to be about all

children in the classroom and not just those with identified disabilities?

Interviews

Interviews are another source of data teachers may find useful in evaluating social relationships among students. In fact, interviews provide a source of insight about how students perceive their relationships, which may be uniquely valuable to teachers and other adults, who often have only partial understanding of the students' point of view. Some disadvantages of interviews include the time-consuming nature of conducting and analyzing the interviews and the difficulty in using these data to document student progress.

If you choose to use interview, the type of questions you ask will affect the usefulness of the information you receive. We have found that interview protocols that begin with an open-ended question asking for description rather than evaluation of "what's going on" in relation to the student with disabilities or others in the classroom are the most effective. We also attempt to establish trust with the interviewee by assuring them that they do not have to answer every question and that they can stop whenever they want. Using an open-ended interview strategy allows the adult or student being interviewed an opportunity to bring up issues of concern that the interviewer may not know to ask about. This information may be of great value to teachers and others who are trying to develop a richer understanding of the social experiences and relationships of students with severe disabilities for the purpose of designing interventions as well as monitoring and evaluating change.

Analyzing and Evaluating Narrative Data

The value of narrative (qualitative) data as a source of information about what is going on in the social lives of students with disabilities is enhanced to the extent that these data are read and analyzed regularly. Simply jotting down observational notes or excerpts from conversations with children and others will not in itself necessarily lead to greater understanding of what is going on in the classroom. But the reflection involved in regular and systematic analysis of the data does. This analytic process need not be highly formal, but it should be ongoing. Furthermore, it should involve all the members of the team, including the special educator, general educator, parent(s), and any

other individuals providing services to the student (e.g., paraeducator, physical therapist). The use of a reflective journal may add considerably to the depth of this process of "re-searching" the data for patterns of behavior, context events, or other factors affecting social relationships. Hubbard and Powers (1991) describe a variety of specific techniques teachers have used for analysis of narrative data, such as looking for common themes across journal entries or identifying information that doesn't seem to fit to bring up possible issues *of concern*.

Blending Traditional and Alternative Data Collection Strategies

When discussing assessment and data collection, it is helpful to go back to the basics. The basic idea of assessment is to collect information that will help you answer a question. In special education, one can think of IEP objectives as the questions and data on child performance as the information we collect to attempt to answer those questions. Therefore, it is important that the type of data you collect is informed by the question you are asking (Schwartz & Olswang, 1996). In terms of child behavior, we can ask questions about how frequently behavior happened, how long it lasted, who was around when it happened, whether the child needed help, and even whether the child appeared to be happy when they were demonstrating the behavior. All this information could be important to answer questions about a child's social competence; however, the most important characteristic of the data we collect must be that it answers the question we are asking. For example, if I am interested in the fluency of a specific behavior, then knowing how long it lasted may help me answer my question. If I am interested in generalization, knowing that a child can name pictures at a rate of 35 a minute is not helpful.

The challenge of data collection, whether it is using quantitative or qualitative methods, is to match data collected to the question being asked. Figure 3–4 presents a matrix that can be used to help plan instruction and data collection. This sample matrix displays targeted behaviors by social domain across the activities of a typical school day for Sean. Although much instruction is embedded across the day and teachers are always encouraged to take advantage of teachable moments, this matrix indicates when teachers will include specially designed instruction and data collection. Teachers can also use the matrix to help

FIGURE 3–4
Planning and Data Collection Matrix

Student's Name: Sean		Week of: February 22, 2004	
Daily Schedule	**Membership**	**Relationships**	**Skills**
Arrival/transitions	Sign in and check job chart (frequency)	Greet peers by name (frequency) Respond to greetings (frequency)	Manage materials independently (count number of teacher prompts)
Journal writing	Share journal with his small group (count number of teacher prompts) Participate at his assigned seat (1–5 rating scale)	Hand out journal to group members (count number of teacher prompts) Ask peers for assistance (frequency)	Writing short sentences Drawing picture to match stories (work sample)
Reading	Participate in teacher-led and student-led groups (1-5 rating scale)	Assist other students with reading (duration of engagement) Work with peer on completing a book (duration of engagement)	Improve reading fluency (weekly probes) Improve comprehension (weekly probes)
Class meeting	Follow teacher-directed activity (count number of teacher prompts) Participate in group discussions and problem solving (frequency of turns)	Work collaboratively with peers (duration of engagement)	Conversation skills (number of turns) Question-answering skills (frequency) Problem solving (decrease in challenging behavior)
Math	Work on problems in teacher-assigned groups (count number of teacher prompts) Select partner for small-group work (count number of teacher prompts)	Receive or provide assistance to partners (frequency)	Understanding of basic arithmetic facts Basic concepts (weekly probes)
Lunch	Eat lunch with student-selected group (narrative)	"Hang out" with peers (narrative)	Manage materials independently (count number of teacher prompts)
Social studies	Participate in teacher-selected group (narrative)	Work with partner (narrative)	Basic concepts Language comprehension(weekly probes)
Independent work			Fluency of previously acquired skills (work samples) Self-regulation (decrease in challenging behaviors)
Choice	Participate in student-selected group (duration of engagement)	Participate in appropriate leisure skills with partner (duration of engagement)	Conversation skills (number of turns)
Recess	Participate in student-selected group (duration of engagement)	Participate in appropriate leisure skills with partner (duration of engagement)	Conversation skills (number of turns plus narrative to comment on content)

them keep track of what data have and have not been collected. This type of tool can also be extremely helpful in lesson planning and developing class activities.

Nondisabled Students and Severely Disabled Peers: All True Benefits Are Mutual

Facilitating the social relationships of people with severe disabilities has become a greater priority in recent years. Why, when general education is seemingly obsessed with high-stakes testing on traditional academic subjects, have professionals working with students with severe disabilities worked even harder on social relationships? One reason may be that family members, educators, and researchers value the role that satisfying social relationships play in the quality of life for people with disabilities and their families. It follows, then, that other people will also benefit from the improved social skills and social relationships of people with severe disabilities. Research and development work related to social relationships between children with severe disabilities and their nondisabled peers has been focused almost exclusively on the functions of these relationships in the lives of children with disabilities (Haring, 1991; Meyer et al., 1998; Strully & Strully, 1985). One of the most robust phenomena we have observed in our inclusive schools research is the positive value many nondisabled students place on their relationships with peers who have severe disabilities. Indeed, the relatively few studies that have been carried out to evaluate the impact of these relationships on nondisabled students are quite consistent in their findings (Staub & Peck, 1994–1995). Specifically, it is clear that nondisabled students are perceived by themselves, their parents, and their teachers as benefiting in a variety of ways from their relationships with peers who have severe disabilities. These include the following:

1. Increased understanding of how other people feel
2. Increased acceptance of differences in appearance and behavior
3. Increased sense of self-worth in contributing to the lives of others
4. Increased sense of commitment to personal principles of social justice (Biklen, Corrigan, & Quick, 1989; Helmstetter, Peck, & Giangreco, 1994; Murray-Seegert, 1989; Peck, Carlson, & Helmstetter, 1992; Peck, Donaldson, & Pezzoli, 1990; Staub, 1998; Staub et al., 1994)

In addition, the academic progress of nondisabled students is not harmed by the inclusion of students with severe disabilities in regular classes (Hollowood, Salisbury, Rainforth, & Palombaro, 1995; Peck et al., 1992; Sharpe, York, & Knight, 1994).

Perhaps most exciting is the reciprocity of outcomes between students with and without moderate and severe disabilities that emerged from many of the relationships we observed over the course of our follow-along research. Three outcomes that we perceived to be mutually beneficial included (a) warm and caring companionships, (b) increased growth in social cognition and self-concept, and (c) the development of personal principles and an increased sense of belonging (Staub, 1998).

Companionship

One of the most important functions of relationships is to enable us to feel safe, loved, and cared for. When Karly and Deanne first became acquainted in their K–2, multiage class, each needed a friend. Both were shy, hesitant, and often intimidated by the activity that surrounded them. By becoming companions, they found comfort in each other's presence in an overwhelming situation.

> *Deanne is truly a friend for Karly. They hang out, they comfort each other, and they are always hugging and holding hands. Karly and Deanne truly have a "bud" friendship. You don't want to be friends with everyone in the classroom necessarily, but everyone has a need for at least one buddy. That's what they provide to each other. (Karly's and Deanne's teacher)*

Growth in Social Cognition and Self-Concept

We found that several of the nondisabled children who participated in our research identified as "connected" to their peers with disabilities became more aware of the needs of their disabled peers. These children became skilled at understanding and reacting to the behaviors of their classmates with disabilities. Stacey, a nondisabled peer of Carrie's who attended class with Carrie for many years, was perceived to have benefited from her long-standing relationship with Carrie.

I think Stacey is at a point where she looks at Carrie as a friend, and I think inclusion, overall, has benefited Stacey in the sense that Stacey will never judge someone by their mental ability, whether they have Down syndrome or are developmentally delayed. I think she's come to a point where later on in life, if she has a chance to hire someone that could do the job with a disability, she would be the first one to say "yeah." (Carrie's and Stacey's teacher)

Likewise, having a relationship with Stacey was very important to Carrie's own sense of self-worth. Stacey not only provided Carrie with a model for how to socialize appropriately but also helped Carrie feel better about herself.

Stacey has had an enormous impact on Carrie's behavior. Carrie wants to do the "right thing" in front of Stacey, and you can really tell that she feels reinforced when Stacey compliments her on her behavior or actions. (Carrie's mother)

Development of Personal Principles

Children are extremely vigilant about the way vulnerable peers are treated by other children and by adults (Bukowski, Newcomb, & Hartup, 1996). While the risks of vulnerability, including social rejection and exclusion, are commonly recognized for children with disabilities, the meanings that nondisabled students may construct about the experiences they observe in relation to their peers with disabilities have received little empirical attention from researchers and little practical attention from educators. We believe that there may be considerable risks for nondisabled students that are constituted by their belief that it is not safe to be weaker than others in our society. Significantly, the likelihood of children drawing this conclusion appears to be compounded, not reduced, when vulnerable peers are sent away (to other classes or to other schools).

Viewed from this perspective, the inclusion of children with severe disabilities in regular classes creates both risk and opportunity for all children. The creation of classroom and school communities in which developmental differences are accepted and in which vulnerability is not observed to produce exclusion may represent one of our most powerful opportunities to make schools psychologically safer and more humane places for all children. The social relationships that develop between children with disabilities and their nondisabled peers thus constitute a wonderful opportunity for all educators. For the benefits of these relationships to be realized, it is essential that educators, parents, and other adults concerned with the well-being and development of children recognize the deep ways in which our relationships with people with disabilities offer us possibilities to see and to redefine who we are.

Brittany [Sean's nondisabled classmate] definitely keeps us on our toes. One day last week, Sean was really having a hard time—lots of screaming and fussing. I asked his teaching assistant to take him for a walk. I was stressed that the kids were getting stressed. Brittany came up to me and said, "I think we should ignore Sean's screaming and find something that he wants to do in class. Think how bad he feels being sent out of the room." Well, how do you respond to that? What it did was force me to push for a better communication system on his part, and the special education staff have really responded positively. But really, it caused me to look at Sean differently, not as a child with disabilities but as a classmate, a peer. (Sean's teacher)

Summary

This chapter highlights the importance of social relationships in the lives of all children. The level of importance and value that teachers place on supporting and facilitating their students' relationships will influence greatly their successful development. It is our hope that this chapter has provided ideas and tools for teachers to use in this important capacity.

Suggested Activities

1. Plan to spend at least 40 minutes in an inclusive classroom to observe a target student's interactions with his or her peers. Write down your observations in an objective fashion (e.g., provide a running account of what you observe without comment or judgment). After your observation, read over your notes and write your responses to the following:

   a. What looked "right" about the interactions I observed? (For example, nondisabled students were treating student with severe disabilities respectfully, student with severe disabilities was included in conversations.)

b. What looked "uncomfortable" about the interactions I observed? (For example, nondisabled students were not treating the student with severe disabilities as a member of their class.)

c. What was working well in the classroom environment for promoting peer interactions? (For example, the arrangement of desks allowed for easy conversation among students, the teacher used cooperative learning activities to promote interactions.)

d. What barriers were evident in the classroom environment that interfered with students' interactions? (For example, a class rule was that students were not to talk with one another during activities.)

2. Looking back over your responses to the items in question 1, develop an action plan that specifies how the classroom environment could be arranged to facilitate more appropriate peer interactions. What are things the teacher(s) could do? What environmental changes would you recommend? What types of activities would facilitate more peer interactions?

References

Apolloni, T., & Cooke, T. P. (1975). Peer behavior conceptualized as a variable influencing infant and toddler development. *American Journal of Orthopsychiatry, 45*, 4–17.

Baer, D. M., Wolf, M. M., & Risley, T. R. (1987). Some still-current dimensions of applied behavior analysis. *Journal of Applied Behavior Analysis, 20*, 313–327.

Baumgart, D., Brown, L., Pumpian, I., Nisbet, J., Ford, A., Sweet, M., et al. (1982). The principle of partial participation and individualized adaptations in educational programs for severely handicapped students. *Journal of the Association for Persons with Severe Handicaps, 1*, 17–27.

Biklen, D., Corrigan, C., & Quick, D. (1989). Beyond obligation: Student's relations with each other in integrated classes. In D. Lipsky & A. Garnter (Eds.), *Beyond separate education: Quality education for all* (pp. 207–222). Baltimore: Paul H. Brookes.

Billingsley, F., Gallucci, C., Peck, C., Schwartz, I., & Staub, D. (1996). "But those kids can't even do math": An alternative conceptualization of outcomes for inclusive education. *Special Education Leadership Review, 3*, 43–56.

Bogdan, R., & Biklen, S. (1992). *Qualitative research for education: An introduction to theory and methods.* Boston: Allyn & Bacon.

Breen, C., & Haring, T. G. (1991). Effects of contextual competence on social initiations. *Journal of Applied Behavioral Analysis, 24*, 337–347.

Bronfenbrenner, U. (1979). *The ecology of human development.* Cambridge, MA: Harvard University Press.

Brown, W. H., Odom, S. L., & Conroy, M. A. (2001). An intervention hierarchy for promoting young children's peer interactions in natural environments. *Topics in Early Childhood Special Education, 21*(3), 162–175.

Bruner, J. (1990). *Acts of meaning.* Cambridge, MA: Harvard University Press.

Bruner, J. (1996). *The culture of education.* Cambridge, MA: Harvard University Press.

Bryant, B. K. (1998). Children's coping at school: The relevance of failure and cooperative learning for enduring peer and academic success. In L. H. Meyer, H. S. Park, M. Grenot-Scheyer, I. S. Schwartz, & B. Harry (Eds.), *Making friends: The influences of culture and development* (pp. 353–368). Baltimore: Paul H. Brookes.

Bukowski, W. M., Newcomb, A. F., & Hartup, W. W. (1996). *The company they keep: Friendship in childhood and adolescence.* New York: Cambridge University Press.

Cohen, E. (1986). *Designing groupwork: Strategies for the use of heterogeneous classrooms.* New York: Teachers College Press.

Cole, M. (1996). *Cultural psychology: The once and future discipline.* Cambridge, MA: Harvard University Press.

Copeland, S. R., Hughes, C., Agran, M., Wehmeyer, M. L., Fowler, S. E. (2000). An intervention package to support high school students with mental retardation in general education classrooms. *American Journal on Mental Retardation, 107*, 32–45.

Epstein, J. L., & Karweit, N. (1983). *Friends in school: Patterns of selection and influence in secondary schools.* New York: Academic Press.

Ferguson, D. L. (1987). *Curriculum decision making for students with severe handicaps: Policy and practice.* New York: Teachers College Press.

Ferguson, D. L. (1994). Is communication really the point? Some thoughts on interventions and membership. *Mental Retardation, 32*, 7–18.

Ferguson, D. L., & Baumgart, D. (1991). Partial participation revisited. *Journal for the Association for Persons with Severe Handicaps, 16*, 218–227.

Fisher, M. (2001). Andre's story: Frames of friendship. In M. Grenot-Scheyer, M. Fisher, & D. Staub (eds.), *At the end of the day: Lessons learned in inclusive education.* Baltimore: Paul H. Brookes.

Fiske, A. P. (1992). The four elementary forms of sociality: Framework for a unified theory of social relations. *Psychological Review, 99*, 689–723.

Gallucci, C., Staub, D., Peck, C., Schwartz, I. & Billingsley, F. (1996). *But we wouldn't have a good class without him: Effects of a peer-mediated approach on membership outcomes for students with moderate and severe disabilities.* Seattle: University of Washington.

Garfinkle, A. N., & Schwartz, I. S. (2002). Peer imitation: Increasing social interactions in children with autism and other developmental disabilities in inclusive preschool classrooms. *Topics in Early Childhood Special Education, 22*, 26–38.

Gaylord-Ross, R., Haring, T., Breen, C., & Pitts-Conway, V. (1984). Training and generalization of social integration skills with autistic youth. *Journal of Applied Behavior Analysis, 17*, 229–247.

Gaylord-Ross, R., & Peck, C. A. (1985). Integration efforts for students with severe mental retardation. In D. Bricker & J. Filler (Eds.),

Serving students with severe mental retardation: From research to practice (pp. 185-207). Reston, VA: Council for Exceptional Children.

Geertz, C. (1973). *Interpretation of cultures.* New York: Basic Books.

Giangreco, M., Edelman, S., Luiselli, T., & MacFarland, S. (1997). Helping or hovering? Effects of instructional proximity on students with disabilities. *Exceptional Children, 64*, 7-18.

Gibbs, J. (2000). *A new way of learning and being together.* Windsor, CA: Center Source Systems.

Greenwood, C. R., Maheady, L., & Delquadri, J. (2002). Classwide peer tutoring programs. In M. R. Shinn, H. M. Walker, & G. Stoner (Eds.), *Interventions for academic and behavior problems II: Preventive and remedial approaches* (pp. 611-650). Bethesda, MD: National Association of School Psychologists.

Grenot-Scheyer, M., Fisher, M., & Staub, D. (2001). *At the end of the day: Lessons learned in inclusive education.* Baltimore: Paul H. Brookes.

Grenot-Scheyer, M., Staub, D., Peck, C. A., & Schwartz, I. S. (1998). Reciprocity and friendships: Listening to the voices of children and youth with and without disabilities. In L. H. Meyer, H. S. Park, M. Grenot-Scheyer, I. S. Schwartz, & B. Harry (Eds.), *Making friends: The influences of culture and development* (pp. 149-168). Baltimore: Paul H. Brookes.

Grigg, N. C., Snell, M., & Lloyd, B. (1989). Visual analysis of student evaluation data: A qualitative analysis of teacher decision making. *Journal of the Association for Persons with Severe Handicaps, 14*, 23-32.

Haring, T. G. (1991). Social relationships. In L. Meyer, C. Peck, & L. Brown (Eds.), *Critical issues in the lives of people with severe handicaps* (pp. 195-217). Baltimore: Paul H. Brookes.

Haring, T. G. (1992). The context of social competence: Relations, relationships and generalization. In S. Odom, S. McConnel, & M. McEvoy, (Eds.), *Social competence of young children with disabilities: Issues and strategies for intervention* (pp. 307-320). Baltimore: Paul H. Brookes.

Haring, T. G., & Breen, C. G. (1992). A peer-mediated social network intervention to enhance the social integration of persons with moderate and severe disabilities. *Journal of the Association for Persons with Severe Handicaps, 13*, 20-27.

Hart, B. M., & Risley, T. R. (1996). *Meaningful differences in the everyday experiences of young American children.* Baltimore: Paul H. Brookes.

Hartup, W. W. (1983). Peer relations. In E. M. Hetherington (Ed.), *Handbook of psychology: Vol. IV. Socialization, personality, and social development* (pp. 103-196). New York: Wiley.

Hedeen, D., Ayres, B., & Tate, A. (2001). Charlotte's story: Getting better, happy day, problems again! In M. Grenot-Scheyer, M. Fisher, & D. Staub (eds.), *At the end of the day: Lessons learned in inclusive education.* Baltimore: Paul H. Brookes

Helmstetter, E., Peck, C. A., & Giangreco, M. F. (1994). Outcomes of interactions with peers with moderate or severe disabilities: A statewide survey of high school students. *Journal of the Association for Persons with Severe Handicaps, 19*, 263-276.

Hollowood, T. M., Salisbury, C. L., Rainforth, B., & Palombaro, M. M. (1995). Use of instructional time in classrooms serving students with and without severe disabilities. *Exceptional Children, 61*, 242-253.

Hubbard, R., & Powers, B. (1991). *The art of classroom inquiry.* Portsmouth, NH: Heineman.

Hughes, C., Rodi, M. S., Lorden, S. W., Pitkin, S. E., Derer, K. R., Hwang, B., & Cai, X. (1999). Social interactions of high school students with mental retardation and their general education peers. *American Journal on Mental Retardation, 104*, 533-544.

Hunt, P., Alwell, M., & Goetz, L. (1988). Acquisition of conversation skills and the reduction of inappropriate social interaction behaviors. *Journal of the Association for Persons with Severe Handicaps, 13*, 20-27.

Janney, R., & Snell, M. (1996). How teachers use peer interactions to include students with moderate and severe disabilities in elementary general education classes. *Journal of the Association for Persons with Severe Handicaps, 21*, 72-80.

Janney, R. E., & Snell, M. E. (1997). How teachers include students with moderate and severe disabilities in elementary classes: The means and meaning of inclusion. *Journal of the Association for Persons with Severe Handicaps, 22*, 159-69.

Jones, V., & Jones, L. (2000). *Comprehensive classroom management.* Boston: Allyn & Bacon.

Joseph, G. E., & Strain, P. S. (2003). Comprehensive evidence-based social-emotional curricula for young children: An analysis of efficacious adoption potential. *Topics in Early Childhood Special Education, 23*, 65-76.

Kaye, K. (1982). *The mental and social life of babies: How parents create persons.* Chicago: University of Chicago Press.

Kennedy, C. H., Horner, R., & Newton, S. (1989). Social contacts of adults with severe disabilities living in the community: A descriptive analysis of relationship patterns. *Journal of the Association for Persons with Severe Handicaps, 14*, 190-196.

Kennedy, C. H., & Itkonen, T. (1994). Some effects of regular class participation on the social contacts and social networks of high school students with severe disabilities. *Journal of the Association for Persons with Severe Handicaps, 19*, 1-10.

Lave, J., & Wenger, E. (1991). *Situated learning: Legitimate peripheral participation.* New York: Cambridge University Press.

Lieber, J. (1994). Conflict and its resolution in preschoolers with and without disabilities. *Early Education and Development, 5*, 5-17.

Lipsky, D. K., & Gartner, A. (1998). Taking inclusion into the future. *Educational Leadership, 56*, 78-81.

McBride, B. J., & Schwartz, I. S. (2003). Effects of teaching early interventionists to use discrete trials during ongoing classroom activities. *Topics in Early Childhood Special Education, 23*, 5-18.

McConnell, S. R., Missall, K. N., Silberglitt, B., & McEvoy, M. A. (2002). Promoting social development in preschool classrooms. In M. R. Shinn, H. M. Walker, & G. Stoner (Eds.), *Interventions for academic and behavior problems II: Preventive and remedial approaches* (pp. 501-536). Bethesda, MD: National Association of School Psychologists.

McGregor, G., & Vogelsberg, T. (1998) Inclusive schooling practices: Pedagogical and research foundations. A synthesis of the literature that informs best practices about inclusive schooling. Allegheny Univ. of the Health Sciences, Pittsburgh, PA.

Meyer, L., & Evans, I. (1993). Science and practice in behavioral intervention: Meaningful outcomes, research validity and usable knowledge. *Journal of the Association for Persons with Severe Handicaps, 18*, 224-234.

Meyer, L. H., Park, H. S., Grenot-Scheyer, M., Schwartz, I. S., & Harry, B. (1998). Participatory research approaches for the study of the social relationships of children and youth. In L. H. Meyer, H. S. Park, M. Grenot-Scheyer, I. S. Schwartz, & B. Harry (Eds.), *Making friends: The influences of culture and development* (pp. 3–30). Baltimore: Paul H. Brookes.

Murray-Seegert, C. (1989). *Nasty girls, thugs, and humans like us: Social relations between severely disabled and nondisabled students in high school*. Baltimore: Paul H. Brookes.

Nelson, J., Lott, L., & Glenn, H. (1993). *Positive discipline in the classroom*. Rocklin, CA: Prima.

Odom, S. L., McConnell, S. R., McEvoy, M. A., Peterson, C., Ostrosky, M., Chandler, L., et al. (1999). Relative effects of interventions supporting social competence of young children with disabilities. *Topics in Early Childhood Special Education, 19*, 75–91.

Ohtake, Y. (2003). Increasing class membership of students with severe disabilities through contribution to classmates' learning. *Research and Practice for Persons with Severe Disabilities, 28*, 228–231.

Peck, C. A., Carlson, D., & Helmstetter, E. (1992). Parent and teacher perceptions of outcomes for typically developing children enrolled in integrated early childhood programs: A statewide survey. *Journal of Early Intervention, 16*, 53–63.

Peck, C. A., Donaldson, J., & Pezzoli, M. (1990). Some benefits non-handicapped adolescents perceive for themselves from their social relationships with peers who have severe handicaps. *Journal of the Association for Persons with Severe Handicaps, 15*, 241–249.

Peck, C., Gallucci, C., Staub, D., & Schwartz, I. (1998, April). *The function of vulnerability in the creation of inclusive classroom communities: Risk and opportunity*. Paper presented at the annual meeting of the American Educational Research Association, San Diego.

Peck, C. A., Schwartz, I., Staub, D., Gallucci, C., White, O., & Billingsley, F. (1994, December). *Analysis of outcomes of inclusive education: A follow-along study*. Paper presented at the annual meeting of the Association for Persons with Severe Handicaps, Atlanta.

Pernat, D. (1995). Inclusive education and literacy: Engaging a student with disabilities into language arts activities in a sixth grade classroom. *Network, 4*(4), 12–19.

Putnam, J. (Ed.). (1993). *Cooperative learning and strategies for inclusion*. Baltimore: Paul H. Brookes.

Rogers, S. J. (2000). Interventions that facilitate socialization in children with autism. *Journal of Autism and Developmental Disorders, 30*, 399–410.

Routman, R. (1994). *Invitations: Changing as teachers and learners in K–12*. Portsmouth, NH: Heineman.

Salisbury, C., Gallucci, C., Palombaro, M., & Peck, C. (1995). Strategies that promote social relationships among elementary students with and without severe disabilities in inclusive schools. *Exceptional Children, 62*, 125–137.

Salisbury, C., & Palombaro, M. M. (1998). Friends and acquaintances: Evolving relationships in an inclusive elementary school. In L. H. Meyer, H. S. Park, M. Grenot-Scheyer, I. S. Schwartz, & B. Harry (Eds.), *Making friends: The influences of culture and development* (pp. 81–104). Baltimore: Paul H. Brookes.

Sameroff, A., & Chandler, M. (1975). Reproductive risk and the continuum of caretaking casualty. In F. Horowitz, M. Hetherington, S. Scarr-Scalapatek, & G. Siegel (Eds.), *Review of research in child development* (Vol. 4, pp. 197–243). Chicago: University of Chicago Press.

Sandall, S. R., Hemmeter, , Smith, B. J., & M. E. McLean (Eds.). (2004). *DEC recommended practices in early intervention/early childhood special education*. Longmont, CO: Sopris West.

Sandall, S. R., & Schwartz, I.S. (2002). *Building blocks: A comprehensive approach for supporting young children in inclusive placements*. Baltimore: Paul H. Brookes.

Sapon-Shevin, M. (1992). Student support through cooperative learning. In W. Stainback & S. Stainback (Eds.), *Support networks for inclusive schooling* (pp. 65–80). Baltimore: Paul H. Brookes.

Schneider, E. (1996, September). Giving students a voice in the classroom. *Educational Leadership*, pp. 22–26.

Schnorr, R. (1990). Peter? He comes and he goes . . . First graders' perspectives on a part-time mainstreamed student. *Journal of the Association for Persons with Severe Handicaps, 15*, 231–240.

Schwartz, I. S. (2000). Standing on the shoulders of giants: Looking ahead to facilitate membership and relationships for children with disabilities. *Topics in Early Childhood Special Education, 20*, 123–128.

Schwartz, I. S., & Baer, D. M. (1991) Social validity assessments: Is current practice state of the art? *Journal of Applied Behavior Analysis, 24*, 189–204.

Schwartz, I. S., & Olswang, L. B. (1996). Evaluating child behavior change in natural settings: Exploring alternative strategies for data collection. *Topics in Early Childhood Special Education, 16*, 82–101.

Schwartz, I. S., Staub, D., Gallucci, C., & Peck, C. A. (1995). Blending qualitative and behavior analytic research methods to evaluate outcomes in inclusive schools. *Journal of Behavioral Education, 5*, 93–106.

Sharpe, M. N., York, J. L., & Knight, J. (1994). Effects of inclusion on the academic performance of classmates without disabilities. *Remedial and Special Education, 15*, 281–287.

Shonkoff, J. P., & Phillips, D. A. (Eds.). (2000). *From neurons to neighborhoods: The science of early childhood development*. Washington, DC: National Academy Press.

Snell, M.E., & Janney, R. E. (2000). Teachers' problem-solving about children with moderate and severe disabilities in elementary classrooms. *Exceptional Children, 66*, 472–90.

Staub, D. (1998). *Delicate threads: Friendships between children with and without special needs in inclusive settings*. Bethesda, MD: Woodbine House.

Staub, D., & Hunt, P. (1993). The effects of a social interaction training on high school peer tutors of schoolmates with severe disabilities. *Exceptional Children, 60*, 41–57.

Staub, D., & Peck, C. A. (1994–1995). What are the outcomes for nondisabled kids? *Educational Leadership, 52*, 36–40.

Staub, D., Schwartz, I. S., Gallucci, C., & Peck, C. A. (1994). Four portraits of friendship at an inclusive school. *Journal of the Association for Persons with Severe Handicaps, 19*, 314–325.

Staub, D., Spaulding, M., Peck, C.A., Gallucci, C., & Schwartz, I.S. (1996). Using nondisabled peers to support the inclusion of students with disabilities at the junior high school level. *Journal of the Association for Persons with Severe Handicaps, 21*, 194–205.

Strain, P., Cooke, T., & Apolloni, T. (1976). *Teaching exceptional children: Assessing and modifying social behavior*. New York: Academic Press.

Strully, J., & Strully, C. (1985). Friendship and our children. *Journal of the Association for Persons with Severe Handicaps, 10*, 224-227.

Sugai, G., Horner, R. H., & Gresham, F. M. (2002). Behaviorally effective school environments. In M. R. Shinn, H. M. Walker, & G. Stoner (Eds.), *Interventions for academic and behavior problems II: Preventive and remedial approaches* (pp. 315-350). Bethesda, MD: National Association of School Psychologists.

Voeltz, L. M. (1982). Effects of structured interactions with severely handicapped peers on children's attitudes. *American Journal of Mental Deficiency, 86*, 380-390.

Vygotsky, L. (1978). *Mind in society*. Cambridge, MA: Harvard University Press.

Williams, L. J., & Downing, J. E. (1998). Membership and belonging in inclusive classrooms: What do middle school students have to say? *Journal of the Association for Persons with Severe Handicaps. 23*, 98-110.

Wolf, M. M. (1977). Social validity: The case for subjective measurement or how applied behavior analysis is finding its heart. *Journal of Applied Behavior Analysis, 11*, 203-214.

Wolfberg, P. J. (1999). *Play and imagination in children with autism*. New York: Teachers College Press.

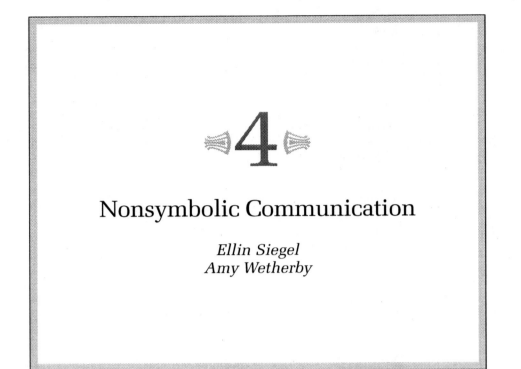

4

Nonsymbolic Communication

Ellin Siegel
Amy Wetherby

Although people communicate with each other in many ways, talking is the most common way. Spoken words are a symbolic mode of communication because they rely on forms that represent, or stand for, something else. For example, the spoken word "shoe" is a symbol that refers to things that you put on your feet. Similarly, the sign for shoe and a picture of a shoe are also symbols because they represent or refer to the class of objects that we know as shoes. Language is a system for combining symbols with shared meaning using formal rules of grammar and conversation. A child who says "shoe off" is using symbolic communication to ask for his or her shoe to be taken off. While most children immersed in a language-rich environment learn to talk without being formally taught,

children with disabilities may face significant challenges learning to talk, which may affect their ability to understand what others say or their ability to express themselves with words. Many individuals with severe disabilities have limited ways of expressing themselves or understanding those around them; they may communicate symbolically or nonsymbolically. Using the shoe example, a child can use nonsymbolic communication to request help in tying by moving her untied shoe toward another person, rubbing the shoe and moaning, or just crying. While symbolic communication may be much more explicit than nonsymbolic communication, there are many different ways to communicate without symbols, and nonsymbolic communication can be very powerful.

Marina is 3 years old and began attending an early intervention center last year. At age 1, she was not walking or talking but laughed frequently and always wanted to be near the "action" of her two older siblings and her parents. Marina's parents became very skilled at noticing and interpreting her subtle movements and facial expressions.

FIGURE 4–1

Marina enjoys interactions with her mother. They have learned how to read each other's expressions, and their enjoyment in this familiar peek-a-boo game is obvious

She smiled often as her head bobbed up and down. Her parents helped her learn to make choices by directing her gaze toward desired items. Her family learned to understand when Marina's body movements meant that she wanted a favorite game or event to occur (see Figure 4–1). For example, Marina would rock back and forth in a wagon to get her brother to pull it and reach up and climb on her mother's back to get a ride.

By age 2, Marina began having seizures, and her parents sought further medical testing, which led to the diagnosis of Angelman syndrome. This syndrome was first identified by Dr. Harry Angelman in 1965. Major clinical characteristics include microbrachycephaly (small head with a flattened occiput), abnormal results on electroencephalogram (EEG), an awkward gait, severe language impairment (usually without speech), excessive laughter, a protruding tongue, the mouthing of objects, and intense curiosity (Clayton-Smith & Pembrey, 1992; Dooley, Berg, Pakula, & MacGregor, 1981; Williams & Frais, 1982; see

http://www.angelman.org for information about Angelman syndrome).

A great deal of familiarity with Marina and her subtle ways of communicating was needed before the intervention staff could readily interpret her behaviors. The onset of her seizures led Marina to regress. Now, medication controls her seizures but makes her fatigue easily and her abilities fluctuate. The staff members are trying not only to interpret Marina's behaviors but also to encourage her to use the behaviors that she was using before the Angelman syndrome progressed. They want to solidify Marina's communication by developing her awareness of the effects that her communicative behaviors have on other people. In addition, the staff and her family are trying to get Marina to use more conventional gestures (giving an object, raising her arms to be picked up, holding an object up to show it, and reaching) and to expand her use of eye gaze so she will be more understandable and readable to people who are less familiar with her.

Ryan

When Ryan sees you approach him, he usually smiles, reaches toward you to shake hands, and vocalizes. He is a 16-year-old teenager who has limited peripheral vision and a mild hearing loss. He enjoys attention and expresses his interest by smiling at familiar people, extending his fisted hands toward objects or people, and making eye contact. Because of severe motor impairments, Ryan relies on others to move him. He has a variety of

supported positions: sitting in different adapted chairs, side lying, and sitting in a motorized wheelchair. It is difficult for Ryan to maintain his head erect for very long when seated and needs adaptations. He must be moved to new positions every hour.

Ryan attends the local high school in his community, where he rotates through many different subjects and spends part of the day in the community. He has developed some friendships with his peers, especially since he began assisting the football team. Paired with other assistants assigned to the football team, Ryan takes care of the team towels (i.e., laundering, folding, handing them). He also helps with getting drinks to the players.

Ryan tends to wait for others to interact with him but will indicate his interest in maintaining interactions by increasing his vocalizations or body movements. He turns his head away or is quiet when he wants to terminate or deter an interaction.

Nonsymbolic Skills

This chapter focuses on individuals who do not use or understand symbols and the rules of language. To communicate, these individuals rely on their own bodies and information from their current contexts or activities. Their communication may include facial expressions, body movements, gazing, gesturing, and touching. This communication has been referred to by many different terms, such as prelinguistic, prelanguage, and nonverbal. The authors of this chapter prefer the word "nonsymbolic" in order to focus on what individuals are doing. *Nonsymbolic behavior* is viewed as a legitimate form of communication, not just a transition to another stage. Because some individuals with severe disabilities rely primarily on nonsymbolic skills, it is crucial to recognize each individual's current communication repertoire and to expand it. Intervention that meets best practices treats the person with dignity and focuses on building on what the person can do. The basic right to affect others via communication is central to life (National

Joint Committee for the Communication Needs of Persons with Severe Disabilities, 1992) (see Box 4-1).

The Impact of the Disability

No single disability or combination of impairments distinguishes which individuals communicate primarily in a nonsymbolic manner. An individual who communicates in this way may have dual sensory impairments, a severe motor impairment, autism spectrum disorder, profound mental retardation, or a cognitive disability combined with a health impairment. Individuals who use nonsymbolic communication form a heterogeneous group. All young children communicate without symbols during the first year of life, and for some this mode continues for many years. Communication partners (school staff members such as teachers and speech-language therapists) must recognize nonsymbolic communication skills and have strategies to enhance these skills for young and older students who use this communication mode (see Box 4-2).

◀ ▶ Box 4–1 National Joint Committee

The National Joint Committee for the Communication Needs of Persons with Severe Disabilities (NJC) focuses on providing information on best practices. In 1992, the NJC established a communication *Bill of Rights* to relay the basic rights every individual has to affect interactions through communication. Everyone has the right to:

- Request what they want
- Refuse what they don't want
- Express preferences and feelings
- Be offered choices and refuse choices
- Request and get another's attention and interaction
- Request and get information about changes in routine or setting
- Get intervention to improve communication
- Get a response to their requests, even if not fulfilled
- Be able to get services and have communication aides at all times
- Be in settings with peers who don't have disabilities
- Be spoken and listened to with respect and courtesy
- Be spoken to directly, not talked about while present
- Have communication that is clear, meaningful, and culturally and linguistically appropriate

Website: **http://professional.asha.org/njc**

Box 4–2

The National Joint Committee for the Communication Needs for Persons with Severe Disabilities (NJC) has created an evidence-based document that can help ensure that all learners who have severe disabilities have access to needed communication supports and services. The NJC document *There Are No Prerequisites* can be accessed at **http://www.asha.org/njc**.

Table 4–1 displays nonsymbolic and symbolic behaviors and examples.

The Trifocus of Intervention

Most school staff and other communication partners expect to observe and respond to verbal or symbolic language. Educators and speech-language pathologists (SLPs) also need to understand the importance of nonsymbolic communication and to broaden the focus of their interventions and improve their responsiveness to nonsymbolic learners. Others' responsivity to child communication is viewed as a central influence on later child communication and language development (Harwood, Warren, & Yoder, 2002). Because most people typically use spoken language to communicate, it may be difficult for school staff as well as other partners to adjust their expressive messages to individuals with severe disabilities. Yet all of us use nonsymbolic expressions. When Mary asks you where Sam has gone, you tip your head in the direction Sam went. When a waitress is at the table next to you, you lift your coffee cup in the air, hoping that she will give you a refill. You may not be fully aware, however, of the many forms of nonsymbolic communication and may not use nonsymbolic communication to enhance your communication skills (Beukelman & Mirenda, 1998; Siegel & Cress, 2002; Stillman & Siegel-Causey, 1989).

Individuals who communicate nonsymbolically can have successful interactions with others. When a child cries, a staff member recognizes this as communication and tries to relieve discomfort. A reach toward the juice conveys the message for more. Nonsymbolic communication plays a key role in most interactions, especially with those who do not use symbols or have limited understanding of symbols (Stillman & Siegel-Causey, 1989).

The trifocus framework (Siegel & Cress, 2002; Siegel-Causey & Bashinski, 1997) incorporates concepts from various fields into three primary components: the learner, the partner, and the environmental context (Figure 4–2). The trifocus framework recognizes that communication partners and learners experience communication interactions mutually and that both parties are reciprocally affected. Because communication is a dynamic process involving at least two people, the willingness of individuals without disabilities to interact may be influenced by the limited behavioral repertoires

TABLE 4–1
Nonsymbolic and Symbolic Forms of Communication

Nonsymbolic	Symbolic
Vocal—Using sounds and utterances produced by voice	Verbal—Using words
Affect—Displaying a feeling or emotion	Sign language—Using system of hand and arm gestures
Tactual—Using touch (stimulation of passive skin receptors and active manipulation and exploration)	Photographs and pictures—Using visual representation or image
Body movement—General motion of body such as leaning, pulling away, or swaying	Representational objects—Using miniature objects to depict real objects or activity; using portions of a real object to depict a real object or activity.
Gestural—Using movement of the limbs or parts of body	Graphic system—Using a method of symbols (Blissymbolics, Rhebus pictures)
Physiological—Displaying functions of body such as alertness or muscle tone	
Visual—Using sense of sight	

Source: Adapted from "Introduction to Nonsymbolic Communication" by R. Stillman and E. Siegel-Causey. In *Enhancing Nonsymbolic Communication Interactions Among Learners with Severe Handicaps* (p. 4) by E. Siegel-Causey and D. Guess (Eds.), 1989, Baltimore: Paul H. Brookes. Reprinted by permission of Paul H. Brookes Publishing Company, P.O. Box 10624, Baltimore, MD 21285-0624.

FIGURE 4–2

The Trifocus Framework

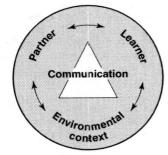

of individuals with severe disabilities. Therefore, one focus of intervention is on enhancing the communication skills of learners with nonsymbolic abilities by expanding their repertoire. A second focus of intervention is on enhancing the skills of communication partners. When interacting with individuals who are nonsymbolic communicators, the partner needs to take a more active role than when interacting with someone who talks. The partner needs to present information in a clear way without relying on symbols and be very responsive to nonsymbolic signals.

This framework recognizes the influence of the environmental context on communication interactions and in particular on the learner. Context encompasses all physical and social aspects of the setting. In order to enhance a student's nonsymbolic communication and responsiveness, partners will pay attention to the physical and social aspects of the environment. Physical refers both to the broad settings (e.g., home, school, and community) and the specific contexts that an intervention occurs within (snack, physical education, or break) as well as to the physical attributes of a setting (lighting, noise level, and materials) (Ault, Guy, Guess, Bashinski, & Roberts, 1995). Social environment includes aspects such as the peers and adults within close proximity of the learner, overall activity level of the setting, and the amount and type of social interaction or contact being provided to the learner by partners (Ault et al., 1995).

Figure 4–3 provides an overview of the trifocus framework. The multiple focus on learner, partner, and environment has considerations that should help the partner more effectively plan assessment and intervention. We organized this chapter using these three

FIGURE 4–3

Overview of Trifocus Framework

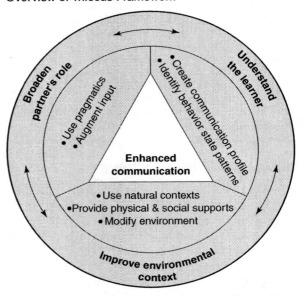

components: understand the learner (assessment), broaden the partner's role (use nonsymbolic input and be responsive to learner's nonsymbolic communication as part of intervention), and improve environmental contexts (modify the environment, use physical and social supports as part of intervention). The next section provides information related to early communication development, including the emergence and the parameters of nonsymbolic communication acquisition.

Early Communication Development

It is sometimes difficult to interpret messages of individuals who use nonsymbolic expressions, especially since most of us function in a world of symbols. Individuals with severe disabilities need to be systematically taught to interact, are likely to learn to communicate first about their own wants and needs, and are most likely to communicate in their familiar environments (Downing, 1999, Siegel & Cress, 2002).

Critical Aspects of Communication

Communication is a developmental process involving reciprocal interactions between individuals (Bates, O'Connell, & Shore, 1987; Duchan, 1995; Dunst, Lowe,

& Bartholomew, 1990; Wetherby, Reichle, & Pierce, 1998). Understanding and enhancing communication requires building on existing nonsymbolic behaviors that are communicative signals or that have the potential to be communicative.

> *When Marina smiled, her parents reacted by lighting up and keeping the activity going. They interpreted her smile as a signal of "I want" within the specific activity and repeated the event. At this early level of communication, Marina did not realize that smiling signaled a message to her family.*

Developmental research shows that infants communicate before they talk and that this ability unfolds during the first few years of life (Bates, 1979; Bloom, 1993; Bruner, 1981; Dore, 1986; McLean & Snyder-McLean, 1978, 1999; Siegel-Causey & Downing, 1987; Wetherby et al., 1998). In terms of assessment and instruction, the information compiled from research on the nonsymbolic stage in typical development is particularly relevant to individuals with severe disabilities who communicate in a similar manner. Extensive reviews of the developmental research on nonsymbolic communication and the communicative abilities of children with severe disabilities include Siegel-Causey, Ernst, and Guess (1987, 1989), Siegel-Causey and Guess (1989), Wetherby and Prizant (1992), and Wetherby, Warren, and Reichle (1998).

A Three-Stage Communication Progression

The emergence of communication is a developmental process involving reciprocal interactions between a caregiver and child. Bates and associates (Bates, 1979; Bates, Camaioni, & Volterra, 1975) have provided a theoretical framework to describe the emergence of communication and language. Borrowing terminology from the speech act theory of Austin (1962), they identified three stages in the development of communication. From birth, the infant is in the "perlocutionary stage." The "perlocution" is the effect of the message on the communication partner who must interpret messages. The infant's behavior systematically affects the caregiver and thus serves a communicative function, although the infant is not yet producing signals with the intention of accomplishing specific goals. For example, when an infant cries, this may signal hunger to the caregiver, and the caregiver responds to the crying by holding the child and offering a bottle. The child's

crying serves the function of requesting the caregiver's help although the child may not have deliberately tried to seek that outcome. By about 9 months of age, most children move to the "illocutionary stage" and begin to use preverbal gestures and sounds to communicate intentionally. The "illocution" is the purpose of the message as planned or intended by the speaker. At this stage, the child deliberately uses particular signals to communicate for preplanned effects on others. An example of intentional communication is when a child reaches toward a bottle, grunts, looks at the caregiver, and then looks back at the bottle to signal that he or she wants the bottle. At about 13 months of age, the child progresses to the "locutionary stage" and begins to construct propositions to communicate intentionally with referential words. The "locution" is the referential meaning of the message. At this stage, a child can request his or her bottle by reaching and using a word approximation, such as "baba," to refer to the bottle. Thus, communication and language development can be conceptualized as a three-stage process, involving movement from perlocutionary (preintentional, partner interpreted) communication to illocutionary (intentional nonverbal) communication to locutionary messages (verbal language) used intentionally to communicate. This model has been adapted for application to the emergence of communication in individuals with severe disabilities (e.g., Beukelman & Mirenda, 1998; McLean & Snyder-McLean, 1988; Musselwhite & St. Louis, 1988; Rowland & Stremel-Campbell, 1987). The speech act theory and its relationship to nonsymbolic behavior are described with examples in Table 4–2.

An important assumption of this three-stage progression is that all individuals communicate in some way. In applying this model to individuals with severe disabilities, communicative partners play a critical role in interpreting behaviors that are communicative. The model also highlights the broad range of communicative abilities spanning the perlocutionary and illocutionary stages. Understanding the developmental progression from perlocutionary to illocutionary communication can help partners detect and enhance progress in subtle but critical aspects of communicative development.

> *When Ryan was a preschooler, he did not intentionally communicate (perlocutionary stage). During this period, Ryan often interacted with nondisabled peers at preschool. On one such occasion, Tom, a peer,*

TABLE 4–2
Speech Act Theory and Nonsymbolic Behaviors

Definition	Nonsymbolic messages	Interpretation or meaning	Speech act messages	Interpretation or meaning
Perlocution (Partner interpreted communication): the effect or function of the message on the listener; interpretation of behaviors as if they were intentional	Ryan's first moves toward his book bag.	His friend interprets this to mean that Ryan wants the book bag and says, "Hey, you want some help buddy?"	Says "mm" after he swallows a bite of his sandwich.	His teacher assumes that he wants another bite and says, "Here's your sandwich."
Illocution (Intentional communication): the meaning of the message as planned by the speaker; using behaviors and conventional gestures with the intent of affecting the behavior of others	Ryan looks at his friends when the bell rings before gym class.	Ryan wants his friend to push him to gym class.	Andy says "nn" and turns his head away when the teacher puts the sandwich toward his mouth.	Andy is full.
Locution (Intentional symbolic communication): using words with the intent of affecting the behaviors of others			Andy smiles and says "yes" when his teacher extends his cup of juice toward him.	Andy uses words to convey wanting a drink.

Source: Based on *How to Do Things with Words* by J. Austin, 1962, Cambridge, MA: Harvard University Press, and *The Emergence of Symbols: Cognition and Communication in Infancy* by E. Bates, 1979, New York: Academic Press.

and Ryan were seated across from each other at a table. On the table was a large switch connected to a toy that had sound and movement linked to many small, colorful toy birds. Ryan squealed in delight each time Tom used the switch to make the toy movements occur. Ryan's vocal expressions became a humming sound when the toy's noises and movements stopped. Tom, with help from staff, learned to react to the humming as if Ryan expressed "I want more." Later Ryan was taught to hum and look at Tom to signal "more," and he also was taught to use the switch.

It is important for communication partners to understand how communication emerges because nonsymbolic communication may be the primary or only means used by individuals with severe disabilities. Communicative interactions are rooted in early social and emotional development in infants. Gaze, the expression of emotion, body movement, and orientation are signals (or forms) that guide infants' responses and

regulate social interactions. The caregiver's ability to interpret and respond contingently to the preintentional communicative signals of infants plays an important role in the child's development of intentional communication (Dore, 1986; Dunst et al., 1990; Harwood et al., 2002; Yoder, Warren, McCathren, & Leew, 1998). Early social interactions involving shared experiences lead to awareness of the effects that their behaviors have on others (Bruner, 1981; Corsaro, 1981). Thus, the responsiveness of communicative partners to learners' preintentional communicative behaviors plays a major role in developing communication skill.

Intentional Behavior
Behavior is intentional if an individual has an awareness of or a mental plan for a desired goal as well as the means to obtain the goal (Piaget, 1952). For example, if a child wants a toy on a shelf out of reach, the child may pull a chair over to the shelf, climb on the chair, and get the toy. This example demonstrates cognitive intentional

behavior. Parallels in the development of cognitive intentionality are seen in the social domain. For instance, the child may pull on the caregiver's pant leg, point to the toy, and vocalize until the caregiver gets the toy.

The constructs of intention and function are significant to a discussion of nonsymbolic communication. Since communication involves a dyadic interaction between a sender and a receiver, communicative intent must be considered in relation to the function of communication. *Intention* refers to the plan of the message sender, and *function* refers to the purpose of the act as interpreted by the message receiver. Look at Figure 4-4 and read about the following nonsymbolic communication act.

> *Marina looks at and reaches toward her ball, looks at her mother, looks back at the ball, and looks up at her mother. As a result, her mother tips the basket so that Marina can reach the ball. Marina's plan was to get the ball and play with Mom. The function of Marina's signal was to request an action, and her mother interpreted the signal as intended by Marina. The success of a communicative act depends on whether the sender's intention is appropriately interpreted by the receiver of the message. Marina's interaction with her mother was successful.*

Wetherby and Prizant (1989) suggested that intentional communication develops along a continuum beginning with automatic, reflexive reactions. Children then develop awareness of goals but do not have plans to achieve the goals. As children gain more experience,

they learn to coordinate their behaviors to pursue their goals. Further development in intentionality is evident in the use of *repair strategies* (i.e., strategies used to clarify one's intentions when communicative attempts are unsuccessful). Rudimentary efforts to repair involve repeating a signal to persist in achieving a goal. For example, if a child reaches to request a bottle and the caregiver does not respond, the child may reach again. More sophisticated efforts involve modifying the form of the signal. Using the same example of reaching to request a bottle, a child may repair by reaching again and adding a vocalization and eye gaze. A child's ability to use simple plans, coordinated plans, and alternative plans to achieve goals develops from 9 to 18 months of age, during Piaget's sensorimotor stages V and VI (Bates et al., 1975; Harding, 1984; Wetherby, Alexander, & Prizant, 1998). The ability to repair is evidence of intentionality and would indicate illocutionary communication.

> *Ryan has developed repair strategies. For example, his friend Matt is helping him get to their next class, art. As they enter the room, his teacher points to Matt's project and says, "Ryan, where is your project?" Ryan looks at her and vocalizes, "Ehh." "Don't worry, Matt can take you back to your locker." The teacher did not understand his message, so Ryan has to add to it using a repair strategy. Ryan's repair strategy is to look at the art teacher, vocalize louder, and pull his head to the right side of his wheelchair. "Oh, is it in your backpack?" she says as she points to his backpack. Ryan smiles.*

FIGURE 4–4
In the photo at left, Marina reaches toward the toy basket to request her ball (intention). In the photo (right), Marina's mother interprets the action to mean that Marina wants a toy (function) and tips the basket so that Marina can reach inside.

Chapter 4

Communication Roles

Communication involves taking turns between being a sender of a message (expressive role) and being a receiver (receptive role). Communicative partners interacting with nonsymbolic learners must be aware of these dual roles. Individuals with disabilities also must function as senders and receivers of messages. Figure 4-5 shows Marina and her mother in these dual communication roles.

While nonsymbolic communicators are individuals who use primarily nonsymbolic communication as senders, their receptive abilities may be comparable to or better than their expressive abilities. Before children comprehend the meaning of words, they use a variety of contextual cues to figure out how to respond, and therefore they may appear as if they comprehend specific words (Chapman, 1978; McLean & Snyder-McLean, 1978; Miller & Paul, 1995). For example, when

FIGURE 4–5
Marina and her mother both act as senders and receivers of messages. Marina is the sender first and reaches toward the jar (top left), and her mother is the receiver and responds to her request by giving her the jar. Marina then gives the jar to her mother to request her to open it (top right), and her mother responds by opening the jar. Her mother is then the sender and shows Marina what is inside the jar, and Marina responds by looking in the jar (bottom left). Marina's mother then blows bubbles and tells Marina to pop them, and Marina responds by popping the bubbles (bottom right).

a child is standing in front of a sink and an adult points to the faucet while saying "wash hands," the child can figure out how to respond from the situation without comprehending the word "wash" or "hands." As children move to the illocutionary stage of communication expression, they begin to comprehend nonverbal cues provided by their caregivers, including gestures, facial expression, and directed eye gaze (e.g., an adult pointing to or looking at an object "means" the child should give or attend to that object). Children may also respond to intonation cues (i.e., the melody or tone of speech) to determine how to respond (e.g., mom's loud, deep voice "means" angry). At this stage, children also may respond to situational cues by using the immediate environment and knowledge of what to do with objects to respond (e.g., observe what others do in the situation, knowing that you drink from a cup, knowing to put objects in a container). As children progress to the locutionary stage of expression, they begin to comprehend the meanings of familiar words but continue to be guided by the context. It is easy to overestimate a child's comprehension of language if one is not aware of the nonverbal, intonation, or situational cues that the child may be using to determine how to respond. The development of response strategies serves as a bridge to the comprehension of word meanings: contextual cues give children strategies for responding and guidance to the meanings of words.

Recognizing Nonsymbolic Communication

Nonsymbolic communication is a reciprocal interaction involving understanding or reception and signaling others or expression (Figure 4–6). The overlapping circles depict the communication partner's abilities to use both nonsymbolic and symbolic behavior.

For nonsymbolic learners, it is necessary to identify the observable behaviors that may serve a communicative function. The first parameter to identify is *how* the learner communicates, or what *forms* of communication are used. Nonsymbolic communication may be conventional in form if the meaning of the behavior is shared by many partners and is generally recognizable. Examples of conventional gestures are giving, showing, reaching, pointing, and open-palm requesting. However, nonsymbolic communication may be unconventional or idiosyncratic and understood only by someone who is very familiar with the individual and the context. Table 4–3 presents examples of forms that nonsymbolic communication may take, including unconventional yet effective forms, such as standing by a sink to request a drink or scratching oneself to protest an action.

A second parameter to identify is the function, or purpose, served by the communicative behavior. Children use presymbolic gestures and vocalizations to communicate for a variety of purposes before they use words (Bates, 1979; Coggins & Carpenter, 1981; Harding & Golinkoff, 1979; Wetherby, Cain, Yonclas, & Walker,

FIGURE 4–6
Reciprocal Nature of Communication Interactions

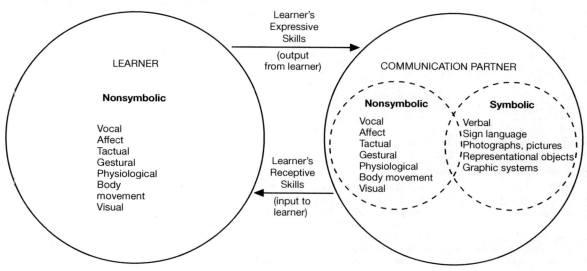

TABLE 4–3

Forms of Learner Nonsymbolic Communication

Generalized movements and changes in muscle tone
- Excitement in response to stimulation or in anticipation of an event
- Squirms and resists physical contact
- Changes in muscle tone in response to soothing touch or voice, in reaction to sudden stimuli, or in preparation to act

Vocalizations
- Calls to attract or direct another's attention
- Laughs or coos in response to pleasurable stimulation
- Cries in reaction to discomfort

Facial expressions
- Smiles in response to familiar person, object, or event
- Grimaces in reaction to unpleasant or unexpected sensation

Orientation
- Looks toward or points to person or object to seek or direct attention
- Looks away from person or object to indicate disinterest or refusal
- Looks toward a suddenly appearing familiar or novel person, object, or event

Pause
- Ceases moving in anticipation of coming event
- Pauses to await service provider's instruction or to allow service provider to take turn

Touching, manipulating, or moving with another person
- Holds or grabs another for comfort
- Takes or directs another's hand to something
- Manipulates service provider into position to start an activity or interactive "game"
- Touches or pulls service provider to gain attention
- Pushes away or lets go to terminate an interaction
- Moves with or follows the movements of another person

Acting on objects and using objects to interact with others
- Reaches toward, leans toward, touches, gets, picks up, activates, drops, or pushes away object to indicate interest or disinterest
- Extends, touches, or places object to show to another or to request another's action
- Holds out hands to prepare to receive object

Assuming positions and going to places
- Holds up arms to be picked up, holds out hands to initiate "game," leans back on swing to be pushed
- Stands by sink to request drink, goes to cabinet to request material stored there

Conventional gestures
- Waves to greet
- Nods to indicate assent or refusal

Depictive actions
- Mimes throwing to indicate "throw ball"
- Sniffs to indicate smelling flowers
- Makes sounds similar to those made by animals and objects to make reference to them
- Draws picture to describe or request activity

Withdrawal
- Pulls away or moves away to avoid interaction or activity
- Curls up, lies on floor to avoid interaction or activity

Aggressive and self-injurious behavior
- Hits, scratches, bites, spits at service provider to protest action or in response to frustration
- Throws or destroys objects to protest action or in response to frustration
- Hits, bites, or otherwise harms self or threatens to harm self to protest action, in response to frustration, or in reaction to pain or discomfort

Source: From "Introduction to Nonsymbolic Communication" by R. Stillman and E. Siegel-Causey. In *Enhancing Nonsymbolic Communication Interactions Among Learners with Severe Handicaps* (p. 7) by E. Siegel-Causey and D. Guess (Eds.), 1989, Baltimore: Paul H. Brookes. Reprinted by permission of Paul H. Brookes Publishing Company.

1988; Wetherby & Prizant, 1993). Bruner (1981) suggests that children use communication to serve three functions during the first year of life (Table 4–4):

- *Behavior regulation:* Communicating to get others to do something or to stop doing something (e.g., request an object or action or protest an object or action)
- *Social interaction:* Communicating to get others to look at or notice oneself (e.g., request a social game, greet, call, showoff)
- *Joint attention:* Communicating to get others to look at an object or event (e.g., comment, request information)

Studies of the communicative functions of individuals with severe disabilities also demonstrate a pattern of relatively strong use of behavior regulation functions and limited use of social interaction and joint attention

functions (Cirrin & Rowland, 1985; Ogletree, Wetherby, & Westling, 1992; Wetherby, Yonclas, & Bryan, 1989; Wetherby, Prizant, & Hutchinson, 1998).

The forms of communication used by individuals with severe to profound mental retardation has been analyzed on the basis of contact gestures versus distal gestures (McLean, McLean, Brady, & Etter, 1991). At about 9 months of age, children first use contact gestures, in which their hands come in contact with an object or person (e.g., giving or showing objects, pushing an adult's hand). By about 11 months, children use distal gestures, in which their hands do not touch a person or object (e.g., open-hand reaching, distant pointing, waving) (Bates et al., 1987). McLean et al. (1991) found that the adolescent and adult participants who used only contact gestures used communication for behavior regulation functions only, while the participants who used distal gestures used communication for

TABLE 4–4
Examples of Nonsymbolic Communicative Functions

Communicative function	Communication form (nonsymbolic examples)
Behavior regulation: to get others to do something or stop doing something	
Request object or action	• Learner *looks* at or *reaches* toward an object that is out of reach • Learner in need of assistance *gives* an object to open or activate it • Learner *holds* up an empty cup to get a refill
Protest object or action	• Learner *pushes* other's hand away to stop being tickled • Learner *cries* in response to a toy's being put away • Learner *throws* undesired object
Social interaction: to draw attention to oneself	
Request social routine	• Learner *taps* other's hand to request continuation of tickling • Learner *looks* at other and laughs to keep a peek-a-boo game going
Request comfort	• When distressed, learner *reaches* toward caregiver to get comforted • Learner *raises* arms to get picked up and comforted • Learner *wiggles* in chair to get other to adjust his or her position
Greet	• Learner *waves* hi or bye • Learner *extends* arm in anticipation of other's shaking to say good-bye
Call	• Learner *tugs* on other's pant leg to get other to notice him or her • Learner *vocalizes* to get other to come to him or her
Show off	• Learner *vocalizes* a raspberry sound, *looks* at other, and *laughs* to get a reaction
Request permission	• Learner *holds* up a cookie to seek permission to eat it
Joint attention: to draw attention to an object or event	
Comment on object or action	• Learner *shows* a toy to get other to look at it • Learner *points* to a picture on the wall to get other to look at it
Request information	• Learner *holds* up a box and *shakes* it with a questioning expression to ask what's inside • Learner *points* to a picture in a book and *vocalizes* with rising intonation to ask what it is

FIGURE 4–7
Marina is using contact gestures successfully with her mother.

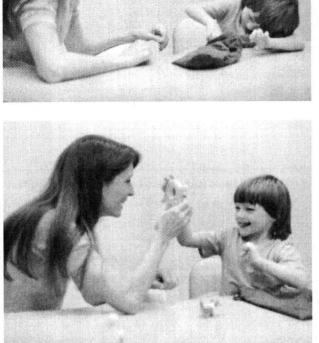

behavior regulation and joint attention functions. That is, the adolescents or adults who used contact gestures communicated by leading others' hands to request actions, while those who used distal gestures drew the attention of others to an object by pointing. Additionally, those using distal gestures attempted to clarify their messages when there was a communication breakdown and communicated at a higher rate than did those using contact gestures. Figure 4-7 shows Marina using contact gestures.

The Capacity for Symbols

Piaget (1952) suggested that sensorimotor cognitive knowledge (i.e., knowledge about how things in the world work) provides the basis for the emergence of using symbols. The ability to use language reflects a child's cognitive capacity to use symbols. There is accumulating evidence of parallels between cognition and the emergence of preverbal communication and first words (Bates & Snyder, 1987; Rice, 1983; Wetherby et al., 1998). In a cross-sectional study of 25 typically developing children, Bates (1979) found that the following sensorimotor skills were correlated with the emergence of language: imitation, tool use, communicative intent, and object use. Thus, the potential for movement toward a symbolic communication system in learners with severe disabilities may be better understood by considering skills that enhance the capacity for symbol use and understanding the developmental progression from nonsymbolic to symbolic skills.

Assessment

This section presents a structure for assessing the nonsymbolic communication of individuals with severe disabilities. Because the learner is interrelated with partners and environments, assessment should address each of these three aspects. Table 4-5 displays the trifocus on learner, partner, and environment with assessment considerations (second column) and an overview of the interventions that are linked to each focus (third column).

Good communication assessment procedures measure typical and spontaneous behaviors, are conducted

TABLE 4–5

Considerations for Assessment and Intervention Focus Using the Trifocus Framework

Focus	Assessment considerations	Intervention focus
1: Understanding the learner who has severe disabilities	*What is the learner's communication profile?* Consider the progression of communicative development Attend to behavior state patterns Identify learner's level of intentionality Identify learner's level of symbolization	View challenging behavior as communication Relate learner's expressions to partners' actions Facilitate alert, responsive state behavior

2: Broadening the communication partner's role	*How can I help the learner communicate better?*
	 How can I communicate better with the learner?
	 Consider the pragmatic perspective
	 Consider opportunities for communication
	 Identify social supports
	 Consider partner interaction style
	 Attend to elements of choice making
	 Consider augmented input
		Use pragmatics:
		   Enhance sensitivity
		   Increase opportunities
		   Sequence experiences
		 Use a continuum of choice formats
		 Augment vocal input:
		   Enhance meaning
		   Facilitate retention

3: Improving the environmental context	*What combination of influences can improve the context of the interaction?*
	 Attend to natural contexts
	 Consider external influences on state behavior
		Provide both physical and social natural supports
		 Use relevant, natural contexts
		 Modify environment:
		   Adjust sensory qualities
		   Alter movement and orientation of the learner's body
		   Change learning atmosphere
		 Modify combinations of environmental influences

Source: Adapted from Siegel-Causey, E., & Bashinski, S. M. (1997). Enhancing initial communication and responsiveness of learners with multiple disabilities: A tri-focus framework for partners. *Focus on Autism and Other Developmental Disabilities*, 12(2), 105–120.

by familiar persons, employ real-life materials and naturalistic activities, use a variety of assessment strategies, and translate information into relevant functional skills. It is important to assess both current and future needs for communication. Assessment strategies include commercially available instruments, communication and language samples, functional behavioral assessment, and oral-motor assessment. Further details about assessment are discussed by Snell (2002) and in chapter 2.

In the next section, we address assessment from the trifocus framework. We discuss in order (a) the learner's profile of communication abilities, (b) the broadening the communication partner's role by assessing their patterns and style, and (c) improving the communication environment.

Assessment: Understanding the Nonsymbolic Communicator

The Learner's Profile

Assessment of nonsymbolic communication should identify not only what individuals cannot do but also what they can do. Assessment should build a profile of student limitations and abilities across cognitive, social, communicative, and motor domains.

Communication partners or team members (educator, SLP) should begin assessment with two assumptions: (a) everyone communicates, and (b) learners with nonsymbolic skills *are* communicating. The purpose of assessment is to identify *how* and *why* an individual uses communication. The profile of the learner's communication in Box 4–3 should guide the

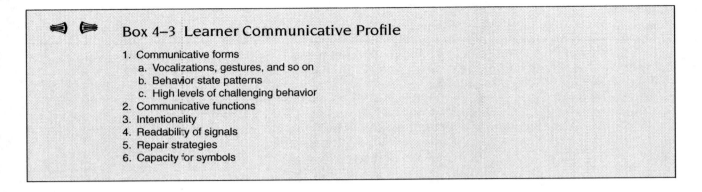

Box 4–3 Learner Communicative Profile

1. Communicative forms
   a. Vocalizations, gestures, and so on
   b. Behavior state patterns
   c. High levels of challenging behavior
2. Communicative functions
3. Intentionality
4. Readability of signals
5. Repair strategies
6. Capacity for symbols

assessment of skills and developmental capacities that are important for intervention planning.

Communicative Forms

The first assessment task is to identify the kinds of forms the learner uses. A person's communication forms give information that will influence how he or she should be taught.

Vocalizations and Gestures The categories of non-symbolic forms in Table 4–3 can guide the assessment process. Team members should be cognizant of both conventional forms and idiosyncratic forms that the learner may use. For gestural communication, contact gestures should be differentiated from distal gestures. Sometimes it can be difficult to distinguish communicative forms from more generalized behaviors in individuals with severe disabilities. Communicative forms need to be linked to specific situations and how the individual uses them to convey messages.

Using the categories from Table 4–3, Marina's communicative forms include generalized movements (e.g., increased hand shaking, moving torso), vocalizations (e.g., undifferentiated vowels, laughs, cries), facial expressions (e.g., smiles, grimaces), orientation with her head and eyes to objects or actions of interest, pauses and acting on objects (reaches toward desired objects, body movement to request action), and withdrawal to avoid activity.

However, many of Marina's forms may not be exhibited by learners with more severe motor impairments than she has.

For Ryan and others with severe motor impairments, partners must be attuned to more subtle movements and a smaller range of movements as

the communicative forms (e.g., increased tone, stop or start of a vocalization, change of expression).

One way to keep track of the learner's current repertoire of communicative forms is by using a gestural dictionary (Beukelman & Mirenda, 1998; Siegel & Cress, 2002) or, as we refer to it, a communication dictionary. This approach, illustrated in part for Ryan in Table 4-6, provides a way to document what the learner communicates, what the family and staff are interpreting each form of communication to mean, and how a partner should react when the form is expressed by the learner. Two considerations need to be addressed in setting up a communication dictionary: (a) how it is organized and (b) how it is displayed. The dictionary should be available for partners to access easily and can be organized in several ways, such as listing each form categorized by body parts starting with head (e.g., head: shaking, movement to side; face: wide open mouth, neutral) or in alphabetical order (e.g.,"aah" sound, arching of back, body movement forward). The selected format should be easy for school staff/communication partners to use. Team members (educators, SLPs) have found it helpful to have the dictionary displayed in more than one way (poster board in classroom, listed on cards in a wallet-photo holder the learner carries, or in a notebook) so that all partners have access to the dictionary during their interaction with the learner. Collecting and revising the communication dictionary is part of assessing the learner's communication and building a communication profile. Periodically updating the communication dictionary documents the changes in forms used by the learner across the school year as more forms are developed or as forms become more conventional.

Behavior state is a physiologic condition that reflects the maturity and organization of an individual's

TABLE 4–6
Communication Dictionary

Student: __Ryan__   Date: __October 1998__

Settings: classes, one-to-one intervention

What the learner does (form)	What it means (function)	How we react (consequence)
Turns head away from activity or person	I don't want to do this or I am done	Respond as if expressed "no" and stop the activity. Tell Ryan what you responded to ("I see that your head turned.")
Increases vocalizations	I like this	Continue activity. Tell him what made you continue. ("I can hear that you like this.")
Eye gaze*	This is the item or person I want	Respond as if he selected what he gazed at. Tell him what made you respond. ("You are looking at Tom. Do you want to go with him?")

* Emerging

central nervous system. The term "behavior state" is also used to refer to an individual's ability to internally and externally mediate interactions with the environment (Rainforth, 1982). Behavior state observations generally include assessment of sleep, drowsiness, awake behavior (e.g., orienting, interacting), agitation (e.g., crying, aggression, self-abuse), and stereotypic behavior. Research suggests that state behavior has a significant influence on alertness and responsiveness of learners who have multiple disabilities and, indirectly, on their learning, development, and overall quality of life ((Guess, Roberts, Siegel-Causey, & Rues, 1995; Guess, Roberts, et al., 1993; Guess, Siegel-Causey, et al., 1993; Guess et al., 1990, 1991; Guy, Guess, & Ault, 1993; Richards & Sternberg, 1992, 1993). These learners' state profiles frequently reveal high occurrences of behaviors that impede progress in educational programs and particularly affect communication intervention (e.g., drowsiness, sleep, stereotypy). Low occurrences of overt responses or little action may be another characteristic of state organizational patterns in learners with

severe disabilities and may further result in an extremely limited response repertoire with reduced fluency in the complex environments of school and community. Learners who display low rates of overt responses, have externally limited response repertoires, and spend significantly less time in alert states than others will need considerable ongoing support to develop effective communication skills.

It is important assess a learner's typical levels of alertness in educational environments. Several authors have extended the research in behavior state and studied assessment strategies for use by educational personnel: (a) the ABLE (Analyzing Behavior State and Learning Environments) model (Ault et al., 1995) and (b) classroom observation methods (Richards & Richards, 1997). For example, both assessment approaches describe ways for team members to observe a student's level of alertness across the school day for its regularity. If irregular patterns are documented (e.g., excessive sleepiness or drowsiness, high rates of self-stimulation), they can be linked to interventions aimed at increasing or decreasing alertness levels. (Intervention is addressed later in regard to environmental considerations.)

High Levels of Alertness and Challenging Behavior An additional consideration is whether any communication forms may be socially inappropriate (e.g., self-injury, aggression). Behavior state research (e.g., Guess, Siegel-Causey et al., 1993) has identified patterns of stereotypy, agitation, aggression, or self-injurious behavior that appear to represent high levels of alertness. These same behaviors have been labeled as "challenging," or "problem," behaviors. If a behavioral state assessment (Siegel-Causey & Bashinski, 1997) was conducted as part of the communication profile, it should be reviewed to see if high level of arousal states were present (e.g., agitation, self-injury, stereotypy). When challenging behavior or high levels of arousal are found, they would be assessed further in terms of their communicative functions.

Whether the behaviors are judged to be part of the behavioral state schema or challenging behaviors, we believe they should be viewed as a form of communication and need to be understood in relation to an individual's entire repertoire of communicative forms. The first step in assessing these forms is to review the communication dictionary and note if any of these behaviors might indicate challenging behaviors (Table 4–6). The checklist in Figure 4–8 includes challeng-

FIGURE 4–8

Checklist of Communicative Functions and Nonsymbolic Forms

Communicative Functions	Nonsymbolic Forms											Challenging Behaviors				
	Acting on/Using Objects	Assuming Positions or Moving to Specified Places	Conventional Gestures	Depicting Actions	Facial Expressions	Generalized Movements or Tone Changes	Orientating or Eye Gaze	Touching or Manipulating Objects	Vocalizing	Withdrawing	Other:	Agitation	Aggression	Self-Injury	Self-Stimulation	Other:
Behavior Regulation																
Request Activity or Help																
Protest Object																
Request Access to Tangibles																
Escape Activity or Person																
Social Interaction																
Request Social Routine																
Request Comfort																
Greet																
Call																
Showing Off																
Request Permission																
Request Attention																
Joint Attention																
Comment on Object/Action																
Request Information																
Other Functions																
Sensory																

Student:_____

Date:_____ Setting:_____

Context:_____

_____

Observer:_____

Italicized may be linked to challenging behavior © Siegel & Wetherby, 2004. Reprinted with permission.

ing behavior as forms of communication and can be used in the assessment process.

Communicative Functions

A second goal of assessment is to identify the *reasons* or *functions* that an individual uses communication. If an individual is at a nonintentional level (i.e., does not demonstrate any deliberate, goal-directed communication), assessment should identify any behaviors that serve a communicative function based on others' interpretation of these behaviors. For individuals demonstrating intentional communication, assessment should identify the range of communicative functions

expressed. A useful assessment framework described earlier is based on Bruner's (1981) categories of communicative functions that emerge in development prior to the onset of speech:

1. *Behavior regulation:* Acts used to regulate another's behavior to obtain or restrict environmental goals (e.g., request or demand access to actions, assistance, or activities or protest actions)
2. *Social interaction:* Acts used to draw another's attention to oneself for the purpose of making a social connection (e.g., request social game, attention greet, call, show off)

3. *Joint attention:* Acts used to direct another's attention to an object or event in order to sharing the focus of attention (e.g., comment on object, action, request information)

These categories of communicative functions vary in sociability, with behavior regulation having the least social demands and joint attention having the most. Children with severe disabilities and children with autism spectrum disorders in the early stages of communication have been found to express limited ranges of communicative functions, particularly the more social functions of social interaction and joint attention (Ogletree et al., 1992; Wetherby et al., 1998). Partners should determine whether an individual uses these major functions to convey messages.

> *Marina displays the communicative functions of regulating behavior (e.g., requesting and protesting objects or actions) and engaging in social interaction (e.g., requesting social games, calling) but does not yet communicate for joint attention.*

The Checklist of Communicative Functions and Nonsymbolic Forms Figure 4–8 can help the educational partner link the learner's forms and functions. A first step would be to circle the nonsymbolic forms across the top of the checklist that are known to be in the learner's repertoire; the partner may want to add in the specific types of behaviors the learner uses (e.g., gesture or reaching) or other forms unique to the learner that are not shown. The educator or SLP would then conduct observations in a natural context when the learner is participating in activities with partner(s). As the observation unfolds, the observer identifies (or hypothesizes) the possible function for each nonsymbolic form observed. The observer checks the specific function within each category: behavior regulation, social interaction, joint attention, or other functions. Videotaping oneself interacting with the learner and then completing the checklist is also beneficial in getting a full understanding of forms and functions. The checklist should be completed across a variety of activities and repeated periodically over the school year.

Challenging behaviors can take on functions of behavioral regulation (e.g., requesting item, escaping an action or person) and social interaction (e.g., requesting attention) and also may serve other purposes for the student within these three broad categories of function. The same challenging behavior may serve one or more communicative functions.

> *Ten-year-old Michael often flaps his hands. The assessor observes him during a cooking project. After the cookies are placed in the oven to cook, Michael begins flapping his hands. The paraeducator tells the small group to clean up. Michael's hand flapping continues. Gesturing to the oven, his friend Pete asks, "What's wrong, Michael? We get to eat a cookie when the timer goes off." Michael's hand flapping decreases in intensity. The observer marks "Self-Stimulation" under "Challenging Behaviors" and "Request Access to Tangibles" under "Behavior Regulation." A note is made that Michael may be using hand flapping as a display of agitation and/or as a request for tangibles and that staff should verify this by assessing across activities.*

A number of researchers (e.g., Horner, O'Neill, & Albin, 1991; O'Neill, Vaughn, & Dunlap, 1998; O'Neil et al., 1997; Reichle & Wacker, 1993; Wacker et al., 1990) have considered the impact of challenging behavior in terms of its communicative functions. They agree that much of the challenging behavior exhibited by those with severe disabilities may be a form communicative that serves a specific function or functions (Carr & Durand, 1985; Carr et al., 1994). Using a communicative approach guides the assessor to identify whether a particular communicative form functions to regulate another person's behavior (e.g., as a means to request a desired tangible or escape or avoid a situation) or to request social interaction (to draw attention to self; Brady & Halle, 1997; Carr et al., 1994; Durand & Crimmins, 1992; O'Neill et al., 1997). Thus, assessment with the checklist in Figure 4–8 may indicate a need for functional assessment to verify the function of challenging behavior and provide intervention strategies (also see chapter 2).

The information from the checklist provides a measure of the current repertoire of communicative forms and functions and an overview of the possible intervention: (a) altering or expanding number of forms used, (b) expanding frequency of use, (c) expanding number of functions used, (d) expanding frequency of use of functions, and (e) changing forms that are challenging behaviors.

Intentionality

A third goal of assessment is to identify the degree of intentionality for each communicative function. Recall that communication may range on a continuum from preintentional to intentional. Intentionality cannot be measured directly; it must be inferred from observable behaviors displayed during interactions. A nonsymbolic learner's degree of intentionality can be determined based on behavioral evidence (Bates, 1979; Bruner, 1978; Harding & Golinkoff, 1979), including the following:

1. Alternating gaze between the goal and the listener
2. Persisting in the signal until the goal is accomplished or failure is indicated
3. Changing the signal quality until the goal has been met
4. Ritualizing or conventionalizing the form of the signal over time within specific communicative contexts
5. Awaiting a response from the listener
6. Terminating the signal when the goal is met
7. Displaying satisfaction when the goal is attained or dissatisfaction when it is not

An individual may not display all these behaviors, but the more behaviors displayed, the more likely the behavior is intentional communication. Chris's photo in Figure 4–9 and the following explanation are good examples.

Chris is beginning to show evidence of intentionality in some play situations when he gazes directly at his friend Samantha (the listener). His team is teaching him to alternate this gaze between the listener and the object or event he desires. They know that he will display more intentionality if this skill is present. He does know to wait for Samantha's response of interest in the toy cow.

Learners should be assessed across a variety of activities to determine whether any of the seven intentional behavior indicators are present. The more behaviors present, the more intentional the communicator.

It is important to view intentionality as a developmental process and to evaluate the degree of intentionality in reference to changes in behaviors that indicate anticipation and expectation. Increases in intentionality are evidence of progress for nonsymbolic communicators.

Marina is showing intentionality by alternating her gaze and persisting until a goal is met. She recently began ritualizing communicative forms (e.g., using a brief back-and-forth body movement rather than an exaggerated bouncing movement to request a

FIGURE 4–9
Chris is positioned in the side-lyer next to his peer, Samantha, who holds the toy cow. As an educator assists him in finding the switch, Chris looks toward Samantha (function = engage in social interaction). Samantha smiles to indicate she wants Chris to activate the toy (function = behavior regulation).

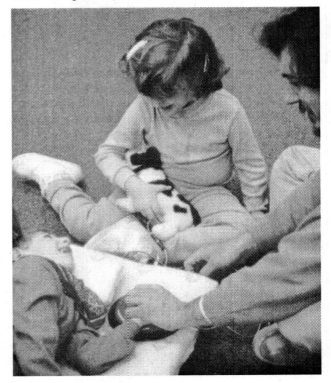

wagon being pulled) and terminating the signal when the goal is met (e.g., ceased the back-and-forth movement once the wagon movement is continued).

Readability of Signals
A fourth goal of assessment is determining how readable nonsymbolic communicative behaviors are. *Readability* refers to the clarity of a communicative signal and ease with which the signal can be interpreted. Readability is influenced by the degree of familiarity of the communication partner with the learner as well as the conventionality of the signal. Ability to use facial expression enhances readability by clarifying the learner's emotional state (Prizant & Wetherby, 1990; Kublin, Wetherby, Crais, & Prizant, 1998). Motor ability greatly influences the use of facial expressions and the clarity of gestural and vocal communication.

Marina's family members find Marina's subtle body movements and facial expressions to be very readable, but less familiar people find Marina's behaviors difficult to interpret.

Repair Strategies

A fifth goal of assessment is identifying repair strategies. Communication breakdowns are frequent when there is limited readability of signals. Thus, it is important for nonsymbolic learners to repair communicative breakdowns (Kublin et al., 1998; Prizant & Wetherby, 1990). An opportunity for repair occurs when a learner initiates a communicative behavior and the partner fails to respond or responds in a manner that violates the learner's intention.

Marina wiggles in her stroller to request out; when her mother fails to respond, this is an opportunity for Marina to repair in order to clarify what she wants. Marina starts vocalizing to communicate that she does not want to stay in the stroller.

In addition to natural opportunities to repair, "holding out" before responding to the learner's communicative intent in order to evaluate the ability to repair can also systematically provide opportunities. It should be determined whether the learner persists by repeating the same signal or by modifying the signal, such as changing the behavior or adding something to the behavior (e.g., adding a gaze or vocalization to a gesture). When learners abandon a communicative goal if it is not immediately achieved, they are lacking in repair strategies. The ability to modify a signal to repair communicative breakdowns allows greater reciprocity and promotes more successful social exchanges.

While Marina occasionally abandons a goal if it is not met immediately, she more often repeats her signals for behavior regulation and is beginning to modify her signals if her goals are not met. For example, if she requests to be pulled by bouncing her body back and forth and her mother does not respond right away, she looks at her mother and vocalizes.

The form provided in Table 4–7 can be used to assess in common situations when learners typically (a) express repairs and (b) do not express repairs but become agitated or withdraw. Those who do not use repair strategies should be taught to do so.

TABLE 4–7
Repair Strategy Assessment

Partner: _____ Activity: _____ Date: _____

Directions: Use this form to assess the learner's repair strategies across a variety of familiar activities. Whenever there is a breakdown in communication, complete columns 1 and 2. If the learner repaired the breakdown, complete column 3. If the learner did not repair the breakdown, complete column 4. Use column 5 to suggest repair strategies the learner could be taught.

1. Learner communicative behavior	2. Partner response	3. Did the learner repair? How?	4. Did the learner withdraw or become agitated? Describe.	5. List possible repair strategies to teach.

Brady, McLean, McLean, and Johnston (1995) studied repairs of 28 individuals with severe to profound mental retardation who resided in an institution. Each participant was provided with five opportunities to repair when adults did not respond to or misunderstood their requests for help or their requests for attention to an object or event. They found that 25 of the 28 participants initiated at least one repair. Significantly more participants repaired when requests for help were misunderstood. The participants who did repair tended to either repeat the same signal or change to a different signal. However, they rarely added information to their signals, suggesting that these repairs are harder to learn. Others have suggested that those who use serious challenging behavior as a form of communication may be using their problem behavior as a repair strategy in instances when their more conventional forms are unsuccessful. Furthermore, the ability to repair with appropriate behavior may lead to reductions in problem behavior (Wetherby, Alexander, et al., 1998).

Capacity for Symbols

A sixth goal of assessment is the learner's capacity for symbol use across activities. By definition, learners who communicate nonsymbolically do not use symbols expressively. However, there may be great variation in terms of their understanding (reception) of symbolic input: speech or graphics (e.g., such as line drawings, photos). Thus, the learner's assessment profile should include information on comprehension.

Knowledge of skill level on cognitive tasks that are correlates of language (i.e., tool use, causality, imitation, object use) can help partners understand the capacity of learners for communication skills. In other words, learners' communicative strategies should be considered in reference to their problem-solving and learning strategies. It is particularly important to consider how learners use objects to obtain a goal, understand the source of actions, observe and attempt to imitate the behaviors of others, and explore the functional uses of objects. For example, a child who attempts to obtain a cracker that is out of reach by scooting to the low cupboard that the cracker box sits on, reaching for the box, pushing it off the shelf, and vocalizing so someone will help open it is demonstrating mental representation skills in tool use.

An understanding of the cognitive skills of learners can provide information about strengths and interests that can be used to develop communication abilities. The transition from nonsymbolic to symbolic activities is a critical milestone that is evident in the use of objects and play. As children are able to symbolize, they show increasing capacity to use objects for specific functions, to engage in pretend actions toward others, and for adding actions during play (Lifter & Bloom, 1998). There is a strong relationship between object knowledge or use in play and the emergence of words. Wetherby and Prutting (1984) describe specific procedures adapted from developmental literature for setting up assessment probes for tool use, causality, imitation, and object use. For individuals with limited motor abilities, microswitches or other adaptive devices are needed to assess cognitive knowledge.

Strategies for Assessing Nonsymbolic Communication

Three strategies help assess nonsymbolic communicative behaviors:

1. Interviewing familiar people
2. Observing in natural contexts
3. Gathering communication samples

Interviews

The first strategy in assessing nonsymbolic communication is to interview people who are very familiar with the learner to document their forms and functions (teachers, care providers). Several guides exist for planning the interview. Peck and Schuler (1987) describe an interview format to identify forms, functions, and repair strategies. The Functional Assessment Interview (FAI) (O'Neill et al., 1997) explained in chapter 2 can be used to collect information about events that influence challenging behavior. Snell (2002) presents another example of an interview format and observation that incorporates the trifocus nonsymbolic framework and may be helpful for the educational team's assessment activities. Communication interviews provide a great deal of information about the learner in a relatively short period of time and may be used to plan further assessment.

Observations in Natural Contexts

A second strategy for assessment is to observe communicative behaviors of learners and partners that occur in natural contexts (Wetherby & Prizant, 1997). Observational checklists, such as Figure 4–8, can help organize recordings from naturalistic observations. Checklists are used most typically while observing children and while observing videotaped naturalistic communicative interactions in several environments.

Communication Sampling

The purpose of the third assessment strategy is to gather a representative sample of communicative behaviors in a relatively short period of time. Although sampling may be done while a school staff person observes, videotaping a communication sample is optimal. Videotapes offer the most objective and the richest data collection procedure for analyzing communicative behaviors. Videotapes also allow repeated observations of behaviors, providing opportunities to note subtle and fleeting behaviors that may be missed during ongoing dyadic interactions.

In contrast to the use of checklists, communication sampling involves designing situations to entice learners to initiate and participate in communicative interactions. Free play within joint-action routines may be used (Snyder-McLean, Solomonson, McLean, & Sack, 1984), but learners must have ample opportunities to initiate a variety of communicative acts. If a learner does not initiate readily, communicative temptations are useful (Wetherby & Prizant, 1989, 1993; Wetherby & Prutting, 1984).

Communicative temptations involve opportunities that entice specific attempts at communication. One example is activating a windup toy, letting it deactivate, and then waiting and looking expectantly at the learner. This gives the learner a chance to request assistance at getting the toy to activate, to protest about the ceasing of action, or to respond in other ways. Another example is giving the learner a block to put away in a box, repeating this several times so that the learner expects a block, and then giving a different object, such as a toy animal or a book. The novel object may tempt the learner to communicate about the unexpected object or to protest over the change in objects. In Figure 4-5, it appears that the bubbles that Marina's mother has deliberately placed out of reach tempt Marina.

Because temptations may be presented nonverbally, they circumvent the problem of a learner's limited comprehension of language. Although each temptation should be designed with at least one particular function in mind, any one temptation may potentially elicit a variety of communicative functions (Wetherby & Rodriguez, 1992). Communicative temptations should not be the only interactive technique used to sample but may be useful as warm-ups or supplements to unstructured interactions.

An accurate assessment of nonsymbolic communication depends on observation of a learner over a period of time in a variety of communicative situations with different partners. Assessment should be viewed as an ongoing process rather than episodic. Furthermore, since communication is a process between at least two people (speaker and partner), assessment must consider the learner's communicative behavior in relation to the interaction styles of communicative partners (Kublin et al., 1998; Mirenda & Donnellan, 1986; Peck & Schuler, 1987) and the characteristics of the environment (Siegel-Causey & Bashinski, 1997). This assessment focus was addressed previously in Table 4-5 (#1).

Assessment: Understanding the Social Environment

Assessment information gained from the "learner communicative profile" is only part of the picture. The team will also assess the communication qualities of the social environment to create the "partner communicative profile." These social qualities might include the following:

1. Opportunities to initiate and respond to communication
2. Social supports present
   a. What is there to communicate about?
   b. Who is available to interact with?
3. Interaction styles of communication partners

These qualities and the structure in Table 4-5 (#2) help us consider ways to assess the broad social aspects of the communication partners' roles.

Opportunities

Educational settings and activities vary a great deal in regard to the quality and quantity of opportunities for communication. School staff partners must ask whether situations and persons give enough opportunities for the learner to initiate and respond using all three major communicative functions. That is, do learners have opportunities to use communication in order to get others to do things (behavior regulation), to draw attention to themselves (social interaction), and to direct others' attention to objects or events (joint attention)?

Opportunities to use communication for behavior regulation generally involve instances when an individual needs to request assistance or objects that are out of reach, to make choices about desired objects or activities (e.g., food items, toys, or play partners), and to indicate undesired objects or activities. Opportunities to regulate behavior should occur throughout activities, not just when materials are first presented or activities are first initiated. An evaluation of behavior regulation opportunities tells team members whether there needs to be more (Peck, 1989).

Opportunities to use communication for social interaction and joint attention are more likely to occur within repetitive, turn-taking interactions. Bruner (1978, 1981) suggests that joint-action routines provide the best chance for communication development and learning to exchange roles in conversation. A joint-action routine is a repetitive turn-taking game or activity in which there are shared attention and participation by both the learner and the caregiver, exchangeable roles, and predictable sequences (Snyder-McLean et al., 1984). A classic example of a joint-action routine for infants and toddlers is the game of peek-a-boo (Bruner & Sherwood, 1976), which caregivers may play hundreds or thousands of times during the first year of a child's life. But joint-action routines exist across all ages. A joint-action routine may include activities involving preparation of a specific product (e.g., painting, food), organization around a central plot (e.g., pretending), or cooperative turn-taking games (e.g., smiling in response to one's name during a song) (Snyder-McLean et al., 1984).

In Ryan's role with helping the football team, there are many repetitive preparations that give structured opportunities for him to communicate. One joint-action routine begins as he and his friend Andy approach the clothes dryer and Andy assists setting up an adaptation that helps Ryan remove the clothes. The adaptation is a slanted board that clips on Ryan's tray and extends into the dryer. There is a large button that is attached to a switch. Each time Ryan hits the switch, it rotates a belt that circulates to draw the clothes to Ryan's tray. Ryan then pushes the clothing item/towel into a basket positioned to his right on the floor. They interact back and forth when Ryan smiles, and then Andy sets the jig each time by placing a clothing item on it to allow Ryan to pull the towels onto his tray and then to push them into the basket to the side of his wheelchair. The routine continues until each dryer is emptied.

In assessment, it is important to consider how the structure of activities influences communication. Snyder-McLean et al. (1984) delineate eight critical elements of successful joint-action routines for the assessment of the communicative environments (Table 4–8). These elements of quality as well as the quantity of joint-action routines should be evaluated. Activities that learners and partners routinely engage in at home, in the classroom, or in the community are potential joint-action routines that should be evaluated for these eight elements.

It is imperative to link these eight critical elements of joint-action routines with the learner's chronological age when selecting materials, settings, and people for the routines. Possible activities at home include eating meals, dressing, bathing, and playing; at school include eating snacks and meals, domestic activities (e.g., doing laundry and preparing meals), and art and leisure activities; and in the community include riding the bus, going shopping, and eating in a restaurant. The elements give joint routines a familiar, predictable structure that allows nonsymbolic learners to anticipate the activity's nature and sequence, participate maximally, and enhance their communication (Duchan, 1995; Kublin et al., 1998; Snyder-McLean et al., 1984).

The following joint-action routine uses these elements:

1. *Obvious unifying theme:* Preparing for football practice.
2. *Requirement for joint focus and interaction:* Both are assigned to get the locker room set up before practice begins.
3. *Limited number of clearly defined roles:* Andy assists with some of Ryan's setup. Ryan completes some tasks alone and some with assistance from Andy. Andy does some tasks on his own.
4. *Exchangeable roles:* For some jobs, it doesn't matter who does what task (shutting the dryer and washer doors).
5. *Logical, nonarbitrary sequence:* The young men proceed logically to wash, dry, fold, and store the locker room towels.
6. *Turn-taking structure:* Ryan's and Andy's turns are dependent on each other, so there is a balance of turns (e.g., Andy sets up the jig and Ryan pulls each item out of the dryer).
7. *Planned repetition:* There is built-in repetition with multiple items that need to be washed, dried, folded, and stored.

TABLE 4–8
Critical Elements of Effective Joint-Action Routines

1. *An obvious unifying theme or purpose* to relate the actions of different individuals engaged in the routine and provide a theme that is meaningful and recognizable to all participants. There are three general types of routines:

   - Preparation or fabrication of a specific product (e.g., food preparation, product assembly)
   - Routines organized around a plot or theme (e.g., daily living routines, pretend play scenarios)
   - Cooperative turn-taking games or routines (e.g., songs with spaces to fill in, peekaboo)

2. *A requirement for joint focus and interaction* to establish need for interaction and negotiation.

3. *A limited number of clearly delineated roles*, but at least two different roles that are definable and predictable (e.g., speaker and listener, giver and receiver).

4. *Exchangeable roles* so that the individual is assigned to more than one role in the same routine.

5. *A logical, nonarbitrary sequence* that is determined by the nature of the activity and can be predicted by the outcome or product.

6. *A structure for turn taking in a predictable sequence* that allows the individual to anticipate when to wait and when to initiate a turn.

7. *Planned repetition* over time to establish role expectancy and sequence predictability, used within a daily time block to offer several turns to each individual.

8. *A plan for controlled variation* that introduces novel elements against a background of familiarity and expectancy to evoke spontaneous comments in the following ways:

   - Interrupt the routine or violate expectations
   - Omit necessary materials
   - Initiate a routine and "play possum"
   - Initiate old routines with new contents
   - Introduce new routines with old contents

Source: Adapted from "Structuring Joint-Action Routines for Facilitating Communication and Language Development in the Classroom" by L.K. Snyder-McLean, B. Solomonson, J. E. McLean, and S. Sack, 1984, *Seminars in Speech and Language 5*(3), 216–218.

8. *A plan for controlled variation:* Natural interruptions or violations occur in their routine, such as finding personal clothes items with the towels or running out of soap. These events allow them to communicate with each other and, of course, goof around, such as when Ryan used his jig to fling a pair of underwear into Andy's pile of towels.

Social Supports

Learners' communication interactions are influenced by the social demands and supports provided in the environment. A nurturing atmosphere fosters warmth and security. Learners need to have responsive interactions with partners over time so that trust and sharing develops between them. Communication interventions should facilitate interactions and relationships with others, particularly with family members, school staff, and peers without disabilities. Assessment should help educators understand from the learner's perspective whether the social environment is positive and conducive to interactions: "What is there to communicate about?" and "Who is available to interact with?" Answering these questions may help staff assess social supports.

For individuals in the perlocutionary stage, social supports mean that structured opportunities are created within familiar activities to attract the learner's interest and give ways to participate and take turns. Partners need to be responsive to the communicative function of subtle behaviors.

When Marina first entered the preschool, staff and peers provided many opportunities for her to express whether she wanted an activity to continue and to choose what would happen next. A staff member watched her reaction, responded to what she seemed to be communicating, and made a record.

If some routines do not met these criteria (repetitive, familiar, and interesting), the assessment process is modified and expanded to examine the opportunities for communication.

As Marina's friend pushed her in the swing, he stopped the swing periodically and asked questions, pausing after each question to watch her response: "Fun, Marina?" "Do you want to swing more?" "Do you want to go on the merry-go-round?"

As individuals move toward the illocutionary stage, they should have social supports that allow them to initiate interactions, maintain interactions, and terminate interactions while realizing that their behaviors affect others.

As Marina learned that staff members and peers understood her expressions, she signaled her needs more readily. As she was swinging, she smiled and vocalized to her friend. When she wanted to stop, she put her head down and stopped vocalizing.

Interaction Style

Communicative behavior is influenced not only by the opportunities for communication but also by the interaction styles partners use in relation to the social supports available. Does a partner foster or inhibit communication? The caregivers' ability to respond contingently to a child's behavior has a major influence on the child's developing communicative competence (Dunst et al., 1990; Yoder, et al., 1998).

School staff partners should think about the unique ways that they talk, gesture, and share "who they are" as they interact with others.

Sam, Ryan's SLP, tends to speak quietly, look directly at his communication partners, and use touch only to emphasize important points. He always wears blue jeans and short-sleeve T-shirts, uses musk cologne, and has glasses. Martha, Ryan's teacher, speaks loudly, uses her tone of voice to convey emotion, and is affectionate and demonstrative with touch and gestures. She usually wears long dresses, wears her hair in a braid, and does not use perfume. Sam and Martha's interaction styles and personal behaviors influence the same learner in different ways.

The learner's ability to understand may be influenced by how communication partners express themselves. A student may receive the most salient information through nonsymbolic means.

Carol, a student who uses nonsymbolic communication, attends to Sam, the SLP, when he touches her or is close enough for her to smell his cologne, although for most of their interactions, she tends not to notice Sam until he redirects her attention by raising his voice and being more animated. She becomes very attentive and animated the moment she hears her teacher Martha's voice and strives to encourage

Martha to interact with her. Ryan, however, prefers Sam's quiet voice and limited touch and tries to avoid Martha's demonstrative nature and loud voice.

Developmental literature provides guidelines for assessing interaction styles of caregivers (Girolametto, Greenberg, & Manolson, 1986; MacDonald, 1989; MacDonald & Carroll, 1992; Yoder et al., 1998). Based on developmental guidelines for children at nonsymbolic stages of communication, interaction styles should be evaluated to determine if the following features are present:

1. Waiting for the learner to communicate by pausing and looking expectantly.
2. Recognizing the learner's behavior (form) as communication by interpreting the communicative function that it serves.
3. Responding to the communicative message (function) of the learner.
4. Matching the communicative level of the learner by expressing oneself with symbolic language paired with nonsymbolic communication.

Table 4–9 provides a format to assess partner interaction styles. Collaboratively conducting assessment allows each team member (and peers) to discover ways to improve their interaction styles. For example, if a learner is requesting an object, does the communicative partner give the desired object immediately?

Marina and her friend Jody, a peer without disabilities, are serving a snack. Jody has the juice pitcher and Marina the cups. Jody looks at Marina as they approach Arturo's place at the table (waiting for communication). Marina smiles and places the cup in front of Arturo. Jody looks at Marina and then at the cup (recognizing and interpreting the communication function). "OK, I pour juice, huh?" and Jody pours the juice (responding contingently and matching the communicative level).

Some interactions do not promote communication:

Marina and Lois, the paraeducator, are serving a snack. Lois smiles and says, "Give Arturo a cup next." This request will help Marina know how to proceed and will speed up the serving process. However, it does not give Marina an opportunity to communicate or allow her to "direct" Lois to pour juice. Thus, Marina's partner did not wait for her to communicate.

TABLE 4–9
Assessing Partner Interaction Styles

Partner: _____   Activity: _____   Date: _____

Directions: Use this form to assess your own (videotape) or other partners' interactions with the learner. Share self- and partner assessments to ensure consistency of instruction.

Features	If present, what was observed?	If not, what alternatives might be used?	Unclear? What might we try next time?
1. Does the partner wait for communication?			
2. Does the partner recognize the learner's form of communication and interpret the function that it serves?			
3. Does the partner respond to the communication function expressed by the learner?			
4. Is the partner's response expressed with symbolic and nonsymbolic behavior that matches the learner's ability?			

Partners must adjust their behaviors to match the communication level of each learner. MacDonald (1989) provides the analogy of being on a staircase with a child so that the partner has one foot on the child's step and the other foot on the next step. In the assessment of a communication partner's interaction style, it is important to consider the balance between the individual and the partner. That is, communicative partners should ask whether the interaction is reciprocal: Does each individual influence and respond meaningfully to the other individual and have a balance of turns?

Assessment: Understanding the Physical Environment

In addition to the social aspects of the environment, the second primary dimension to consider is the effect of physical variables on the communication contexts and interactions. The profile of the physical environment should be assessed in terms of the following:

1. Learner's position in terms of stability, proximity, and access to the interaction
2. Learner's interest in the activity

3. Learner's access to materials given sensory and motor skills
4. Activity level of the immediate environment near the learner's activity

During instruction and interactions, the physical environment influences how well communication is exchanged between the learner and partner (Table 4–5, #3). It has been suggested that changes in behavior state can be improved when environments are intentionally arranged in favorable ways (Ault et al., 1995; Guess et al., 1990). Five primary variables have been documented to influence a person's alert or sleepy states: (a) the attention a learner gives to social contact, (b) a learner's static body position, (c) the type of activity, (d) availability of materials, and (e) activity level in the immediate environment. In addition, behavior state research (Ault et al., 1995) suggests that changing environmental characteristics will directly influence behavior state. A well-engineered environment is associated with learners' display of alert, responsive state behavior. Conversely, this study also demonstrated that when educational staff did not systematically manage environmental characteristics, learners displayed more behavior states that were

TABLE 4–10
Assessing the Physical Environment

Partner: _____   Activity: _____   Materials: _____   Date: _____

Directions: Use this form to assess routines and activities via videotape or in real time. Share results within team to improve consistency of instruction.

Features	If present, what was observed?	If not, what alternatives might be used?	Unclear? What might we try next time?
1. Is the learner supported adequately: A. Stable? B. Can access the activity materials?			
2. Is the activity of interest?			
3. Are the materials matched to learner's sensory and motor skills?			
4. Is the activity and noise level near the learner conducive to attending and interacting?			

nonoptimal for learning (i.e., sleep, drowse, daze, agitation). Systematic instructional application of the environmental techniques yielded significant decreases in nonoptimal behavior states.

There are some simple ways to assess these variables while also assessing partners' interaction styles. Team members can use Table 4–10 to observe familiar routines and activities that take place across the person's school day and assess the presence or absence of facilitative communication strategies and the ways that the physical structure of activities influences the learner's communication.

Teaching

Methods to Promote Communication

Traditionally, intervention has focused on promoting speech and language development. Speaking and communicating have been viewed as synonymous (Calculator, 1988). Efforts were focused on remediation, including drilling in discrimination and teaching speech as a behavior within one-to-one isolated therapy sessions (Bedrosian, 1988; Musselwhite & St. Louis, 1988).

This focus on speech excluded many students with severe disabilities who were described as "not ready" for communication development or enhancement. Previously, the belief was held that before a child could benefit from augmentative and alternative communication interventions, a criterion level of cognitive ability was necessary (Rice & Kemper, 1984). Such beliefs are no longer supported (National Joint Committee for the Communication Needs for Persons with Severe Disabilities, 1992; Snell et al., 2003). The current trend is to teach communication in ways that match the learner's skills regardless of the mode of expression. Current research and theory suggest the following:

1. Focus teaching on interactions that are learner centered in natural home, school, and community environments
2. Use responsive and nondirective systematic instruction
3. Use intervention strategies that enhance early communication, such as naturalistic teaching procedures, including time delay (Halle, Marshall, & Spradlin, 1979), mand model (Warren, McQuarter & Rogers-Warren, 1984), and incidental teaching (Hart & Risley, 1975) (see chapter 5)

4. Use a communication dictionary so that partners respond to idiosyncratic gestures consistently (Beukelman & Mirenda, 1998; Mirenda, 1988; Siegel & Cress, 2002)

5. Use scripted routines (Beukelman & Mirenda, 1998)

6. Use joint-action routines (Snyder-McLean et al., 1984)

7. Provide choice-making opportunities (Brown, Belz, Corsi, & Wenig, 1993; Downing, 1999; Guess, Benson, & Siegel-Causey, 1985; Peck, 1989)

8. Use augmented input (Romski & Sevcik, 1993; Rowland, Schweigert, & Prickett, 1995; Wood, Lasker, Siegel-Causey, Beukelman, & Ball, 1998)

9. Use interrupted behavior chains (Allwell, Hunt, Goetz, & Sailor, 1989; Goetz, Gee, & Sailor, 1985; Hunt, Goetz, Alwell, & Sailor, 1986)

Next we describe intervention strategies that facilitate communication interaction between both learners and their partners and synthesize many intervention methods. An overview of the intervention methods is shown in Figure 4–10.

A Reciprocal Assessment Focus That Leads to Intervention

The assessment strategies described earlier in this chapter help educational partners recognize the effect of communication interactions on both the learner and his or her partner(s) and target areas that might be enhanced through instruction. Communication intervention is best viewed as a reciprocal process between a partner and a learner. The learner may be the responder

FIGURE 4–10
Intervention Guidelines in Relation to the Context of the Environment

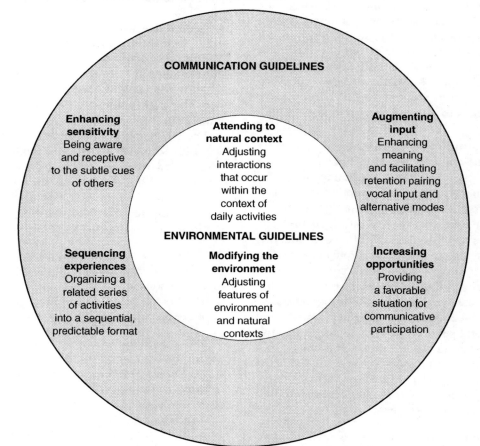

Source: Adapted from "Procedures for Enhancing Nonsymbolic Communication" by E. Siegel-Causey, C. Battle, and B. Ernst. In *Enhancing Nonsymbolic Communication Interactions Among Learners with Severe Handicaps* (p. 25) by E. Siegel-Causey and D. Guess (Eds.), 1989, Baltimore: Paul H. Brookes.

and thus influenced by how clearly he or she understands (responder-receptive understanding). In this case, intervention might focus on improving the partner's expressions. Alternately, the learner may be the initiator, in which case the partner's understanding is influenced by how clearly the learner expresses him- or herself (initiator-expressive competence). Intervention might focus on improving the learner's expressions and improving the partners' responsiveness and consistency. Interactions are influenced by what both the initiator and the responder do rather than assuming that either partner has deficits to remediate.

Using Functional, Systematic Methods in Natural Routines

As educational partners deliver communication instruction, they must incorporate systematic instructional methods regardless of the intervention approach. All communication instruction should occur within the routines of the day and natural environments (within the home, school, or community) so that learners not only communicate better or more but also recognize that communication always serves a purpose. This approach uses a collaborative model of service delivery, with all staff members working together to establish goals and facilitate cross-disciplinary training.

Potential Communication Content and Environmental Intervention Focus

In addition to being aware of the influence that partners' interactional styles have on receptive understanding, school staff partners should consider how the environment influences communication instruction. The center of Figure 4–10 displays the two environmental guidelines for teaching communication: (a) attend to natural contexts and (b) modify the environment to promote communication. To use these guidelines, the team will address several questions. What activities are conducive to joint-action or turn-taking segments? Are staff members and peers conducting activities that use these attributes? From the learner's perspective, what is there to communicate about in each familiar activity? Such questions may help partners discover potential communication content and interventions that focus on environmental arrangement(s).

Using an adaptation that facilitates handling and transferring, Ryan hands out towels to the team at the football games. This activity provides his team with many possible communication opportunities: Ryan

indicates to a peer that he is ready with a towel, that he recognizes individual friends and favorite players, that he wants to move his wheelchair or change his position, that he has finished the job, that he wants to start a conversation, and so on.

By answering these questions, school partners will identify a wide range of teaching targets and may develop additional targets to generalize to other natural activities. Then the educational team can prioritize the targets that are most functional and will generalize across people, events, and settings.

Communication Intervention Guidelines

Four guidelines for improving communication intervention are shown in the outer circle of Figure 4–10: (a) enhance sensitivity, (b) sequence experiences, (c) augment input, and (d) increase opportunities. These guidelines evolved as part of an overall intervention for interacting with learners who have severe handicaps (see Siegel, in press; Siegel-Causey & Bashinski, 1997; Siegel-Causey & Guess, 1989). The guidelines are not arranged in a sequential manner; rather, educational partners should incorporate the relevant components of the guidelines during any individual communicative interaction.

The six guidelines in Figure 4–10 and their corresponding strategies form a philosophy of intervention based on two assumptions: (a) partners should expect learners to communicate and, (b) improving the partner's communication will positively influence interactions. Using this approach, partners should enhance the following (Figure 4–11):

1. Their use of nonsymbolic and symbolic expressions
2. Their understanding of the learner's nonsymbolic expressions
3. Their enhancement of communication contexts and attention to influences on the learner's state behavior

Jack, Ryan's friend, expects that Ryan will communicate as they take off their coats on entering the room. This allows Jack to be ready to respond to Ryan's initiations and expressions. Since Jack has had a variety of interactions with Ryan, he is familiar with Ryan's nonsymbolic ways of communicating, can predict what this activity will be like, and is alert to opportunities that occur naturally in their routine. (Jack uses the guideline of increasing opportunities and enhancing sensitivity.)

FIGURE 4-11
Intervention Guidelines and Corresponding Strategies

Enhancing the partners' nonsymbolic and symbolic expressions to the learner

Increase opportunities
- Create need for requests
- Facilitate alert, responsive state behavior
- Provide choices
- Provide opportunities to interact
- Use time delay

Sequence experiences
- Encourage participation
- Establish routines
- Provide turn-taking opportunities

Augment input
- Enhance meaning
- Facilitate retention

Enhancing the partners' understanding of the learner's nonsymbolic communication

Enhance sensitivity
- Recognize individual's readiness for interaction
- Recognize nonsymbolic behaviors
- Respond contingently at the learner's level of communication
- Respond to expressions and challenging behavior as communicative behavior

Enhancing the learner's communication contexts and attending to external influences on the learner's state behavior

Attend to natural contexts
- Provide physical supports
- Provide social supports

Modify environment
- Adjust sensory qualities
- Alter movement and orientation of learner
- Change learning atmosphere

Note: Based on Siegal-Causey, E., Battle, C., & Ernst, B. (1989). Procedures for enhancing nonsymbolic communication. In *Enhancing Nonsymbolic Communication Interactions Among Learners with Severe Handicaps* (p. 25) by E. Siegel-Causey and D. Guess (Eds.), Baltimore: Paul H. Brookes; and Siegel-Causey, E., & Bashinski, S.M. (1997). Enhancing initial communication and responsiveness of learners with multiple disabilities: A tri-focus framework for partners. *Focus on Autism and Other Developmental Disabilities,12*(2), 105–120.

An initial focus of some communication interventions is to encourage learners to convey messages. Some learners are discouraged from communicating because of the great physical or cognitive effort required, while others have had infrequent opportunities to communicate (Downing, 1999; MacDonald, 1985; Musselwhite & St. Louis, 1988). Still others are at the perlocutionary stage and do not understand that their behaviors can affect others. Thus, a better focus may be to teach learners that they can affect people and events. We believe that all the guidelines and strategies in this section can help learners progress on a continuum of development from perlocutionary to locutionary to illocutionary expressions. In addition, the strategies allow learners to control interactions as they initiate, maintain, and terminate communication exchanges. When using the intervention guidelines, remember to do the following:

1. Use relevant and functional tasks and age-appropriate methods and materials and intervene within natural contexts and activities
2. Expect communication

Intervention Guidelines to Enhance Partners' Nonsymbolic and Symbolic Expressions
The first intervention guidelines we will review are listed in the top section of Figure 4-11: enhancing partners' expressions to the learner. The three strategies are to increase opportunities, sequence experiences, and augment input.

Increasing Opportunities
Creating situations that empower learners to communicate can promote their participation in interactions. The strategies to increase opportunities include (a) creating need for requests; (b) facilitating alert, responsive behavior; (c) providing choices; (d) providing opportunities to interact; and (e) using time delay (Halle, 1984; Siegel-Causey & Bashinski, 1997; Siegel-Causey & Guess, 1989).

Requests As learners move to a more illocutionary level, they can direct attention to an object or event (e.g., get peers' attention on the waves in a pool), seek to initiate social interaction, and attempt to create changes in actions or objects. If a need is created, these skills can be shaped into requests.

> *When Marina finishes her juice, her teacher acts "busy." Thus, if Marina wants more to drink, she will need to get the partner's attention so that he will pour the juice.*

Responsive State Behavior Intervention to facilitate state behavior at the perlocutionary level will focus on establishing the relationship between what the learner expresses and the actions of other people and environmental events. Perlocutionary nonsymbolic behaviors generally include relaxing or stiffening of the body; total body movement; arm, leg, or hand gestures or movements; and vocalizations (e.g., crying, cooing, noise making).

> *The peer stops the country music CD that he and Chris are listening to and starts to play another CD. Chris's legs stiffen, and he begins to vocalize. His peer looks over, attending to the change in Chris's expression. "Hey buddy, you want to hear it still?" He reactivates the music, and Chris relaxes and quiets down.*

When partners notice a learner's level of alertness and change an activity accordingly, they can facilitate responsive behavior.

Choices The right to choose is highly valued. Offering opportunities to choose has been shown to be a powerful intervention (e.g., Bambara & Koger, 1996; Bannerman, Sheldon, Sherman, & Harchik, 1990; Brown et al., 1993). Siegel-Causey and Bashinski (1997) suggested that choice making involves (a) displaying preferences and (b) making decisions. To display a preference, the learner recognizes that options exist, has a propensity (liking) toward something, and makes a communicative expression (choice) about that item or occurrence.

> *Ryan is given the opportunity to choose which peer he wants to work with during football practice tasks. To choose, he needs to recognize that there are peers present to choose from, to prefer being with one of them (propensity), and to convey this preference by gazing at the peer he prefers.*

For choice making to be effective, it is important to consider the learner's level of receptive understanding

and symbolization, and it may be necessary to teach choice making. A simpler level of choice making applicable to learners who communicate nonsymbolically is the active or passive choice system with two options (Beukelman & Mirenda, 1998). The learner gets choice "X" when passive (for doing nothing) and choice "Y" when active (for doing something). A slightly more difficult option is two-item active choice making using real objects (Beukelman & Mirenda, 1998). The types of items in the two-choice array can be (a) two preferred options (Writer, 1987), (b) one preferred and one nonpreferred option, or (c) one preferred option and a "blank" or "distracter" option (Reichle et al., 1991; Rowland & Schweigert, 1990). Choice items should be used that will promote the learner's understanding that his or her behavior influenced the choice. Learning to make choices should be a positive experience; thus, starting with two preferred options is usually favored. Partners analyze each routine to identify the options for choice-making that exist during a scheduled class period or school day (for more information, refer to Brown et al., 1993).

Daily routines and activities in the school setting have many opportunities for choice making. Brown et al. (1993) presented a model of *choice diversity* that expands traditional choice-making options by analyzing opportunities for choices within specific routines. Seven categories of choice are available within the context of most daily routines. These categories include offering choices between activities and within activities, as well as giving students choices of refusing an activity, of terminating an activity, and when, where, and with whom an activity is performed.

> *During a leisure activity routine, Marina can be given the opportunity to choose listening to music or to have a book read to her (a choice between two activities). If Marina chooses to listen to music, she can be given the opportunity within that activity to choose listening to either rock or country music (choice within activity). Marina can also be given the opportunity to choose where (either lying on the mat or sitting in a rocking chair) and with whom to listen to music (either with Paul or with her friend Jody). Marina could choose not to listen to music or be read a book (refusal) and choose to end the activity when she wants (terminate). The educational team decides which aspects of these options would be implemented in the leisure routine with Marina.*

Opportunities to Interact Providing opportunities for the learner to interact and communicate is a central strategy of intervention. The learner who is building intentional behavior will use nonsymbolic behavior to affect actions of people and the environment. Partners can provide opportunities for the learner to use their behaviors within natural routines or activities that occur. Nonsymbolic behaviors used purposefully in the early stages of intentionality generally include actions such as approaching or avoiding people, materials, or activities; contacting or pushing or pulling people, materials, or activities; smiling; and pointing. Partners will provide opportunities for the learner to use these behaviors.

The learner who communicates at a nonsymbolic level is limited to expressions focused on his or her current behavior state or on something that can be touched, looked at, or directly perceived. Opportunities are enhanced when the partner provides materials within interactions that can form concrete input to a learner and gives meaningful content to communicate about. The preintentional and intentional behaviors may appear very similar in form and may affect the partner similarly whether the expressions were reactions (perlocutionary, partner interpreted) or actions displayed intentionally by the learner to get desired effects from the partner (illocutionary, intentional).

Time Delay School staff partners can insert pauses (time delay) in interactions so that learners can initiate a change in the interchange, maintain the interchange, or terminate it. Giving learners clear opportunities (with a delay) for them to take "their turn" and emit an expression can be beneficial to learners at both the perlocutionary and the illocutionary stage.

At the perlocutionary stage, partners can help learners recognize that they have signals. Thus, partners convey information with the behaviors expressed by the individual.

At a snack table with Marina and other children, the juice pitcher is passed around the table. John (the SLP) used Marina's own behavior, fluttering his hands and saying, "Abga," as the juice pitcher gets closer to him. To expand the communication opportunities, John increased his vocalizations and looked at Marina (pausing rather than pouring the juice). Marina then had an opportunity to jointly attend to the juice pitcher, request juice herself, or terminate the interaction.

Sequencing Experiences

Learners at the perlocutionary level do not realize that they can control their own behaviors or that their behaviors affect a game or routine. However, sequencing experiences allows them to experience maintaining and terminating interactions. As learners develop more illocutionary skills, they anticipate steps in a sequence and initiate parts of a routine or game. The second guideline for enhancing the partner's nonsymbolic and symbolic expressions to the learner is to sequence experiences; three strategies are used: (a) encourage participation, (b) establish routines, and (c) provide turn-taking opportunities.

Participation Partners can analyze routines that are already familiar and provide a role for the learner in the sequential components. Partners may select dialogues, scripted routines, or routine components to help sequence the experiences for the learner and thus encourage more participation and communication.

Routines Routines such as self-care, leisure, and transition between activities and places provide redundancy and reoccurrence across the day. These recurring events across environments can be structured to encourage the learner to anticipate what may occur next. Planned "dialogues" (Siegel, in press; Siegel-Causey & Guess, 1989) can structure routines for the multiple partners so that communication is expected and consistent reciprocal roles between the learner and partners is promoted. (An example dialogue within a routine is provided later in this chapter [Table 4–11].) Similarly, "scripted routines" delineate the specific verbal and touch cues the partner should provide and the pauses and the precise actions of the partner within natural events (Beukelman & Mirenda, 1998).

Turn Taking Games and familiar routines often have a component of "your turn, my turn," which helps learners realize that they can express themselves.

Marina helps pour juice for the class with her friend Jody. Each time that Jody moves the pitcher forward, Marina moves a cup toward the pitcher. This interchange occurs repeatedly.

Since many routines and games have built-in roles of receivers and senders of communication, *turn taking* can be enhanced and emphasized as well as combined with increased opportunities.

TABLE 4–11

Dialogue Before Snack in Marina's Classroom

This classroom has students with disabilities and typical peers who are 3 to 5 years of age. It is time for snack, and each student has a role. The teacher, Rachel, has paired Marina and Jody together for many classroom activities. Marina has missed school for the last month because of hospitalizations for extensive seizures. Jody is a typical peer, who is extremely quiet and reluctant to interact with other children. Rachel feels that Jody can benefit from helping Marina get back into the school routine and from having structured interactions to communication about.

Intervention guidelines and strategies	Interventionist	Learner and peer
Opportunity: Provide opportunities to interact	Rachel says to the group, "Class, it is time to prepare for snack. You will find a job and a partner on the snack picture board here." Rachel points to the bulletin board that displays photographs of student pairs and a photograph of the job each pair is to complete. "Who wants to find a job?" Rachel *pauses* and *looks* around the circle. A few students raise their hand, and Rachel calls them up to find their picture. "What job did Andy and Josh find?" Rachel extends the photo that Andy and Josh found under their pictures and shows it to the children. She pauses in front of Jody. "What job is in this picture?"	
		Jody whispers, "Tablecloth."
	"Great, Jody. That's right, it is a tablecloth. Pass the photo to Marina. Marina, get ready." Rachel knows that Jody will barely extend the photo to Marina. Thus, Marina will have to reach out to get it. Rachel wants Marina to practice reaching out for items so that she can learn that this is a good way to request things she wants.	
Sequencing: Encourage participation	"Where is the photo, Marina?" Rachel says as she *looks quizzically and extends her palms upwards.*	
		Marina looks at Rachel's hands and laughs.
Sensitivity: Respond to the individual's level of communication	"You're happy! Let's find the photo." Rachel *guides Jody to extend the photo toward Marina.*	
		Marina laughs again and reaches toward the photo that Jody has extended in front of her.
Sensitivity: Recognize nonsymbolic behavior	"*Marina, you want the photo!*" Rachel exclaims.	*Marina takes the photo.*
Augmenting: Enhance meaning	Rachel points out the tablecloth in the photo that Marina now holds and *gestures, as if laying it out as she says*, "Put out tablecloth?"	
		Marina touches the photo. Jody looks over at the snack area, where the tablecloths are stacked on a shelf.
Sensitivity: Recognize nonsymbolic behaviors	"Yes, Jody, I see you looking at the snack area. Andy and Josh are going to put the tablecloth out." Rachel continues to call students up to find their snack jobs on the photo board. Soon, it is Marina and Jody's turn.	
Sequencing: Encourage participation	"*Who wants a job?*"	
		Jody looks at the photos of her and Marina.
Sensitivity: Respond contingently	"*Right, Jody, your picture is still here*," Rachel says as she points to the photos of Jody and Marina.	

TABLE 4–11 (*Continued*)

Intervention guidelines and strategies	Interventionist	Learner and peer
Sequencing: Encourage participation	"Who is in the picture with you?" Rachel *asks*.	
		Jody looks at Marina. *Marina laughs.*
Sequencing: Provide turn taking	Rachel *extends the photo* toward the girls.	
		Marina turns toward the photo.
Sensitivity: Recognize non-symbolic behaviors	"*Yes, Marina, this is your job,*" says Rachel.	
		Jody moves toward Rachel, and Marina crawls to follow her. Jody takes the photo from Rachel.
	Rachel encourages Jody to show the photo to Marina in the same manner as they did with the photo of the tablecloth.	
Sequencing: Encourage participation	Rachel asks, "*What job is in the picture?*"	
		Jody whispers, "Napkins."
Sensitivity: Respond to the individual's level of communication.	"Napkins!" Rachel *says* as she *gestures toward Jody and Marina and pretends to hand out napkins.*	
Augmenting: Enhance meaning		
		Jody watches. Marina laughs and touches Rachel's hands.
Opportunity: Provide opportunities to interact	"Marina, where are the napkins?" Rachel *asks as she shrugs her shoulders and looks around the room.*	
		Marina turns toward the shelves and begins to crawl to them.
Sensitivity: Respond contingently	"*Marina sees the napkins,*" Rachel *says with a loud and happy tone in her voice.* "Are you going to help with your job, Jody?" Jody slowly follows Marina to the shelf.	
		Marina giggles and watches Jody follow her.
	Rachel continues to guide the girls as needed to complete their job of putting out the napkins and encourages them to interact as opportunities arise.	

Augmenting Input

The last intervention guideline for enhancing the partners' nonsymbolic and symbolic expressions to the learner is to augment input by enhancing meaning and facilitating retention.

Enhance Meaning The use of verbal input paired or "augmented" with another mode of communication may improve the learner's understanding. This commonly used strategy may help learners receive information more clearly because verbal input is elaborated on with another mode (such as concrete gestures, touch cues, real objects, photographs, or pictures).

Facilitate Retention Learners have better recall of events and messages through objects, gestures, or photographs than simply another's words. Thus, object schedules or calendar boxes may facilitate a learner's recall and anticipation of familiar activities (Blaha, 2001; Downing, 1999; Rowland & Schweigert, 1990).

When it is time to go to physical education class (PE), the teacher says "line up at the door." Harris, a learner with autism, notices the movement of his classmates and picks up his pencil (the object that signals writing tasks he was working on). He walks over to his object schedule and puts the pencil in the "finished" box. The next object in his schedule boxes are two wristbands that signal PE class. Harris puts them on his wrists. These objects help Harris recall the next event in his day.

Intervention Guidelines to Enhance the Partner's Understanding of the Learner's Nonsymbolic Expression: Enhance Sensitivity

If partners don't know what learners are communicating, there is a breakdown. The key guideline for improving partners' understanding is for partners to become sensitive to the nonsymbolic expressions of learners. In the middle section of Figure 4–11, five strategies help partners concentrate on what learners do: (a) recognizing readiness for interaction, (b) recognizing nonsymbolic behaviors, (c) responding contingently, (d) responding to expressions and challenging behavior as communicative, and (e) responding to the individual's level of communication.

Recognize Readiness for Interaction The learner's assessment profile and gestural dictionary are not strategies per se but sets of information that equip partners with concrete ways to understand both what the learner expresses and the alert, responsive behaviors that can be responded to in a consistent manner. Recognizing these alert behavior states helps the partner notice the learner's *readiness* for interaction. Thus, sensitivity is enhanced by being familiar with the learner's range of communication forms and by assigning meaning to those expressions.

Paul, a school staff partner, waits for Chris to indicate interest in activating the switch (increasing opportunities to create a need for requests) (Figure 4–12). When Chris smiles and vocalizes at Paul (his signals that communicate behavior regulation and social interaction), Paul helps position Chris's arm so that he can more easily engage the switch (enhancing sensitivity by responding contingently).

Recognize Nonsymbolic Behaviors At the perlocutionary stage, learners do not realize that their behaviors can affect others, so the intervention focus is on always noticing and responding to the learners' expressions. As learners express themselves in a more illocutionary manner (with intentionality), partners can note nonsymbolic behaviors that display a readiness for interaction and respond with expressions that

FIGURE 4–12
Paul is following the intervention guidelines and strategies to enhance Chris's communicative expressions.

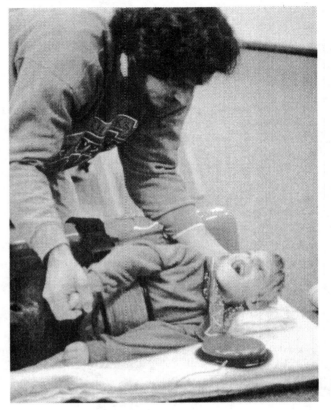

are at the same level. Regardless of the level of intentionality, partners can enhance their sensitivity to learner expressions and capitalize on opportunities for communication by thoroughly knowing the learner's current nonsymbolic behavior. Gestural dictionary (Beukelman & Mirenda, 1998) or communication dictionary (Siegel & Cress, 2002) is the best way to apply this strategy (Table 4–6 provides a format to report nonsymbolic and symbolic behavior).

Respond Contingently and at the Learner's Level of Communication Another aspect of being sensitive is for partners to *respond contingently* to nonsymbolic behaviors using a communicative level matched to the learner's understanding. Again, the dictionary is useful because it not only describes the learner's current forms of expression and their meanings but also gives suggestions for how to respond appropriately (what partners should consistently do). The dictionary also can guide partners to use the learners' behaviors to augment their own messages, making them more likely to be understood by the learner.

The music teacher, Anne, turns her head away from Ryan and says "no" to convey that she does not want to play the tambourine that is on the tray. Turning away is a nonsymbolic behavior Ryan uses to express "no," and the word "no" is a symbolic form that Anne pairs with her use of that nonsymbolic expression.

Respond to Expressions and Challenging Behavior as Communicative Behavior In the assessment of forms and functions, we described forms of challenging behavior (aggression, self-stimulation, self-abuse) as having potential communicative function (Table 4–8). As one considers intervention at the nonsymbolic level, partners should respond to all the learner's expressions. This includes assessing the function(s) of a learner's challenging behavior (escape, attention, tangible, sensory) and then responding to that communicative function by teaching an appropriate form that can serve the same function for the learner using functional communication training (chapter 2).

Intervention Guidelines to Enhance the Learner's Communication Contexts and Attend to Influences on the Learner's State Behavior
The final guideline in Figure 4–11 focuses on contexts and environment of the learner using the strategies of (a) attending to natural contexts and (b) modifying the environment.

Attend to Natural Contexts If interactions occur naturally or as part of daily activities and routines, then it is easier for partners to use the learner's communication interests and participation needs. At these times, partners embed their direct instruction, thereby highlighting for the learner the relationship of stimulus, response, and consequences (Noonan & Siegel, 2003). The milieu teaching techniques, described in chapter 5, embrace this approach by systematically teaching skills when they are needed and relevant.

Chris is relaxing on the floor after he has been taken out of his wheelchair for a short break. He notices the rest of his class putting away their materials. He vocalizes and moves his head toward the students' desks.

Paul sees Chris's communication and squats down near him on the floor. "I hear you Chris, what do you want?" and pauses, looking at Chris. Chris vocalizes again and scoots closer to his switch and puts his arm on it. Once activated, the Big-Mack switch relays "Help me." Paul responds to Chris's communication by saying, "OK, Chris, I'll give you a hand so you can be ready for story time," and initiates lifting him back into his wheelchair, which is positioned at the front of the room, where his peers are gathering to hear a story.

Physical Supports The partner may need to change the *physical supports* to increase the learner's performance. For example, physical supports that may enhance participation include adding interesting and manipulable materials, adapting the activity materials, or increasing personal assistance.

Social Supports Social supports may also enhance learner motivation and improve instruction. Examples include involving peers as facilitators, using group project activities, and teaching social communication strategies within the activity.

Modify the Environment Sometimes team members need to modify the environment so that the learner can interact with others in a functional manner while displaying more alert, responsive state behavior. Ault et al. (1995) validated techniques for improving alert, responsive behaviors and found three characteristics that most influenced responsive behaviors: (a) sensory qualities, (b) movement and orientation of the learner's body, and (c) learning atmosphere. These data suggest a direct relationship between changing environmental characteristics and influencing behavior state.

Adjust Sensory Qualities A range of sensory qualities can be modified: visual, auditory, tactile, gustatory, and olfactory stimuli. The partner determines whether certain features of sensory stimuli in the activity (or that could be added) would have an activating or soothing effect on the learner. For example, direct versus indirect light, materials highlighted with bright or neutral backgrounds, or a change from light to deep pressure may produce responsive behavior in the learner.

Alter Movement and Orientation Similarly, the partner can evaluate the effects of movement and orientation of the learner's body. Team members may consider tempo or movement of the learner's body parts or the learner's body tilt and position when on various adaptive equipment.

Change Learning Atmosphere The final consideration involves assessing the *learning atmosphere*. For example, what effects do secondary noise, location changes, and nearby activity level have on an individual learner? Making minor changes or manipulations in these environmental characteristics can easily be implemented within an activity in conjunction with partner strategies from this chapter (for more, refer to Ault et al., 1995).

Using the Intervention Guidelines: Examples

Intervention guidelines should be incorporated into natural routines, as displayed in the photo sequence in Figure 4–13.

> *Jona, a paraeducator, tells Chris that it is time for music. She waits for his vocal and hand movements*

FIGURE 4–13
Jona, an interventionist, uses intervention strategies within the naturally occurring event of moving Chris to a new position.

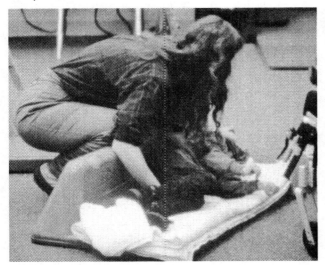

that signal that he agrees, then she picks him up. Once he is face to face, she asks who he wants for a music buddy, says the name of two peers, and then repeats their names, pausing after each name for his response. He vocalizes to choose one peer, and she places him in his chair. She pauses before strapping his feet and looks at him; this is Chris's cue to move his foot into place; Jona thanks him.

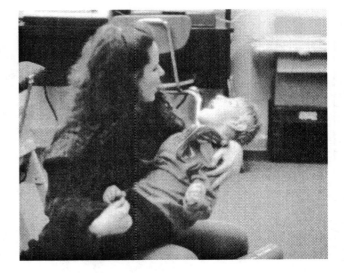

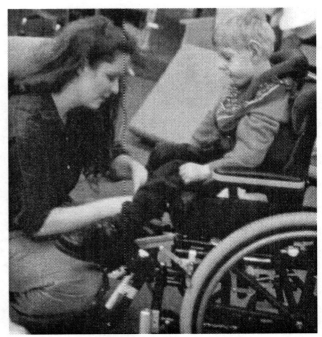

The dialogue in Table 4-11 illustrates ways to incorporate intervention into the daily context of interactions. The left-hand column of this table identifies partner behaviors and the intervention guideline or strategy being used. The italics in the middle column denote the partner's use of a specific intervention within the dialogue. Italics in the learner and peer column designate their communications.

Summary

The assessment and intervention methods in this chapter can help school staff members become effective communication partners with the learners who use nonsymbolic communication. Researchers and practitioners in the field of severe disabilities and speech-language pathology have only begun to recognize the broad spectrum of communication intervention needs of individuals who have disabilities. A new emphasis on and inclusion of instructional methods and procedures for enhancing the primary repertoire of communication forms a foundation for the development of symbolic and augmentative communication. The goal is to use methods that incorporate students' nonsymbolic skills and to build on their repertoires of communication skills so that they can understand and use more sophisticated symbolic skills.

Suggested Activities

1. Select a learner who uses primarily nonsymbolic communication. Write down the activities that occur with partners (peers or adults). Select one activity that you participate in and analyze the interaction using the following table:

Learner Behavior	What I Think it Means	How I Respond	Effectiveness of Interaction	Possible Changes

What intervention strategies will you apply based on your analysis?
2. Think about your personal style of interacting with learners who have severe disabilities.
   a. Pick one of these learners.
   b. Who are his or her favorite peers?
   c. Who are his or her favorite adults?
   d. What information can you gather that will help determine what interactional style this learner prefers?
   e. What is your interaction style, and how does it match the learner's preferences?
3. Select a learner and an activity that you engage in with that learner. Analyze the activity in terms of the naturally occurring opportunities for the learner to communicate. Which opportunities do you respond to? Are there any opportunities that you inadvertently preempt? Write a dialogue to enhance the activity.

References

Alwell, M., Hunt, P., Goetz, L., & Sailor, W. (1989). Teaching generalized communicative behaviors within interrupted behavior chain contexts. *Journal of the Association for Persons with Severe Handicaps, 14,* 91-100.

Ault, M. M., Guy, B., Guess, D., Bashinski, S., & Roberts, S. (1995). Analyzing behavior state and learning environments: Application in instructional settings. *Mental Retardation, 33,* 304-316.

Austin, J. (1962). *How to do things with words.* Cambridge, MA: Harvard University Press.

Bambara, L. M., & Koger, F. (1996). *Opportunities for daily choice making.* Washington, DC: American Association on Mental Retardation.

Bannerman, D. J., Sheldon, J. B., Sherman, J. A., & Harchik, A. E. (1990). Balancing the right to habilitation with the right to personal liberties: The rights of people with developmental disabilities to eat too many doughnuts and take a nap. *Journal of Applied Behavior Analysis, 23,* 78-89.

Bates, E. (1979). *The emergence of symbols: Cognition and communication in infancy.* New York: Academic Press.

Bates, E., Camaioni, L., & Volterra, V. (1975). The acquisition of performatives prior to speech. *Merrill-Palmer Quarterly, 21,* 205-226.

Bates, E., O'Connell, B., & Shore, C. (1987). Language and communication in infancy. In J. Osofsky (Ed.), *Handbook of infant development* (pp. 149-203). New York: Wiley.

Bates, E., & Snyder, L. (1987). The cognitive hypothesis in language development. In I. Uzgiris & J. Hunt (Eds.), *Infant performance and experience* (pp. 168-204). Chicago: University of Illinois Press.

Bedrosian, J. L. (1988). Adults with mildly to moderately severe mental retardation: Communicative performance, assessment and intervention. In S. N. Calculator & J. L. Bedrosian (Eds.), *Communication assessment and intervention strategies* (pp. 265-307). Boston: College-Hill.

Beukelman, D. R., & Mirenda, P. (1998). *Augmentative and alternative communication: Management of severe communication disorders in children and adults* (2nd ed.) Baltimore: Paul H. Brookes.

Blaha, R. (2001). *Calendars for students with multiple impairments including deaf blindness.* Austin: Texas School for the Blind and Visually Impaired.

Bloom, L. (1993). *The transition from infancy to language.* New York: Cambridge University Press.

Brady, N. C., & Halle, J. W. (1997). Functional analysis of communicative behaviors. *Focus on Autism and Other Developmental Disabilities, 12*(2), 95–104.

Brady, N. C., McLean, J. E., McLean, L. K., & Johnston, S. (1995). Initiation and repair of intentional communication acts by adults with severe to profound cognitive disabilities. *Journal of Speech and Hearing Research, 38,* 1334–1348.

Brown, F., Belz, P., Corsi, L., & Wenig, B. (1993). Choice diversity for people with severe disabilities. *Education and Training in Mental Retardation, 28,* 318–326.

Bruner, J. (1978). From communication to language: A psychological perspective. In I. Markova (Ed.), *The social context of language* (pp. 17–48). New York: Wiley.

Bruner, J. (1981). The social context of language acquisition. *Language and Communication, 1,* 155–178.

Bruner, J., & Sherwood, V. (1976). Early rule structure: The case of peekaboo. In J. Bruner, A. Jolly, & K. Sylva (Eds.), *Play: Its role in evolution and development* (pp. 277–285). London: Penguin.

Calculator, S. N. (1988). Exploring the language of adults with mental retardation. In S. N. Calculator & J. L. Bedrosian (Eds.), *Communication assessment and intervention strategies* (pp. 523–547). Baltimore: University Park Press.

Carr, E. G., & Durand, V. M. (1985). Reducing behavior problems through functional communication training. *Journal of Applied Behavior Analysis, 18,* 111–126.

Carr, E. G., Levin, L., McConnachie, G., Carlson, J., Kemp, D., & Smith, C. (1994). *Communication-based intervention for problem behavior: A user's guide for producing positive change.* Baltimore: Paul H. Brookes.

Chapman, R. (1978). Comprehension strategies in children. In J. Kavanagh & W. Stragne (Eds.), *Speech and language in the laboratory, school and clinic* (pp. 308–330). Cambridge, MA: MIT Press.

Cirrin, F., & Rowland, C. (1985). Communicative assessment of nonverbal youths with severe/profound mental retardation. *Mental Retardation, 23,* 52–62.

Clayton-Smith, J., & Pembrey, M. E. (1992). Angelman syndrome. *Journal of Medical Genetics, 29,* 412–415.

Coggins, T., & Carpenter, R. (1981). The communicative intention inventory: A system for observing and coding children's early intentional communication. *Applied Psycholinguistics, 2,* 235–251.

Corsaro, W. (1981). The development of social cognition in preschool children: Implications for language learning. *Topics in Language Disorders, 2,* 77–95.

Dooley, J., Berg, J., Pakula, Z., & MacGregor, D. (1981). The puppet-like syndrome of Angelman. *American Journal of Disordered Children, 135,* 621–624.

Dore, J. (1986). The development of conversation competence. In R. Scheifelbusch (Ed.), *Language competence: Assessment and intervention* (pp. 3–60). San Diego: College-Hill.

Downing, J. E. (1999). *Teaching communication skills to students with severe disabilities.* Baltimore: Paul H. Brookes.

Duchan, J. (1995). *Supporting language learning in everyday life.* San Diego: Singular.

Dunst, C., Lowe, L. W., & Bartholomew, P. C. (1990). Contingent social responsiveness, family ecology, and infant communicative competence. *National Student Speech Language Hearing Association Journal, 17,* 39–49.

Durand, V. M., & Crimmins, D. B. (1992). *The motivation assessment scale (MAS) administration guide.* Topeka, KS: Monaco.

Girolametto, L. E., Greenberg, J., & Manolson, H. A. (1986). Developing dialogue skills: The Hanen early language parent program. *Seminars in Speech and Language, 7,* 367–382.

Goetz, L., Gee, K., & Sailor, W. (1985). Using a behavior chain interruption strategy to teach communication skills to students with severe disabilities. *Journal of the Association for Persons with Severe Handicaps, 10,* 21–30.

Guess, D., Benson, H. A., & Siegel-Causey, E. (1985). Concepts and issues related to choice making and autonomy among persons with severe disabilities. *Journal of the Association for Persons with Severe Handicaps, 10,* 79–86.

Guess, D., Roberts, S., Siegel-Causey, E., Ault, M. M., Guy, B., Thompson, B., et al. (1991). Investigations into the state behaviors of students with severe and profound handicapping conditions (Monograph No. 1). Lawrence, KS: University of Kansas Department of Special Education.

Guess, D., Roberts, S., Siegel-Causey, E., Ault, M. M., Guy, B., Thompson, B., et al. (1993). An analysis of behavior state conditions and associated environmental variables among students with profound handicaps. *American Journal on Mental Retardation, 97,* 634–653.

Guess, D., Roberts, S., Siegel-Causey, E., & Rues, J. (1995). Replication and extended analysis of behavior state, environmental events, and related variables in profound disabilities. *American Journal on Mental Retardation, 100,* 36–51.

Guess, D., Siegel-Causey, E., Roberts, S., Guy, B., Ault, M. M., & Rues, J. (1993). Analysis of state organizational patterns among students with profound disabilities. *Journal of the Association for Persons with Severe Handicaps, 18,* 93–108.

Guess, D., Siegel-Causey, E., Roberts, S., Rues, J., Thompson, B., & Siegel-Causey, D. (1990). Assessment and analysis of behavior state and related variables among students with profoundly handicapping conditions. *Journal of the Association for Persons with Severe Handicaps, 15,* 211–230.

Guy, B., Guess, D., & Ault, M. M. (1993). Classroom procedures for the measurement of behavior state among students with profound disabilities. *Journal of the Association for Persons with Severe Handicaps, 18,* 52–60.

Halle, J. (1984). Arranging the natural environment to occasion language: Giving severely language-delayed children reason to communicate. *Seminars in Speech and Language, 5*(3), 185–197.

Halle, J. W., Marshall, A. M., & Spradlin, J. E. (1979). Time delay: A technique to increase language use and facilitate generalization in retarded children. *Journal of Applied Behavior Analysis, 12,* 431–439.

Harding, C. (1984). Acting with intention: A framework for examining the development of the intention to communicate. In L. Feagans, C. Garvey, & R. Golinkoff (Eds.), *The origins and growth of communication* (pp. 123–135). Norwood, NJ: Ablex.

Harding, C., & Golinkoff, R. (1979). The origins of intentional vocalizations in prelinguistic infants. *Child Development, 50,* 33–40.

Hart, B., & Risley, T. R. (1975). Incidental teaching of language in the preschool. *Journal of Applied Behavioral Analysis, 8,* 411–420.

Harwood, J., Warren, S. F., & Yoder, P. (2002). The importance of responsivity in developing contingent exchanges with beginning communicators. In J. Reichle, D. R. Beukelman, & J. Light (Eds.), *Exemplary practices for beginning communicators* (pp. 59–95). Baltimore: Paul H. Brookes.

Horner, R. H., O'Neill, R. E., & Albin, R. W. (1991). *Supporting students with high intensity problem behavior.* Unpublished manuscript, University of Oregon, Eugene.

Hunt, P., Goetz, L., Alwell, M., & Sailor, W. (1986). Using an interrupted behavior chain strategy to teach generalized communication responses. *Journal of the Association for Persons with Severe Handicaps, 11,* 196–204.

Kublin, K. S., Wetherby, A. M., Crais, E. R., & Prizant, B. M. (1998). Using dynamic assessment within collaborative contexts: The transition from intentional to symbolic communication. In A. Wetherby, S. Warren, & J. Reichle (Eds.), *Transitions in prelinguistic communication* (pp. 285–312). Baltimore: Paul H. Brookes.

Lifter, K., & Bloom, L. (1998). Intentionality and the role of play in the transition to language. In A. Wetherby, S. Warren, & J. Reichle (Eds.), *Transitions in prelinguistic communication* (pp. 161–195). Baltimore: Paul H. Brookes.

MacDonald, J. D. (1985). Language through conversation. In S. Warren & A. Rogers-Warren (Eds.), *Teaching functional language* (pp. 89–122). Baltimore: University Park Press.

MacDonald, J. D. (1989). *Becoming partners with children: From play to conversations.* Chicago: Riverside.

MacDonald, J., & Carroll, J. (1992). Communicating with young children: An ecological model for clinicians, parents, and collaborative professionals. *American Journal of Speech-Language Pathology, 1,* 39–48.

McLean, J., McLean, L., Brady, N., & Etter, R. (1991). Communication profiles of two types of gesture using nonverbal persons with severe to profound mental retardation. *Journal of Speech and Hearing Research, 34,* 294–308.

McLean, J., & Snyder-McLean, L. (1978). *A transactional approach to early language training.* New York: Merrill/Macmillan.

McLean, J., & Snyder-McLean, L. (1988). Applications of pragmatics to severely mentally retarded children and youth. In R. L. Schiefelbusch & L. L. Lloyd (Eds.), *Language perspectives: Acquisition, retardation and intervention* (pp. 255–288). Austin, TX: PRO-ED.

McLean, J., & Snyder-McLean, L. (1999). *How children learn language.* San Diego: Singular.

Miller, J., & Paul, R. (1995). *The clinical assessment of language comprehension.* Baltimore: Paul H. Brookes.

Mirenda, P. (1988, August). *Instructional techniques for communication.* Paper presented at the Annual Augmentative and Alternative Communication for Students with Severe Disabilities Special Education Innovative Institute, Fremont, CA.

Mirenda, P. L., & Donnellan, A. M. (1986). Effects of adult interaction style on conversational behavior in students with severe communication problems. *Language, Speech and Hearing Services in the Schools, 17,* 126–141.

Musselwhite, C. R., & St. Louis, K. W. (1988). *Communication programming for persons with severe handicaps: Vocal and augmentative strategies* (2nd ed.). San Diego: College-Hill.

National Joint Committee for Communication of Persons with Severe Disabilities. (1992). Bill of rights. Retrieved January 5, 2004, from **http://www.asha.org/njc/bill_of_rights.htm**

Noonan, M. J., & Siegel, E. (2003). Special needs of young children with severe handicaps. In L. McCormick, D. Loeb, & R. Schiefelbusch (Eds.), *Supporting children with communication difficulties in inclusive settings: School-based language intervention* (2nd ed., pp. 405–432). Boston: Allyn & Bacon.

Ogletree, B., Wetherby, A., & Westling, D. (1992). A profile of the prelinguistic intentional communicative behaviors of children with profound mental retardation. *American Journal on Mental Retardation, 97,* 186–196.

O'Neill, R. E., Horner, R. H., Albin, R. W., Sprague, J. R., Storey, K., & Newton, J. S. (1997). *Functional assessment and program development for problem behavior: A practical handbook.* Pacific Grove, CA: Brookes/Cole.

O'Neill, R., Vaughn, B., & Dunlap, G. (1998). Comprehensive behavioral support: Assessment issues and strategies. In A. Wetherby, S. Warren, & J. Reichle (Eds.), *Transitions in prelinguistic communication* (pp. 313–341). Baltimore: Paul H. Brookes.

Peck, C. A. (1989). Assessment of social communicative competence: Evaluating environments. *Seminars in Speech and Language, 10,* 1–15.

Peck, C. A., & Schuler, A. L. (1987). Assessment of social/communicative behavior for students with autism and severe handicaps: The importance of asking the right question. In T. L. Layton (Ed.), *Language and treatment of autistic and developmentally disordered children* (pp. 35–62). Springfield, IL: Charles C Thomas.

Piaget, J. (1952). *The origins of intelligence in children.* New York: Basic Books.

Prizant, B., & Wetherby, A. (1990). Assessing the communication of infants and toddlers: Integrating a socioemotional perspective. *Zero to Three, 11,* 1–12.

Rainforth, B. (1982). Biobehavioral state and orienting: Implications for educating profoundly retarded students. *Journal of the Association for the Severely Handicapped, 6,* 33–37.

Reichle, J., & Wacker, D. (Eds.). (1993). *Communication and language intervention series: Vol. 3. Communicative alternatives to challenging behavior: Integrating functional assessment and intervention strategies.* Baltimore: Paul H. Brookes.

Rice, M. (1983). Contemporary account of the cognition/language relationship: Implications for speech-language clinicians. *Journal of Speech and Hearing Disorders, 48,* 347–359.

Rice, M. L., & Kemper, S. (1984). *Child language and cognition: Contemporary issues.* Baltimore: University Park Press.

Richards, S., & Richards, R. (1997). Implications for assessing biobehavioral states in individuals with profound disabilities. *Focus on Autism and Other Developmental Disabilities, 12*(2), 79–86.

Richards, S. B., & Sternberg, L. (1992). A preliminary analysis of environmental variables affecting the observed biobehavioral states of individuals with profound handicaps. *Journal of Intellectual Disability Research, 36,* 403–414.

Richards, S. B., & Sternberg, L. (1993). Corroborating previous findings: Laying stepping stones in the analysis of biobehavioral states in students with profound disabilities. *Education and Training in Mental Retardation, 28,* 262–268.

Romski, M.A., & Sevcik, R.A. (1993). Language learning through augmented means: The process and its products. In A. Kaiser & D. Gray (Eds.), *Enhancing children's communication: Research foundations for intervention* (pp. 85–104). Baltimore: Paul H. Brookes.

Rowland, C., & Schweigert, P. (1990). *Tangible symbol systems: Symbolic communication for individuals with multisensory impairments.* Tucson, AZ: Communication Skill Builders.

Rowland, C., Schweigert, P. D., & Prickett, J. G. (1995). Communication systems, devices, and modes. In K. M. Huebner, J. G. Prichett, T. R. Welsch, & E. Joffee (Eds.), *Hand in hand: Essentials of communication and orientation and mobility for your students who are deaf-blind* (pp. 219–259). New York: American Foundation for the Blind.

Rowland, C., & Stremel-Campbell, K. (1987). Share and share alike: Conventional gestures to emergent language for learners with sensory impairments. In L. Goetz, D. Guess, & K. Stremel-Campbell (Eds.), *Innovative program design for individuals with dual sensory impairments* (pp. 49–75). Baltimore: Paul H. Brookes.

Siegel, E. (in press). *Enhancing nonsymbolic communication for learners with severe disabilities and autism.* Baltimore: Paul H. Brookes.

Siegel, E., & Cress, C. (2002). Overview of the emergence of early AAC behaviors: Progression from communicative to symbolic skills. In J. Reichle, D. R. Beukelman, & J. Light (Eds.), *Exemplary practices for beginning communicators* (pp. 25–57). Baltimore: Paul H. Brookes.

Siegel-Causey, E., & Bashinski, S. (1997). Enhancing initial communication and responsiveness of learners with multiple disabilities: A tri-focus framework for partners. *Focus on Autism and Other Developmental Disabilities, 12*(2), 105–120.

Siegel-Causey, E., & Downing, J. (1987). Nonsymbolic communication development: Theoretical concepts and educational strategies. In L. Goetz, D. Guess, & K. Stremel-Campbell (Eds.), *Innovative program design for individuals with dual sensory impairments* (pp. 15–48). Baltimore: Paul H. Brookes.

Siegel-Causey, E., Ernst, B., & Guess, D. (1987). Elements of nonsymbolic communication and early interactional processes. In M. Bullis (Ed.), *Communication development in young children with deaf-blindness: Literature review III* (pp. 57–102). Monmouth, OR: Communication Skills Center for Young Children with Deaf-Blindness.

Siegel-Causey, E., Ernst, B., & Guess, D. (1989). Nonsymbolic communication in early interactional processes. In M. Bullis (Ed.), *Communication development in young children with deaf-blindness: Literature review IV* (pp. 69–122). Monmouth, OR: Communication Skills Center for Young Children with Deaf-Blindness.

Siegel-Causey, E., & Guess, D. (Eds.). (1989). *Enhancing nonsymbolic communication interactions among learners with severe handicaps.* Baltimore: Paul H. Brookes.

Snell, M. E. (2002). Using dynamic assessment with learners who communicate nonsymbolically. *Alternative and Augmentative Communication, 18,* 163–176.

Snell, M. E., Caves, K., McLean, L., Mineo Mollica, B., Mirenda, P., Paul-Brown, D., et al. (2003). Concerns regarding the application of restrictive "eligibility" policies to individuals who need communication services and supports. *Research and Practice for Persons with Severe Disabilities, 28,* 70–78.

Snyder-McLean, L. K., Solomonson, B., McLean, J. E., & Sack S. (1984). Structuring joint-action routines for facilitating communication and language development in the classroom. *Seminars in Speech and Language, 5*(3), 213–228.

Stillman, R., & Siegel-Causey, E. (1989). Introduction to nonsymbolic communication. In E. Siegel-Causey & D. Guess (Eds.), *Enhancing nonsymbolic communication interaction among learners with severe disabilities* (pp. 1–13). Baltimore: Paul H. Brookes.

Stremel-Campbell, K., & Rowland, C. (1987). Prelinguistic communication intervention: Birth-to-2. *Topics in Early Childhood Special Education, 7*(2), 49–58.

Wacker, D. P., Steege, M. W., Northup, J., Sasso, G., Berg, W., Reimers, T., et al. (1990). A component analysis of functional communication training across three topographies of severe behavior problems. *Journal of Applied Behavior Analysis, 23,* 417–429.

Warren, S. F., McQuarter, R. J., & Rogers-Warren, A. K. (1984). The effects of mands and models on the speech of unresponsive socially isolated children. *Journal of Speech and Hearing Disorders, 47,* 42–52.

Wetherby, A., Alexander, D., & Prizant, B. (1998). The ontogeny and role of repair strategies. In A. Wetherby, S. Warren, & J. Reichle (Eds.), *Transitions in prelinguistic communication* (pp. 135–160). Baltimore: Paul H. Brookes.

Wetherby, A., Cain, D., Yonclas, D., & Walker, V. (1988). Analysis of intentional communication of normal children from the prelinguistic to the multi-word stage. *Journal of Speech and Hearing Research, 31,* 240–252.

Wetherby, A., & Prizant, B. (1989). The expression of communicative intent: Assessment issues. *Seminars in Speech and Language, 10,* 77–91.

Wetherby, A., & Prizant, B. (1992). Profiling young children's communicative competence. In S. Warren & J. Reichle (Eds.), *Causes and effects in language assessment and intervention* (pp. 217–253). Baltimore: Paul H. Brookes.

Wetherby, A., & Prizant, B. (1993). *Communication and symbolic behavior scales—Normed edition.* Chicago: Applied Symbolix.

Wetherby, A., & Prizant, B. (1997). Communication, language, and speech disorders in young children. In S. Greenspan, J. Osofsky, & S. Wieder (Eds.), *Handbook of child and adolescent psychiatry* (pp. 473–491). New York: Wiley.

Wetherby, A., Prizant, B., & Hutchinson, T. (1998). Communicative, social-affective, and symbolic profiles of young children with autism and pervasive developmental disorder. *American Journal of Speech-Language Pathology, 7,* 79–91.

Wetherby, A., & Prutting, C. (1984). Profiles of communicative and cognitive-social abilities in autistic children. *Journal of Speech and Hearing Research, 27,* 364–377.

Wetherby, A., Reichle, J., & Pierce, P. (1998). The transition to symbolic communication. In A. M. Wetherby, S. F. Warren, & J. Reichle (Eds.), *Transitions in Prelinguistic Communication* (pp. 197–230). Baltimore: Paul H. Brookes.

Wetherby, A., & Rodriguez, G. (1992). Measurement of communicative intentions during structured and unstructured contexts. *Journal of Speech and Hearing Research, 35,* 130–138.

Wetherby, A., Warren, S., & Reichle, J. (Eds.). (1998). *Communication and language intervention series: Vol. 7. Transitions in prelinguistic communication*. Baltimore: Paul H. Brookes.

Wetherby, A., Yonclas, D., & Bryan, A. (1989). Communicative profiles of handicapped preschool children: Implications for early identification. *Journal of Speech and Hearing Disorders, 54,* 148-158.

Williams, C., & Frais, J. (1982). The Angelman ("happy puppet") syndrome. *American Journal of Medical Genetics, 11,* 453-460.

Wood, L., Lasker, J., Siegel-Causey, E., Beukelman, D., & Ball, L. (1998). Input framework for augmentative and alternative communication. *Augmentative and Alternative Communication, 14,* 261-267.

Writer, J. (1987). A movement-based approach to the education of students who are sensory impaired/multihandicapped. In L. Goetz, D. Guess, & K. Stremel-Campbell (Eds.), *Innovative program design for individuals with dual sensory impairments* (pp. 191-223). Baltimore: Paul H. Brookes.

Yoder, P., Warren, S., McCathren, R., & Leew, S. (1998). Does adult responsivity to child behavior facilitate communication development? In A. M. Wetherby, S. F. Warren, & J. Reichle (Eds.), *Transitions in prelinguistic communication* (pp. 39-58). Baltimore: Paul H. Brookes.

5

Teaching Functional
Communication Skills

Ann P. Kaiser
Joan C. Grim

Communication skills are essential for everyday social and learning interactions. Most students with severe disabilities need systematic instruction to learn communication forms and strategies that are easily understood by others. Efficiently teaching functional skills so that students can participate in everyday interactions is the primary goal for systematic instruction in communication. Functional communication skills are dependable, consistent forms used in a manner that informs listeners of students' needs, wants, interests, and feelings. Such skills may take many different forms, including words, phrases and sentences, signs, gestures, and the use of augmentative devices. Functional communication skills allow students to participate in social interactions by giving them a means to express their intentions and to respond to others. For the majority of learners with severe disabilities, functional communication skills are acquired most easily when they are taught in everyday interactions and routines to achieve specific social goals with familiar conversational partners.

Naturalistic Approaches to Teaching Communication

During the past three decades, naturalistic strategies for teaching functional communication have been demonstrated to be effective for increasing everyday communication by students with severe disabilities across school, home, and work settings. Naturalistic teaching strategies begin with the student's intention to communicate and systematically provide models of appropriate communication forms and meaningful social consequences for communication attempts. These strategies are designed to teach new forms of language while simultaneously promoting social communication in everyday conversational contexts. By embedding instruction in ongoing interactions and everyday activities, students may immediately use the forms being taught to express their needs and wants and experience the functional consequences of their communication (see Table 5-1).

TABLE 5–1
Key Terms

Key terms	Definition	Examples
Functional communication	Communication acts that have the intended effect on the listener; that is, acts that achieve the goals of the speaker by gaining the desired response from others. Any communicative act, in any mode, can be functional, depending on the response of the communication partner.	• Student verbally requests assistance • Student points to picture for "help" • Student signs "help" and adult responds with indicated assistance
Form	The mode of communication and, within modes, the topography and systematic organization of symbol or sign use.	• Words • Signs • Grammar • Computer vocal output • Pictures
Function	The social purpose of a communication event and, especially, the actual effect of the individual's communicative act. Function is established by the consequences experienced by the communicator. Functional communication has the intended effect on the listener.	• Greeting • Protest • Comment • Agree
Naturalistic communication intervention strategies	Techniques for teaching communication in the context of ongoing daily activities, using the social and physical context, the need for communication, and natural consequences as an integral part of the teaching episode. Teaching is incidental, dispersed across the day, and embedded in activities rather than occurring in massed practice trials for specifically teaching a skill.	• Responsive interaction • Milieu teaching • Enhanced milieu teaching • Prelinguistic milieu teaching • Incidental teaching
Social communication	Exchange of information, including expression and understanding of expressed needs, wants, and feelings, between two persons.	• Verbal conversations • Hugging • Mutual gaze • Gesturing that is understood by partner
Augmentative and alternative communication (AAC)	Use of an integrated system of components (symbols, aids, strategies, and techniques) to support communication by persons with severe impairments in verbal communication. The system may include visual, auditory, or tactile representations of concepts and includes gestural communication; multimodal communication is most common.	• Gestures • Signs • Pictures • Printed words • Computer-based technologies • Using any of the above with speech

Naturalistic teaching is grounded in social communication. That is, teaching occurs when two persons have a shared goal of exchanging information within a social interaction. One person (e.g., the teacher) supports social communication or the construction of a shared meaning by conversational partners in a communicative interaction by modeling, prompting, or cuing communication for the less skilled partner. Typically, social communication is verbal and linguistic (i.e., uses words and sentences), but communication can also be nonverbal, symbolic, or gestural. Naturalistic teaching supports effective social communication by responding to and expanding the students' current form and mode of communication. Thus, students' use of words, signs, natural gestures, or simple or complex augmented communication modes will be responded to with meaningful communication, and models of more complex forms will be provided. The goal of naturalistic teaching is to make the student's current form of communication functional in the ongoing interaction and also to provide models of more complex forms. Sharing information and sustaining meaningful interaction between partners co-occur with instruction about communication form. Thus, naturalistic teaching emphasizes both function and form while using everyday communicative context for teaching.

Naturalistic approaches to teaching communication skills build on principles of behavioral teaching technology that have been used to teach specific skills to individuals with limited language for more than 30 years. Teaching functional communication skills to students with severe disabilities requires an approach to

intervention that emphasizes useful communication and promotes generalization and maintenance of newly learned skills. Limited generalization is a major barrier to acquisition of a functional communication repertoire (Kaiser, Hester, & McDuffie, 2001). Both longitudinal analysis (Warren & Rogers-Warren, 1983) and specific experimental analyses (Anderson & Spradlin, 1980) have demonstrated that limited generalization of newly learned language skills by individuals with severe disabilities is a typical training outcome when training occurs outside the settings where the newly learned skills are required.

Case Studies

Lizabeth

Lizabeth is a 4-year-old with autism. At this time, she has no spoken words but is learning to use the Picture Exchange Communication System (PECS) to signal her requests to her teachers. She has learned to use pictures to request her favorite stuffed toy, food, or activity; to ask for help; to indicate she needs to use the bathroom; and to say no. She will soon be learning to use more pictures for other preferred items and activities. Lizabeth has attended a preschool sponsored by her family's church since age 3. She is the only child with a disability in a class of 12 children. An itinerant special education teacher visits the classroom 4 days a week, and a speech-language pathologist (SLP) visits 2 days a week. Both work with Lizabeth in the classroom. The special education teacher consults with the SLP and the two classroom teachers. The two most challenging issues for her teachers are understanding Lizabeth's needs and wants and engaging her in the activities of the classroom.

Kristi

Kristi is a bright-eyed 9-year-old with a charming smile and lots of energy. She is a full participant in the third-grade classroom she attends in her neighborhood school. Along with 20 other children, she receives academic instruction that is designed to fit her developmental needs in the context of cooperative learning groups, individualized tutoring, and classroom activities. Kristi's special education teacher collaborates with her classroom teacher in planning and implementing instruction. In addition, Kristi works with an SLP and a physical therapist 3 days each week. Kristi has multiple disabilities: a vision impairment corrected with glasses, a moderate level of motor control that limits her mobility, and cognitive delays. Although she is socially engaging and frequently smiles and gestures at adults and peers, her formal communication skills are limited. Only when prompted does Kristi currently

use the four pictures on her StepTalk™ (Voice Output Communication Aide, VOCA) that she learned in one-to-one training with her speech therapist. Kristi does not yet use the device with peers or initiate communication. Her parents are interested in learning ways to facilitate her use of the VOCA at home, and her teachers want to enhance her participation.

Carter

Carter is a 10-year-old boy with autism. His spoken language is limited to one- and two-word utterances, but he understands longer sentences if the topic is concrete. Carter's favorite activities include visiting his grandparents and looking at family picture albums. He is a fan of all kinds of sports, and he likes to throw a football with his older brother. Carter is sometimes echoic (e.g., repeats the last word or two) of phrases directed to him. His mother, Catherine, has been taught to use responsive interaction and milieu teaching during interactions with him at home. She is careful to respond to Carter's verbal and nonverbal initiations, expand his utterances into short sentences, and prompt him to verbalize choices when appropriate.

Michael

Michael is a 15-year-old student with mental retardation and a moderate hearing loss. He uses a wheelchair. His communication skills include single words and two-word phrases. He struggles to articulate sounds clearly because of his hearing loss. It is important to maintain face-to-face visual contact with Michael when speaking to him so that he can see as well as hear what is being said. Michael uses a DynaMyte™ (an electronic VOCA with three levels) and his voice, especially with peers who have difficulty understanding him. Michael is socially responsive to peers and enjoys participating in a variety of activities.

Michael is enrolled in a multiability, prevocational high school program where much of the instruction takes place in community settings. Michael has several different teachers across a typical school day. His teachers and SLP work together to individualize his vocational and academic instruction to fit his communication abilities.

For students like Kristi and Lizabeth, emphasizing functional communication skills translates into (a) selecting an alternative mode of communication (e.g., a VOCA or the PECS book) (Frost & Bondy, 1994, 1996) that is easier for them to acquire than the verbal mode, (b) teaching responses that have an immediate use in indicating needs and wants, and (c) providing specific training to promote generalized use of new skills in everyday conversational contexts. To ensure that skills are functional and generalized, training occurs in several different settings where communication is needed. Dinner at home, recess on the playground with peers, lunch in the cafeteria, and bus rides to school are settings for training in addition to the regular education classroom and the speech therapy room. Teaching[1] communication is a collaborative process, involving regular and special educators, SLPs, other professionals, family members, and peers and friends who are conversational partners. Before teaching new skills, the team must assess the student's needs for communication and the demands for communication across settings.

Overview of Enhanced Milieu Teaching

This chapter discusses one method of naturalistic teaching, enhanced milieu teaching (EMT) (Kaiser, 1993). EMT is the third generation of naturalistic teaching strategies. It builds on the principles of incidental teaching (Hart & Risley, 1968) and milieu teaching (Hart & Rogers-Warren, 1978) and adds systematic principles for responsive conversational style. EMT is a naturalistic approach to teaching communication skills

in everyday communication contexts based on (a) responding to the meaning of students' communication while providing models of elaborated communication, (b) embedding supportive prompts for elaborated communication within ongoing social interactions, and (c) providing functional consequences for students' communicative attempts. Figure 5-1 provides a schematic overview of the components of milieu teaching procedures.

Three Naturalistic Strategies

EMT was designed for use in everyday communication environments by teachers, SLPs, other educational team members, and parents and adult family members. EMT shares an emphasis on social interaction with at least two other prominent naturalistic teaching

FIGURE 5–1
EMT Overview

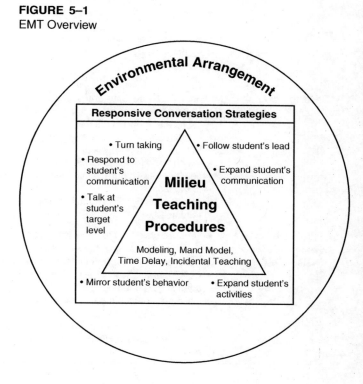

---

[1]Throughout this chapter, the term "teachers" is used to include any adult who teaches new communication skills—special education teachers, regular education teachers, classroom assistants, speech and language therapists, other therapists, parents, friends, assistants, and other adults who interact with students to promote their communication development. Peers can also facilitate and support the use of new communication skills; however, their role will most often be as conversational partners or as a collaborator with an adult rather than as an instructor.

strategies: PECS (Frost & Bondy, 1994, 1996) and Pivotal Response Training (PRT) (Humphries, 2003; Koegel, Koegel, Harrower, & Carter, 1999). These three naturalistic teaching procedures are designed for use in homes and classrooms, with a range of communication partners providing systematic language support, and use behavioral teaching strategies (prompts, shaping responses, facing cues, reinforcement, environmental arrangement). EMT and PECS specifically teach new skills in response to students' immediate interests and

intentions in classroom, community, and home settings. PRT teaches a repertoire of behaviors that help students express their needs and wants and increases their responsiveness to environmental cues for communication. Some portion of PRT training may occur in a clinic-type setting, but the goal is sustained support for communication in everyday settings by persons who typically interact with the student. All three intervention approaches have the goal of spontaneous, initiated social communication (see Table 5-2).

TABLE 5–2
Naturalistic Teaching Procedures Compared

Naturalistic strategies	Training focus	Communicative partners during training	Where training procedures are delivered
Enhanced milieu teaching (EMT)	• Adults arrange the environment to engage child's interests. • Child is taught how to respond during natural communicative exchanges. • Child learns to attend to and respond to socio-communicative cues. • Turn taking is taught through both motor exchanges and verbal exchanges to reinforce reciprocity in social interactions. • Child play behaviors are verbally modeled by teacher. • Reinforcers are directly related to activity. • All attempts by the child to communicate are reinforced.	• Teachers • Parents • Peers	• Clinic and classroom • Training is embedded in daily routines and activities
Pivotal response training (PRT)	• Teaches a repertoire of pivotal behaviors, such as persistence, play, and social exchanges. • Child makes choices during preferred activities. • Tasks are varied to maintain interest. • Mastered tasks are interspersed with new tasks to ensure that child will attempt task again. • Teacher models appropriate social interchanges. • Teacher uses natural reinforcers directly related to the task. • All attempts by the child to respond are reinforced.	• Teachers • Parents • Peers	• Clinic (for initial parent training) • Training is embedded in daily routines and activities
Picture Exchange Communication System (PECS)	• Teaches child how to make requests. • Teaches child to gain the attention of the communicative partner by initiating the request. • Child requests highly desirable items by exchanging a picture for the item. • Child preferences are pretested and ranked throughout the training. • All correct exchanges are reinforced by giving child the requested item, paired with a verbal model.	• Teachers • Parents • Peers	• Clinic and classroom • Training is embedded in daily routines and activities

Considerations for AAC

The principles outlined in this chapter can be applied to teaching communication using alternative and augmented modes of communication as well as verbal communication. An alternative and augmentative communication (AAC) system is "an integrated group of components, including symbols, aids, strategies, and techniques used by individuals to enhance communication" (American Speech-Language-Hearing Association, 1991, p. 10). Multimodal teaching approaches are needed to teach communication through an AAC mode. Thus, when using EMT, teachers will model and respond with both spoken language and the student's AAC mode (e.g., by pointing to a picture in the PECS book or by demonstrating the use of a VOCA).

1. The selection of communication mode should be based on current student and environmental assessments (Beukelman & Mirenda, 1998; Romski & Sevcik, 1992; Wacker & Reichle, 1993) and requires knowledge of the student's physical, cognitive, and intentional communication abilities as well as knowledge of the opportunities for and barriers to communication for the student.

   Kristi is capable of waving and identifying pictures. Therefore, her gestures, combined with pictures on her VOCA (StepTalk™), become functional forms of communication training across her day. She is taught to wave "hi" to her classmates when she enters her classroom at morning arrival time, and her classmates wave or say "hi" in response. While the wave gesture alone works for Kristi in the classroom, when she enters the crowded cafeteria, she is taught to combine her wave gesture with a picture selection to solicit a response from a partner. She may need to wave and point to the picture of her friend Julie to gain her teacher's attention and indicate that she wants to sit with her friend Julie.

   Expert assistance should be sought to evaluate students for their use of AAC modes. The large quantity of AAC devices available ranges from very low technical options, such as picture books, to complex multilayered computer based systems, such as the Freestyle/Speaking Dynamically Pro™. Students may begin with a relatively simple system and move to more complex systems as their communication skills develop.
2. In some cases, students may need exposure to or practice using a new mode of communication in addition to naturalistic teaching. For example, students may require initial practice in operating a computer-based communication system or in learning sufficient motor imitation skills to allow efficient imitation of a simple sign. These practice opportunities can occur concurrent with naturalistic teaching; there is no advantage to waiting until the student is "ready" for teaching in functional contexts.

   Kristi's teacher will need to be sure that Kristi can match the photos of her friends to the actual individuals. She may want to teach photo matching in a more structured classroom activity before she teaches Kristi to use them in the cafeteria.

3. In order for a communication system to be functional, the student's communication partners must have enough knowledge of the system to respond to the student's communicative attempts. Communication partners who are teaching new forms (signs, pictures) need a repertoire of those forms so that they can model and expand in natural contexts.

   Kristi's peers are included in the natural communicative exchanges. They point to pictures on her communication device as they respond to her. Peers are natural sources of content topics for the device. They provide generation-appropriate phrases that can be used on Kristi's communication device.

4. There is no evidence to suggest that using an alternative communication mode reduces a student's chances of learning to speak; in contrast, pairing nonverbal and verbal communicative forms may facilitate learning both forms (Goldstein, 2002; Romski & Sevcik, 1992). Thus, introducing an AAC system as soon as the student demonstrates the minimal cognitive and intentional communication abilities to support the use of the system is highly recommended. Spoken language can always be modeled concurrently to provide opportunities to learn both verbal and alternative forms of communication.

With these caveats in mind, examples of applications with learners who use AAC systems have been included throughout the chapter (see also chapter 4). Table 5-3 illustrates a range of ACC devices suited to naturalistic teaching procedures.

TABLE 5–3
List of AAC Devices

No tech/low tech	Medium-tech devices	High-tech devices
Pictures/photographs/line drawings	6-Level Communicator™	DynaMyte™
Gesture/sign language	Tech Talk™	Freedom 2000/2000Lite™
Written language	Tech Speak™	Head Mouse
PECS	Macaw™	Vanguard™
Simple voice output (VOCA):	Alpha Talker™	Freestyle/Speaking Dynamically Pro™
Big Mac Switch™	Superhawk™	Intellikeys™
Step-by-Step Communicator™	Message mate 8/20/40™	Optimist™
Cheap Talk 4/8™	Hand-Held Voice™	
Twin Talk™	Digivox™	
Chat Box™		
Voice-in-a Box™		
Listen to Me™		
Stepper™		

Low tech: Nonelectronic devices, usually pictures, photographs, or objects representing vocabulary; requires little or no training of teachers or families to use and maintain.

Medium tech: Electric or nonelectric devices, usually battery operated; typically has electronic voice output; accommodates several pictures or words for vocabulary; does not require specialized programming skills but requires some assistance to set up, use, and maintain the device.

High tech: Electronic devices: uses specialized computerized programs to display vocabulary; one symbol represents classes of words embedded in the device; has electronic voice output and some have word prediction capabilities; requires specialized training to program, use, and maintain.

Companies who sell AAC devices:

Mayer-Johnson, Inc.—http://www.mayer-johnson.com

Don Johnston—http://www.donjohnston.com

Enabling Devices—http://www.enablingdevices.com

Naturalistic Teaching Procedures and Students with Autism

Difficulty in acquiring social communication skills is a core characteristic of students with autism (National Research Council, 2001). Intensive intervention to teach functional communication skills that generalize and maintain is essential for these students. There has been much controversy about the timing, amount, and types of intervention that are likely to produce optimal outcomes for students with autism. Although there have been no large clinical studies comparing communication approaches or investigating the parameters of intensity, duration, and timing on the outcomes of milieu teaching approaches with students with autism, there are studies demonstrating the effectiveness of milieu teaching with children who have autism (Goldstein, 2002; Hancock & Kaiser, 2002; Kaiser, Hancock, & Nietfeld, 2000; McGee, Almeida, Sulzer-Azaroff, & Feldman, 1992; McGee, Morrier, & Daly, 1999;

Miranda-Linne & Melin, 1992). Naturalistic teaching approaches, particularly EMT, are appropriate for use with students who have autism for several reasons. First, EMT focuses on teaching functional communication in social contexts; thus, it addresses both the key skill deficit and the problem of use within social interaction that are most difficult for students in autism. Second, EMT embeds the types of behavioral teaching procedures that have been shown to be consistently effective in teaching new skills to students with autism. Third, by teaching functional communication skills across settings and by involving several responsive communication partners, it is possible that EMT promotes generalization across stimuli, settings, and persons that is most difficult for children with autism.

EMT can be used to teach a range of skills, from single words to sequential responses in conversation; thus, it is a technique that may be appropriate for students with widely different skills and for students over a fairly long period of development. Finally, EMT emphasizes the acquisition of spontaneous communication skills that express student needs and communicative intentions. For many students with autism, the transition into spontaneous, initiated communication is very difficult. EMT procedures that systematically reduce the level of prompts and supports may provide a framework for moving from imitation (modeling) to choice making (manding) to spontaneous production (time delay and incidental teaching). As we illustrate in the case examples for Kristi and Michael, EMT can be combined with other strategies to teach communication skills. The choice to use EMT as the primary intervention or as a strategy to promote generalization should be based on students' needs and available teaching resources and teaching contexts.

The Goals of Language Intervention

The overriding goal of language intervention is to increase students' functional communication. As obvious as this goal is, functional communication can be forgotten in classrooms where several students have significant communication needs and teaching new skills requires many trials before a new response is learned. Faced with the many needs and modest skill repertoires of individuals with severe disabilities, it is easy to lose sight of the primary task of language intervention, which is increasing students' abilities to share information, feelings, and intentions with communication partners.

Communication as a Short-Term Target

Functional communication is both a short-term training objective and a long-term goal. Target forms (words, signs, gestures, picture exchanges) should be usable immediately. Although some potential targets may be logical in terms of existing skills, they may not be functional in terms of immediate usefulness. For example, naming colors, an early skill acquired by typical children, may not be immediately functional for students with severe disabilities and limited communication repertoires.

The specific form does not render a target dysfunctional. Instead, the usefulness of the form in the student's everyday communicative environment determines its function. For example, emerging phonemes such as /ba/ and /ma/ are highly functional communication forms for very young children who are developing normally. Caregivers for such young children

attend to new phonetic forms as if those forms had communicative intent. Contrast this with Kristi's team's view.

> *Kristi's team feels that teaching her to articulate early phonemes such as /ba/ and /ma/ will do little to increase her current functional communication skills unless persons in the environment respond to them in functional and systematic ways. Instead, they will use signs, picture selection, or communication using a simple electronic board, as these are forms that Kristi can use immediately to indicate desired objects or activities.*

Making Training Functional

Three steps can be taken to increase the functionality of short-term training targets: (a) select forms known to be functional in a particular setting frequented by the student, (b) teach the student to use new forms in practical ways, and (c) prepare conversational partners to respond to new forms in ways that make these forms useful. Functional forms for training can be determined by observing the settings where students spend time and noting their interactions and the communication needed to participate in those interactions.

> *Kristi's team reflects on her interactions throughout her day and compiles a list of communication opportunities. They decide that Kristi needs greeting skills as she gets on the bus and as she enters the classroom. She needs simple requests to obtain classroom materials and to ask for assistance. She needs to be able to indicate her food preferences at lunch. It would be enjoyable for her to be able to indicate to a peer that she would like to play and to comment on her favorite activities.*

From the list of opportunities, a set of potential target forms can take into account Kristi's preferences. It makes sense to teach generic forms (such as "help"); however, specific forms that allow her to get what she prefers (i.e., a hug, a favorite book, access to a computer game) also should be taught.

Forms become functional only when the environment responds to their use in particular ways. Teaching a form in its functional communicative context gives meaning to an otherwise arbitrary sign or word. Meaning derives from the consequences of attempted communication.

At the lunch table, Kristi combines a waving gesture and selects a picture of Julie on her VOCA that says, "Julie come." Her friend understands Kristi's meaning and joins her at the lunch table.

Ensuring functional use may require intervention to help partners become responsive to the emerging communication skills of students. This is particularly true when students are using an alternative communication mode, have unclear articulation, or have a history of limited language use. Often the greatest barrier that students must overcome is the effectiveness of less desirable strategies, such as hitting others or grabbing materials. If conversational partners respond more quickly and consistently to these behaviors than to emerging forms of "standard" communication, it will be difficult to learn new forms.

Functional Communication

Communication shares feelings, needs, or information. Functional communication (a) begins with a connection between people, (b) does not depend on the specific form of communication, but (c) does depend on shared understanding or meaning.

In Kristi's case, signaling her request for a friend to come is not functional unless her friend responds to the request. Her friend may need support from a teacher (such as a prompt to respond to Kristi's gesture and VOCA) to understand and respond to Kristi's attempt to communicate.

Training parents, classroom aides, community members (i.e., bus driver), and peers to pay attention and respond to communication attempts is often critical for functional language intervention.

Effective social communication interventions, such as EMT, require increasing the interaction skills of the target students and their conversational partners (Hunt, Alwell, & Goetz, 1988; Kaiser, Hancock, McLean, & Stanton-Chapman, 2001; Ostrosky, Kaiser, & Odom, 1993). Coaching peers to initiate communication and to respond to students' communication attempts may be nearly as important as teaching new forms. Similarly, supporting conversational interaction by providing a common topic (e.g., a photo album containing pictures of a student's family and favorite activities [Hunt et al., 1988]) or providing toys or activities enjoyed both by students with disabilities and by their peers (Ostrosky et al., 1993) may be a necessary modification.

Lizabeth's 4-year-old classmates easily learned words for the pictures in her PECS communication book when their teacher used a large-group time to talk about ways to communicate. The teacher first asked the children to name some ways they let people know what they want. They talked about using words and about pointing, nodding heads, and taking things they wanted. The teacher showed them Lizabeth's book and asked them to name each picture. Some pictures were easy to name (i.e., potty, toy); others were a little harder (i.e., more, no, help). They practiced pointing to and naming the pictures. The teacher told them that Lizabeth was just learning to use these pictures to communicate. She suggested that they watch very carefully when Lizabeth attempted to give them a picture and that they say the name of the picture so Lizabeth could hear the word. Every day for 2 weeks after the initial large-group activity, the teacher asked the children to name a time when they had helped Lizabeth use her book. During play and snack, the teacher set up opportunities for Lizabeth to communicate with peers and used the EMT strategies to prompt peer-directed communication.

EMT Strategies

EMT refers to language and communication training procedures that are (a) brief and positive in nature, (b) carried out in the natural environment as opportunities for teaching functional communication occur, and (c) occasioned by student interest in the topic. EMT provides specific instruction about the form, the function, and the social use of language. Instruction takes place using a responsive conversational style, and the environment is arranged to support student communication. Naturalistic modeling of what, how, and when to communicate is combined with systematic prompts and consequences for communication. Teaching opportunities that are embedded in the context of meaningful social interaction between partners with shared interests are most likely to result in learning new, functional communication forms.

Guidelines for Using EMT

- Teach when the student is interested
- Teach what is functional for the student at the moment

- Stop while both the student and the teacher are still enjoying the interaction

There are important differences between traditional direct instruction to teach language and EMT. In traditional direct instruction, the basic structure of the teaching interchange is predetermined by the adult's agenda for training. Specific discrete trials are constructed to provide massed practice with particular linguistic forms, and standard consequences are selected to reinforce or correct the responses of students. Discrete-trial training focuses on teaching the student to respond to specific cues or stimuli in exact ways. For example, students may be taught to label objects ("chair") or to respond precisely to pictures with short descriptive phrases ("boy sits chair"). Trials are grouped together to give students intensive practice with consistent feedback for their performance. Teaching occurs in one-to-one or small-group settings in order to help students focus their attention and to limit interference from ongoing activities or other students. Potentially, discrete-trial training can be used effectively to establish an initial repertoire of sounds or acquisition of motor responses needed for operating an electronic communication device. The controlled and systematic sequencing of stimuli, responses, and consequences in discrete-trial training promotes rapid acquisition of relatively narrow responses but does not readily facilitate generalized use of new forms for social communication. See Table 5–4 for comparison of teaching principles and procedures of four intervention language procedures.

For example, during a 20-minute session, a student might be presented with 30 opportunities to name common objects. Each time, the teacher holds up the object and says, "What is this?" When the student responds, the teacher praises her; if the student gives an incorrect answer or does not answer at all, the teacher models the correct response. Although EMT shares some of these features, it differs in important ways. EMT occurs in the natural environment in response to the interests of students and incorporates functional consequences. Successful EMT more closely resembles a conversation than a rote instructional episode. During EMT, teachers or peers and the student communicate in a meaningful, responsive way.

Effective use of EMT requires that teachers do the following:

1. Arrange the environment as a context for conversation

2. Communicate with students using a responsive, interactive style and model language at the student's target level
3. Be able to fluently use the four core EMT techniques (i.e., model, mand model, time delay, and incidental teaching)
4. Be skilled in assessment and planning for EMT
5. Be sufficiently skilled in classroom management to ensure classroom time, space, and opportunities for communication
6. Collaborate with other communication team members

Why EMT Is Effective for Learners with Severe Disabilities

EMT procedures are well suited for teaching functional language skills to students with severe disabilities.

Michael is a 15-year-old student with mental retardation and a moderate hearing loss. When teaching Michael new language skills, his teachers match his intentions (e.g., greeting, answering, requesting, commenting) and the complexity of his language (e.g., single words with some simple two-word requests). They model appropriate new vocabulary and two- and three-word phrases when his attention is focused on something of interest to him (e.g., a favorite material, an activity, a peer), when he has a specific need or desire, or when he can make a choice. Because Michael's speech is difficult to understand, he uses both verbalizations and his DynaMyte to communicate; teachers model using language and his DynaMyte.

Teachers try to match their requests for language and their models to Michael's emerging skills. They teach forms that are just slightly more advanced than his current spontaneous language. Since Michael uses a few two-word utterances, such as "want" plus a noun (e.g., "want Coke") to make requests, the teachers work to expand his requesting repertoire by modeling a variety of new nouns in combination with the verb "want" and by adding a pronoun (e.g., "I want chips"). Modeling a new form occurs as Michael attends to the specific aspect of the environment that the new form describes. Teachers encourage increasingly complex skills, increased vocabulary, and Michael's use of the DynaMyte by pointing to the pictures representing new labels while verbally modeling the complete utterance.

Successful EMT occurs when a student's communication works to control the immediate environment.

TABLE 5–4
Comparison of Language Teaching Procedures

	Core principles	How taught	Where technique occurs	Who teaches
Enhanced milieu teaching	• Naturalistic approach to teaching communication • Focus is on child's interest. • Increase student's functional communication. • Pragmatic outcomes for child and communicative partner.	• Environmental arrangement • Responsive style • Model, mands, and time delay • Incidental teaching	• Everyday contexts • Natural routines • Preplanned playtimes	• Everyone who comes into contact with the child • Support provided for each component of the procedure
Picture Exchange Communication System	• Focus of communication is on the exchange with the communicative partner, not the referent. • Children learn to use reliable methods to request. • Spontaneous, nonprompted communication is the goal. • Children learn to persist in establishing communication with a partner.	• Environmental arrangement • Errorless learning and correction strategies • Time delay • Prompt fading • Correspondence checks • Interrupted chains	• Everyday contexts • Natural routines • Preplanned training environments	• Any persons trained to implement the PECS system • Training completed after multiday didactic instruction
Pivotal response training	• Teaches children pivotal behaviors that spread across all areas of their behavioral repertoire. • Focus on improving children's motivation, responsivity to cues in the environment, and self-management. • Emphasis on generalization of treatment. • Designed to address specific behavioral characteristics of autism spectrum disorder.	• Target behaviors taught • Direct and natural reinforcement • Interspersed easy and difficult tasks • Child responds to multiple cues • Systematic fading of reinforcement and adult supervision	• Clinic for initial parent training • Home • Preplanned training environments	• Parents and peers after 15 hours of training
Discrete-trial teaching	• Goal of communication is on responding to teacher-chosen referents. • Focus is on child's verbal response followed by adult-delivered consequences. • Therapist holds up stimulus item; item not functional within interaction.	• Numerous discrete skills taught by repeated trials • Verbal prompts • Direct reinforcement • Prompt fading	• Clinic • Isolated room in home • Designated classroom areas	• Any person trained to implement the program with intense (usually weekly) training • Child receives daily (20 to 40 hours per week) directing teaching

First, teaching new requesting forms is most effective when a student has indicated the desire for a specific object or a specific activity. Initiations and requests signal when a student has specific communicative intentions and has already made discriminations among many aspects of the communication context (e.g., what he wants, presence of a cooperative partner, that language is needed to communicate). Prompting or modeling language that matches the student's intentions help her learn how language functions to control the environment. Furthermore, requiring elaborated language also teaches the student that specific forms work more effectively than general or incomplete ones.

Modeling a New Form in a Functional Context

MICHAEL: (Reaching for a CD that has fallen on the floor)

TEACHER: Want CD. [verbal model plus activates the pictures for "want" and "CD" on his DynaMyte]

MICHAEL: Want (activates "want" on VOCA). [incomplete response]

TEACHER: Say "Want CD." [corrective model plus activates "want" and "CD" on Dynamyte]

MICHAEL: Want CD (activates "want" and "CD"). [complete response]

TEACHER: Oh, you want the CD. (Activates the pictures) Let me get it for you. (Picks up CD from the floor and hands it to him)

EMT also may help students develop strategies that increase their naturally occurring language learning. Michael is being taught to attend to both the presence of a conversational partner and his own needs as opportunities to talk. When he initiates, his verbal behavior results in specific consequences. Thus, EMT is likely to increase Michael's initiations and positive interactions with adults.

EMT promotes establishment of groups of related responses composed of functionally equivalent communication forms (response classes). In EMT episodes, Michael hears at least two utterances that serve the same purpose: the original form he produces and the elaborated form that is modeled by the teacher. He also has the forms modeled in speech and on his DynaMyte.

When Michael requests more milk at lunch by saying "milk" and/or selecting the picture of milk on his DynaMyte, his teacher models a slightly more elaborate request, "milk, please." Michael has an opportunity to equate his existing single-word request with a more polite form of requesting. When teachers and his parents provide Michael with another container of milk accompanied by additional descriptive talk (e.g., "it's chocolate milk" or "yes, you can have more milk"), several forms are paired with the same function in a brief interaction.

Finally, teaching in communicative contexts facilitates generalization to other conversational interactions. Teaching incorporates a variety of stimuli that occur in naturalistic contexts. Thus, students are not likely to become "stimulus bound" to the same extent observed after traditional one-to-one training. Teaching in response to Michael's attention to a specific object or event increases the likelihood that Michael will learn new labels and simple request forms without the use of massed trials and intensive practice or teacher-selected reinforcers that may mitigate against generalization.

Core Milieu Teaching Procedures

This section describes four core milieu teaching procedures: (a) modeling, (b) mand model, (c) time delay, and (d) incidental teaching. Table 5–5 summarizes these teaching techniques.

Modeling Procedure

Modeling is used during the initial stages of teaching a new form (e.g., a new sign, word, or picture) when a student has not acquired independent use of the form. Modeling may be considered the most fundamental milieu teaching process. The four primary goals of child-directed modeling are (a) building turn-taking skills, (b) training generalized imitation skills, (c) establishing a basic vocabulary, and (d) participating in conversations that occur outside the training context. Modeling can be used in environments that are arranged to facilitate communication by students. The teacher first establishes joint attention, meaning that the teacher will focus attention on the student *and* on what the student is interested in. Next, the teacher presents a verbal or gestural model that is related to the student's immediate interest. If the student imitates the model correctly, immediate positive feedback (which includes an expansion of the student's response) and the material of interest are offered to the student. Then the teacher expands the student's response to present a more complex communication form.

TABLE 5–5
Core EMT Teaching Techniques

Modeling procedure	Mand-model procedure
• Use the modeling procedure to teach new forms. • Note student interest. • Establish joint attention. • Present a verbal model related to the student's interest. • A correct student response receives immediate praise, verbal expansion, and (when material is being withheld) access to material. • An incorrect or absent student response is followed by a corrective model. • A correct student response receives immediate praise, verbal expansion, and access to material. • An incorrect or absent response to the corrective model is followed by corrective feedback plus access to material.*	• Use the mand-model procedure to prompt functional use of emerging forms. • Note student interest. • Establish joint attention. • Present a verbal mand related to student interest. • A correct student response receives immediate praise, verbal expansion, and (when material is being withheld) access to material. • An incorrect or absent student response is followed by a second mand (when student attention is high and when the student is likely to know the answer) or a model (when student interest is waning and the student is unlikely to know the answer). • A correct response to a mand or model is followed by immediate praise, verbal expansion, and access to material. • An incorrect student response to the corrective mand or model should be followed with the steps of the model procedure IF the child remains interested*.

Time delay procedure	Incidental teaching procedure

• Use time delay to teach more spontaneous use of emerging forms.
• Identify occasions when a student is likely to need materials or assistance.
• Establish joint attention.
• Introduce time delay.
• A correct student response (i.e., student communicates what he or she needs) receives immediate praise, verbal expansion, and materials or assistance.
• An incorrect or absent student response is followed by application of the mand-model procedure (if student interest is high and the student is likely to know the answer) or application of the model procedure (if student interest is waning and the student is unlikely to know the answer).*
	• Use incidental teaching whenever the student requests.
	• Identify occasions when a student is verbally or nonverbally requesting materials or assistance.
	• Establish joint attention.
	• Use the occasion to teach more intelligible, complex, or elaborated language/communication skills by applying steps of the following:
	  a. Model procedure (use to train new or difficult forms or structures or to improve intelligibility)
	  b. Mand-model procedure (use to train complexity and conversational skills)
	  c. Time delay procedure (use to train a student to initiate verbal or nonverbal communicative behavior about environmental stimuli)

* If the child loses interest (reaches for another toy, starts playing with something else) before any prompting procedure is "completed," discontinue that episode (set the requested material aside in case the child becomes interested again—do not give it to them!) and follow the child's lead, watching for other opportunities. Child interest is paramount to functional and meaningful milieu teaching.

If the student does not respond to the initial model or responds with an unintelligible, partial, incorrect, or unrelated response, the teacher establishes joint attention again and presents the model a second time (a corrective model).

A correct student response results in immediate positive feedback, expansion of the student's utterance, and access to the material. If an incorrect response follows the corrective model, the teacher provides corrective feedback by stating the desired response and then gives the topic material to the student. All milieu procedures have a modeling component that includes the steps described here. Figure 5–2 contains a flowchart showing the steps of the modeling procedure.

Modeling Language That Matches the Student's Intention

MICHAEL: (Touching the front of his jacket and looking at the teacher)

TEACHER: Say, "New jacket." [verbal model plus activates pictures on Dynamyte] (Model is followed by a teacher pause to give the student time to respond)

MICHAEL: ...jacket (activates "jacket" picture).

FIGURE 5–2
The Modeling Procedure Flowchart

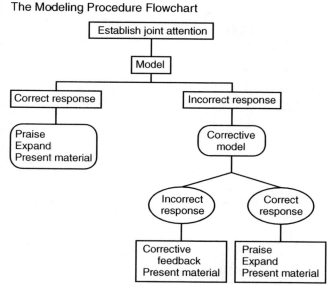

TEACHER: *New* jacket. [verbal model plus activates pictures].

MICHAEL: New jacket (activates "new" and "jacket"). [complete response].

TEACHER: Oh, I like your new jacket! Let me see the back.

Modeling may be used to increase the complexity of Michael's requesting.

Michael and two peers are taking CDs from the shelf to play music for the class. Michael looks at his friend, who is holding a favorite CD, and gestures to request the friend to give the CD to him.

TEACHER: Tell Jamie, "Play CD." [verbal model plus activates pictures]

MICHAEL: Play (activates "play" picture). [partial student response]

TEACHER: Play *CD*. [corrective verbal model plus activates pictures]

MICHAEL: Play CD (activates "play" and "CD"). [correct student response]

TEACHER: Right, you want Jamie to play the CD for you. Let's help him put it in. [acknowledgment + expansion + natural consequence]

Mand-Model Procedure

The mand-model procedure was developed by Rogers-Warren and Warren (1980) to actively program for the generalization of language skills from one-to-one

sessions to the classroom. Generalization was facilitated by training classroom teachers to increase the number of opportunities for students to display newly learned language in the classroom. During the mand-model procedure, a variety of interesting materials are provided. When a student approaches a material (a basket containing several toy cars and trucks), the teacher mands (verbally instructs) the student to request what he or she wants (e.g., "Tell me what you want"). If the student gives an appropriate response (e.g., want truck), the teacher responds positively and descriptively (e.g., "Okay, you want the red truck") and provides the requested material. If the student does not respond or gives an incorrect response (e.g., "Points to truck, no verbalization"), the teacher provides a model for the student to imitate. By presenting choices among interesting materials, the teacher allows the student to make language immediately functional in indicating his or her choice.

Use of the mand-model procedure is arranged and initiated by teachers. Teachers are responsive to what students are interested in and present mands only when there is a meaningful opportunity for the student to control the environment through communication. The particular goals toward which the mand-model process is directed are (a) establishing joint attention (topic selection) as a cue for verbalization, (b) teaching turn-taking skills, (c) teaching students to provide information on verbal request or instruction, and (d) teaching students to respond to a variety of adult verbal cues. The mand-model procedure differs from the model procedure by including a nonimitative verbal prompt in the form of a question (e.g., "What do you need?"), a choice (e.g., "We have crayons or paints; which one would you like?") or a request (e.g., "Tell Jamie what you want") rather than providing an initial model. The presentation of corrective models of appropriate responses when a student responds incorrectly or fails to respond to the mand (i.e., question, choice, or request) is identical to the sequence in the model procedure (see flowchart in Figure 5–3).

Choice-making mands are particularly effective variants of the mand-model procedure. Choice-making mands begin with a statement to students about the available choices (e.g., "There are cheese sandwiches and peanut butter sandwiches"). They are followed by asking students to indicate a preference (e.g., "What would you like?"). The subsequent steps are identical to those just described. Asking students to indicate a preference using a familiar question or request form

FIGURE 5–3
The Mand-Model Procedure Flowchart

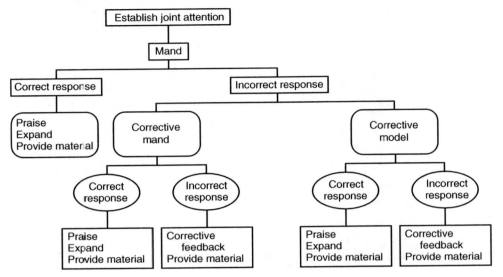

promotes generalization in similar but nonteaching choice situations.

Real questions or real choices form the basis of the mand-model procedure. Real questions and choices allow the student to truly communicate preferences and gain control over the environment. In contrast, questions that test the student's knowledge or seek only to get the student to perform a response are not truly functional communication exchanges because the adult already knows the answer. Use of the mand-model procedure should support both (a) students in becoming more independent and (b) teachers in learning to ask for and respond to student preferences.

Time Delay Procedure

Conversation should involve not only responding to another person's models and mands for verbalization but also initiating communication about various aspects of the environment. The time delay procedure was developed to establish environmental stimuli instead of simply presenting models and mands as cues for verbalization. The effects of the time delay procedure alone were experimentally demonstrated by Halle and his colleagues (Halle, Baer, & Spradlin, 1981; Halle, Marshall, & Spradlin, 1979). Adults in these studies (e.g., caregiving staff members and teachers) were instructed to attend to individual students by introducing a time delay in situations where the students were likely to need assistance or materials. Time delay has also been used in

combination with interrupting a chain of behaviors (Gee, Graham, Goetz, Oshima, & Yoshioka, 1991) and with a systematic reduction in prompting (Gee, Graham, Sailor, & Goetz, 1995). For example, when a student is assembling a pizza box as part of his vocational training, he learns sequential steps: (a) place cardboard, (b) fold along lines, (c) tuck end tabs, (d) secure with tape, and (e) fold down top. A time delay just before step d might be used to prompt the student to request help from his job coach to "hold please."

Steps of the time delay procedure include the following:

1. The teacher is in proximity to and looking at the student.
2. The teacher pauses when student attends to the material (e.g., looks at job coach and then at box) or nonverbally signals his communicative intent (e.g., points to the object).
3. The teacher waits for the student to verbalize.
4. If the student does not respond to the time delay within 5 seconds, the teacher models an appropriate verbal request ("hold please").
5. Positive feedback and immediately offering the desired material or assistance follow student verbalizations.

Michael's teachers decide to use a time delay procedure to prompt his language interactions with persons at school and in the community. His social studies teacher casually will block the door while talking to another student until Michael verbalizes and selects a picture on his DynaMyte. A cafeteria worker may hold on to Michael's tray until he requests it.

Any regular routine (e.g., entering and exiting a classroom, cleaning up after an activity, transitioning into a new task) may be interrupted by pausing between routine steps, focusing attention on the student as a prompt for communication, waiting for a communicative request, and, finally, providing the requested action when the student communicates. Interrupting sequences of behavior by blocking students' next actions should be used infrequently and only when the student already has the desired response in his or her repertoire. The goal is to support spontaneous use of communication and particularly to transfer stimulus control to nonverbal environmental and behavioral cues.

At his work site, Michael is assembling a bicycle gear by taking parts from each of six containers and fitting them together. The second container, which holds washers, is empty.

TEACHER: (Looks at Michael and waits for him to initiate communication) [delay or pause 2 to 5 seconds]

MICHAEL: Washer (activates "washer"). [partial student response]

TEACHER: Say, "Need washers." [corrective verbal model plus activates picture on VOCA]

MICHAEL: Need washers (activates "need" and "washers"). [correct student response]

TEACHER: Yes, Michael, you need more washers. Help yourself. (Giving him a large box of washers to fill his container) [acknowledgment+ expansion+natural consequence]

Time delay alone or in combination with other fading and chaining procedures may be especially useful with students who are echolalic (e.g., frequently imitate or repeat the exact words spoken to them). Students with autistic characteristics may repeat the last words of a prompt. These echoic repetitions can be functional; that is, the student may be communicating a specific intention such as greeting the listener or indicating his or her agreement. By observing the context in which the student uses an echoic utterance, it may be possible to use the occasion to prompt a more standard, spontaneous utterance that serves the same

function. Nonverbal prompting helps avoid the automatic echoing of a response and transfers stimulus control to the social and contextual cues. For Carter, time delays can prompt language without inadvertently eliciting echoic responses.

Teacher stands in the doorway of her homeroom greeting students as they enter the room. She speaks to Carter as he comes down the hall toward his homeroom.

TEACHER: "Good morning, Carter."

CARTER: "Morning, Carter." (Echoic response; may functionally be a greeting)

TEACHER: (Continues to stand in front of the home room door, looks directly at Carter and waits) [time delay]

CARTER: "Hi." (Spontaneous greeting)

TEACHER: "Hi, Carter. I am glad to see you!" (Moves aside to give Carter access) [acknowledgment+natural consequence]

Incidental Teaching Procedure

A fourth strategy has been developed for teaching more elaborate language and improving conversational skills about particular topics. Incidental teaching is used when the student makes a request. The first step in the incidental teaching procedure is to arrange the environment in ways that encourage the student to request materials and assistance. This can be done by displaying potential reinforcers attractively within the student's view but out of reach. A student who verbally or nonverbally requests materials or assistance is identifying what is reinforcing at that moment. The teacher responds by modeling, manding, or delaying for a more elaborated response or for additional information. When the student responds appropriately, the teacher gives the item of interest while affirming and repeating the answer in an expanded fashion (see Figure 5–4).

FIGURE 5–4
The Incidental Teaching Procedure Flowchart

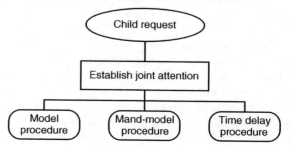

If the student does not respond appropriately to the mand or time delay prompts, the teacher moves to a simpler prompt and instructs the student to imitate a model. The adult then confirms the accuracy of the student's imitation, repeats and expands what the student said, and gives the student whatever he or she requested. Only if the student loses interest does instruction stop.

Because teaching to a reinforcer is possible only as long as the item or event is really of interest to the student, episodes are brief and positive in nature. Ability to request verbally or nonverbally and ability to imitate target forms are the only prerequisite student skills for incidental teaching.

Carter and a peer have been taken to a variety store to purchase a birthday present for a classmate. They are looking at a rack of baseball caps.

CARTER: (Pointing to a blue cap) Cap. [initiation]
TEACHER: Tell me which one you like. [mand]
CARTER: (Continuing to point)
TEACHER: Say, "Blue cap." [corrective model]
CARTER: Blue cap. [correct student response]
TEACHER: Here you go. You like the blue cap. Do you think Jimmy will like this one? [natural consequence + acknowledgment + expansion]
CARTER: (Nodding his head yes)

There is real joy in teaching functional communication forms to a student who is interested and motivated to use the form at the moment. Teaching only when students are highly motivated to respond may reduce the number of teaching episodes, but it ensures that teaching and learning are exciting positive events for both teachers and the students.

When to Use Each of the Four Procedures

Two general guidelines apply when selecting one of the four milieu procedures. First, select the procedure that is the most natural to the ongoing interaction. For example, asking a question (using the mand-model procedure) is natural when a student's intentions or desires are not clear or when asking for specification would be usual (e.g., "Would you like milk or iced tea?"). The modeling procedure is used whenever the student does not know the appropriate response. For example, if the student does not know the name of an object, it is natural to model the label for the student (e.g., "These are Lego blocks").

Second, use the procedure that provides the level of support the student needs to make an appropriate communicative response. Modeling provides maximum support for a student's response. The mand-model procedure provides a middle level of support and can be tailored to fit a student's skills by either asking a question only or providing two named choices followed by a question (e.g., "I have cheese sandwiches and peanut butter sandwiches. What do you want?"). Time delay provides no initial verbal support.

Incidental teaching differs from the other three procedures because it always follows a student request. Thus, incidental teaching should be used only when the student has made a request. Requests can be verbal, vocal, or gestural. How the teacher responds to the student's request in order to prompt elaborated language depends on the level of support the student requires to respond appropriately. In all uses of the milieu procedures, incomplete or incorrect student responses are followed by support for a correct response (i.e., if a student cannot respond to a mand, a model of the correct response is offered). Every episode includes a positive consequence, continuing communication, and modeling of an expanded form of the prompted response. The goals in all the procedures are to ensure that the interaction is as communicative, natural, and positive as possible and that interactions end with the students' gaining the specified reinforcers.

Learning to notice individual students' varied forms of requesting is a challenging task for teachers who want to use incidental teaching. Echoes, rote utterances, repeated gestures, problem behavior, and other behaviors (e.g., banging a hand on the table) and vocalizations with and without gestures may be requests. Systematic observation can help determine if these behaviors are intended to be requests. For students with limited physical mobility, eye gaze and head turns may function as requests. Students with autism and limited verbal skills may have very few obvious requests, but systematic observation can help in identifying their unique forms and reinforcers. *Every student communicates and almost every student requests.* The challenge for teachers is recognizing and responding to these requests as opportunities to teach (see also chapter 4).

Environmental Arrangement Strategies

Using the environment to prompt language involves (a) a focus on making language part of students' routines, (b) including interesting materials and activities in the environment, (c) having adults and peers who encourage students to use language and who respond to their attempts to communicate, and (d) establishing a contingent relationship between language use and access to materials or assistance during some routines and activities. Research suggests that environmental arrangement is an important strategy for teachers who want to promote communication in classrooms (Alpert, Kaiser, Hemmeter, & Ostrosky, 1987; Haring, Neetz, Lovinger, Peck, & Semmel, 1987; Kaiser, Ostrosky, & Alpert, 1993; McCathren, 2000). To encourage the use of language, classrooms and other communication settings require interesting materials and activities. Teachers should intervene by presenting desired materials and activities in response to students' requests and other uses of language (Hart & Rogers-Warren, 1978). Contingent provision of desired materials acts to reinforce language use.

Six strategies have been shown to increase the likelihood that students will show interest in the environment and make communicative attempts and that teachers will prompt language about things of interest to the students (see Table 5–6). The goal of these strategies is to provide clear and obvious prompts, while attractive materials and activities function as both discriminative stimuli and reinforcers for language use.

Interesting Materials

When materials and activities that students enjoy are available, students are most likely to initiate communication about the things that interest them. Thus, increasing interest in the environment increases the likelihood of language use as well as opportunities for language teaching. It may be helpful to assess students' preferences and to arrange settings so that preferred materials and activities are included. Students' preferences

TABLE 5–6
Arranging the Environment to Encourage Communication

1. **Interesting materials.** Students are likely to communicate when things or activities in the environment interest them.

Example: James lay quietly on the rug, with his head resting on his arms. Ms. Davis sat at one end of the rug and rolled a big yellow ball right past James. James lifted his head and looked around for the ball.

2. **Out of reach.** Students are likely to communicate when they want something that they cannot reach.

Example: Mr. Norris lifted a drum off the shelf and placed it on the floor between Judy and Annette, who were both in wheelchairs. Mr. Norris hit the drum three times and then waited, looking at his two students. Judy watched and clapped her hands together. Then she reached for the drum with both arms outstretched.

3. **Inadequate portions.** Students are likely to communicate when they do not have the necessary materials to carry out an instruction.

Example: Mr. Robinson gave every student except Mary a ticket to get into the auditorium for the high school play. He told his students to give their tickets to the attendant. Mr. Robinson walked beside Mary toward the entrance. When Mary reached the attendant, Mr. Robinson paused and looked at Mary. She pointed to the tickets in his hand and signed, "Give me." Mr. Robinson gave her a ticket, and she handed it to the attendant, who said, "Thank you. Enjoy the play."

4. **Choice making.** Students are likely to communicate when they are given a choice.

Example: Peggy's favorite pastime is listening to tapes on her tape recorder. On Saturday morning, Peggy's father said to her, "We could listen to your tapes" (pointing to the picture of the tape recorder on Peggy's communication board) "or we could go for a ride in the car" (pointing to the picture of the car). "What would you like to do?" Peggy pointed to the picture of the tape recorder. "OK, let's listen to this new tape you like," her father said as he put the tape in and turned on the machine.

5. **Assistance.** Students are likely to communicate when they need assistance in operating or manipulating materials.

Example: Tammy's mother always places three clear plastic containers with snacks (cookies, crackers, popcorn) on the kitchen table before Tammy returns from school. When Tammy arrives home and is ready for a snack, she goes to the table and chooses what she wants by handing the container with her chosen snack to her mother. Her mother responds to this nonverbal request by modeling a request form that specifies Tammy's choice (e.g., "Open popcorn").

6. **Unexpected situations.** Students are likely to communicate when something happens that they do not expect.

Example. Ms. Esser was helping Kathy put on her socks and shoes after rest time. After assisting with the socks, Ms. Esser put one of the shoes on her own foot. Kathy stared at the shoe for a moment and then looked up at her teacher, who was smiling. "No," laughed Kathy, "my shoe."

along with age and context appropriateness should be considered.

Out of Reach

Placing some desirable materials within view but out of the students' reach prompts students to make requests to gain access to the materials. Materials may be placed on shelves, in clear plastic bins, or simply across a table during a group activity. Students' requests create opportunities for language teaching. When students request a specific material, he or she is specifying their reinforcer at that moment (Hart & Rogers-Warren, 1978). Thus, a teacher who prompts language and provides the requested material after a communicative response effectively reinforces that response. For students who have limited motor skills, materials should be within their visual field, slightly out of reach, and far enough apart from other materials to allow a teacher or peer to interpret the nonverbal or verbal requests.

At home, Carter's mother keeps three of his favorite objects (a pack of baseball cards, a small trophy from his softball team, and a yo-yo) on the windowsill above the sink. At supper time, Carter likes to be in the kitchen while she cooks dinner and later cleans up. Carter cannot reach over the sink to the window. He initiates by pointing and naming the object he wants. Carter's mother uses this opportunity to prompt a short sentence (e.g., "I want yo-yo") in an incidental teaching episode. Responding to Carter's initiations also reminds his mom to take a few minutes to talk to Carter during this busy time of day. Her attention to his initiations supports his positive behavior at a time of day when he may be challenging.

Inadequate Portions

Providing small or inadequate portions of preferred materials (e.g., blocks, crackers, or turns on a computer game) is another way to arrange the environment to promote communication. During an activity that students enjoy, the teacher can control the materials so that students have only a limited amount. When they have used up the materials, they are likely to request more. When they initiate with requests for more, the adult has the opportunity to model and prompt more elaborate language as well as to provide functional consequences for the communicative attempts.

Teachers may also set up the environment so that students request materials from each other.

Choice Making

On many occasions, two or more options of activities or materials can be presented so that students can make a choice. To encourage students to initiate language, the choice may be presented nonverbally (e.g., by holding up two tools for opening a carton in either hand or by presenting three snack options on a tray). Students may be most encouraged to make a choice when one of the items is much more preferred and the other is much less preferred or disliked.

Lizabeth's teacher sets up a tray with two options at snack time: apples and crackers with peanut butter. She offers each child in the class a choice of snacks. Lizabeth prefers apples and does not like peanut butter. When the teacher holds out the tray with choices and Lizabeth reaches for the apples, the teacher prompts Lizabeth to give her the picture of apples from the communication book and says, "Oh Lizzie, you want apples. Good choice!" After the snack routine is established, the teacher prompts Lizabeth to indicate to a peer what she wants using her book (e.g., the peer will say, "Lizzie, what do you want?," as she waits for Lizabeth to hand her a picture).

Assistance

Creating a situation where students are likely to need assistance increases the likelihood of communication about that need. Attractive materials that require assistance may encourage students to request help. For example, a difficult-to-open container of a preferred food (e.g., chocolate milk) may provide an excellent opportunity to prompt "open" or "help."

Unexpected Situations

The final environmental strategy is to create a need for communication by setting up situations that go against the expectations of students. Children learn routines and expect that things will happen in a particular order. When something unexpected happens, they may be prompted to communicate. Of course, use of this strategy must be tailored to the student's skills and to their familiar routines. At times, students need help recognizing that something is funny or unusual.

Ideally, use of the environmental strategies results in stimulating students' interest and communication.

Teachers should either reinforce acceptable responses that result or use a milieu teaching procedure to (a) prompt a contextually relevant and appropriate response, (b) correct a response, or (c) evoke a more complex response. Nonverbal cues accompanying the environmental arrangement strategies should be faded out over time so that students are responding more to things of interest in the environment and less to arranged cues (Halle et al., 1979). For example, it may be necessary at first for teachers to shrug their shoulders, raise their eyebrows, and tilt their head while extending their hands containing two different materials in order to direct students' attention to the materials and to the opportunity for choice making. As students begin initiating requests, teachers will prompt less often and less overtly.

Environmental strategies must be tailored to each student's cognitive level and responsiveness to the environment. For example, if a student does not notice an unexpected situation created for communication, there is no opportunity to practice a communicative response. Environmental strategies are most effective when they cue communicative responses that are emergent in students' repertoires. Environmental arrangements provide nonverbal cues for communication that may facilitate students' progress toward spontaneous use of their new skills.

Inadequate portions of Kristi's favorite food at lunch serves as a cue to give her PECS card for "more."

When a peer who is handing out passes for the Friday night football game gives Michael only one pass (a planned implementation of inadequate portions), Michael indicates, "I want two" using his DynaMyte.

How teachers and others respond to students' communication attempts when these attempts are elicited by environmental arrangement is extremely important. Immediate attention, feedback, and access to the desired material or requested assistance, as well as a positive response, are essential for reinforcing communication attempts. As in all applications of EMT, episodes that begin with environmental arrangement should be brief, positive, successful for students, and reinforcing for the use of language and social engagement with adults.

The best uses of environmental arrangement are natural opportunities. The strategy of giving choices

can be used naturally in many contexts. Other strategies, such as inadequate portions and out of reach, should not be overused because they can be disliked by students. Environmental arrangement strategies also support peer communication, as peers can provide materials and activities a student requests. It is important to help peers understand the basic principles of EMT if they are going to be prompting specific forms of communication (e.g., teach to the students' interests, be positive, keep episodes short, and always follow through with natural consequences), but increasing responding to student communication may require only brief instructions and feedback to peers.

Using Environmental Arrangements to Promote Peer Interactions

Peer interaction is promoted when the interaction setting is organized so that peers (rather than adults) give assistance or materials contingent on the student's communication. At these times, peers can also present choice-making opportunities and interact more easily with the student in the context of interesting materials (Farmer-Dougan, 1994; McGee et al., 1992). Teachers can mediate interactions with peers by directing the student to communicate with the peer (i.e., provide prompts to the student to address the peer: "Tell Janie, I want another turn shooting the basket"). In addition, peers can be taught simplified milieu strategies to use directly with the student (Hancock & Kaiser, 1996). In Figure 5–5, Elise uses her Dynavox to plan a party with her friend Sarah.

Elise and Sarah are in Elise's backyard—a natural location for the two to play together after school. They are trying to decide who to invite to Elise's birthday party. Elise's mother has given Sarah paper and pencil to write down Elise's ideas for the party. Sarah asks Elise to tell her who to invite and what she wants to eat, and she writes down what Elise tells her.

Responsive Conversational Style

One of the important evolutions in naturalistic communication intervention during the past few years is the greater emphasis on responsive conversational style (Kaiser, Hancock, & Hester, 1998). EMT embeds the milieu teaching procedures into conversational

FIGURE 5–5
Elise using her Dynavox to plan a party with her friend Sarah

interactions by taking advantage of both the turn balance of good conversations and ongoing opportunities for modeling (without requiring a response) the forms and functions of communication (Kaiser, 1993; Kaiser & Hancock, 2000).

Responsive conversational style is a general interaction approach that supports students' communication and greatly enhances the naturalistic qualities of milieu teaching. Responsive conversational style sets a social context for language in the same way that environmental arrangement sets a physical context. Together, responsive conversational style and environmental arrangement create a supportive interactional context for conversation-based teaching. When a responsive interaction is established between teachers and students, communication is ongoing and offers many opportunities for specific but highly natural teaching. Responsive conversational style has four components:

1. Establishment of joint and mutual attention
2. Turn taking
3. Contingent responsiveness
4. Positive affect

As previously defined, *joint attention* occurs when teachers and students are focused on the same activity or material. For example, when a teacher watches closely while a student moves a toy truck back and forth on the floor, the teacher and student are jointly attending to the student's activity. *Mutual attention* occurs when students and teachers look at each other as they talk. In an ideal conversation, there is both joint attention to the student's ongoing activity and mutual attention between the student and the teacher. Joint attention allows teachers to focus their comments and requests for language on the objects and activities that are of immediate interest to the students. Mutual attention helps maintain communicative engagement between the conversational partners and increases the likelihood that students' requests and comments will be understood and responded to appropriately.

Turn taking refers to the exchange of communication turns by students and teachers in a conversation. Ideally, conversational turns are balanced so that each communicator's turns are of similar length and complexity. Turns can be taken nonverbally or verbally. Because many students with severe disabilities initiate infrequently, developing a more even balance of turns may require teachers to talk less, take shorter turns, and attend carefully to the students' ways of taking turns and attempts to communicate. Pausing to allow time for students to respond is an easy way to increase opportunities for students to take their turns. Ending an adult turn with a question can also promote student turn taking, but the adult must ask a question the student understands and then wait for a response.

The following examples illustrate balanced and unbalanced turn taking.

Unbalanced Turn Taking

MR. G.:   Hi there, Markus! What are you doing? Do you like that puzzle? It's a baseball player.

MARKUS: Me ball, too.

MR. G.:   Oh, you like baseball? Do you watch baseball on TV? I never miss a game. I watched three games this weekend. Well, it's time to clean up. Do you need some help? OK, you do it.

Balanced Turn Taking

MR. G.:   Hi there, Markus! (Pause)

MARKUS: Hi!

MR. G.:   Hey, you've got the baseball player. (Pause)

MARKUS: Me ball, too.

MR. G.:   You like baseball?

MARKUS: (Nods yes)

MR. G.:   You like baseball. I bet you watch it on TV. (Pause)

MARKUS: Me. (Nods yes)

MR. G.:   You watch baseball on TV.

Contingent responsiveness means that teachers respond to students' communication attempts quickly and meaningfully. Noticing and responding to student communication attempts are essential in establishing a conversation. Such responsiveness reinforces attempts to communicate and indicates to students that teachers are available as communication partners. Although some attempts will be missed in the context of a busy classroom, teachers should seek to be as responsive as possible to student communication attempts. When students communicate at low rates and there are relatively few potential communication partners in a setting, teacher responsiveness is especially important. Clearly, inclusive settings offer more opportunities for positive communicative interactions with a range of partners; however, teachers' modeling of responsive styles of interaction is often important for both students and other teachers.

To respond in a meaningful way, teachers must try to understand what it is that students intend to communicate and tailor their responses accordingly. The communicative attempts of students with severe language disabilities are not always easily understood. However, when teachers have established joint and mutual attention and have arranged the environment to promote communication, understanding students' messages is easier. The following examples contrast a conversation in which a teacher is contingently responsive with one in which she is not.

Contingently Responsive Conversation

Marci is emptying her backpack (a book, her glasses, a note from her mother, a package of tissues). Her teacher, Mrs. B., is standing by Marci's locker, waiting for Marci to finish.

MARCI: (Takes out her glasses and looks at them)

MRS. B.: Oh, Marci, there are your glasses. (Pause) Shall I help you put them on?

MARCI: (Hands Mrs. B. the glasses and looks at her)

MRS. B.: (Takes the glasses, looks back at Marci, smiles, and then helps Marci put the glasses on)

MARCI: (Takes out the note from her mother and plays with it)

MRS. B.: You brought a note from your mom. (Watches Marci and pauses) Marci, is that note for me?

MARCI: Note. Un-huh.

MRS. B.: (Looks at Marci, extends her hand, and waits)

MARCI: Here. (Gives note)

MRS. B.: Why, thank you, Marci. Let's see what your mom has to say. (Holds note where she and Marci can look at it while she reads it)

Noncontingent Conversation

MRS. B.: Good morning, Marci. Put your things away and come sit down.

MARCI: (Takes out her glasses)

MRS. B.: Hurry, Marci. We're running late.

MARCI: (Takes out a note from her mother)

MRS. B.: (Reaches for note and takes it) Thank you. I'll read this later.

MARCI: Note?

MRS. B.: Hurry. It's late.

Positive affect includes smiling, gentle touching, use of the student's name, a warm tone of voice, and an affirming style of interaction. Students who have limited verbal communication may be particularly sensitive to the nonverbal messages that communication partners send. Teachers who indicate their interest in a student by making themselves physically available and affirming students' attempts to communicate invite conversation. In contrast, adults or peers who speak loudly, do not match their pace and style to that of the students, and are not gentle in their physical contact with students discourage communication even if they do not intend to do so. Positive affect indicates interest, liking, respect, and availability for conversations with students. Positive affect should be an ongoing aspect of interactions with students who have severe disabilities as well as creating a social context for milieu teaching. Responsive, contingent conversation takes time because teachers must focus attention on students, wait for their responses, and pace subsequent comments and responses to match the students' style of communication. The time required is offset by the benefits of connecting and communicating with the student and by setting up opportunities to effectively teach functional communication skills (see also chapter 4).

Michael's job coach is careful to establish physical contact with him at the beginning of a work period. He greets Michael face to face and shakes his hand or touches his shoulder. He expresses his positive regard for Michael with smiles, nods, and gestures as well as words. Because Michael has a hearing loss, his job coach makes sure peers also communicate with Michael with their facial expressions, physical proximity, gentle touching, and gestures.

Peers may need special instructions about the importance of these aspects of communication for students with disabilities. Talking with a warm tone, conveying positive affect, and being relatively gentle in physical exchanges do not come naturally to most children and teens. Teacher modeling of a responsive conversational style with all students and some open discussion of ways in which students can communicate with each other, especially their peers with disabilities, can prompt modest improvements in interactional style.

Research on Milieu Teaching and EMT

Milieu teaching and EMT have a long history of research. More than 50 empirical studies have examined the effects of milieu teaching. Four variants of Hart and Risley's (1968) original model of incidental teaching have been analyzed experimentally: (a) modeling (Alpert & Kaiser, 1992; Alpert & Rogers-Warren, 1985), (b) manding and modeling (Cavallero & Bambara, 1982; Hemmeter, Ault, Collins, & Meyers, 1996; Mobayed, Collins, Strangis, Schuster, & Hemmeter, 2000; Warren, Gazdag, Bambara, & Jones, 1994; Warren, McQuarter, & Rogers-Warren, 1984),), (c) time delay (Angelo & Goldstein, 1990; Charlop & Trasowech, 1991; Charlop & Walsh, 1986; Halle et al., 1979, 1981; Miller, Collins, & Hemmeter, 2002; Oliver & Halle, 1982; Schwartz, Anderson, & Halle, 1988), and (d) incidental teaching (Alpert & Kaiser, 1992; Farmer-Dougan, 1994; Hart & Risley, 1968, 1974, 1975, 1980; Hemmeter & Kaiser, 1994; Hemmeter et al., 1996; Lennox & Brune, 1993). In general, modeling, mand modeling, and time delay are variants of the original incidental teaching model. In these procedures, there is increased adult support for children who are low-frequency initiators and whose language skills are relatively limited. Incidental teaching is simply the use of models, mands, and time delays in response to student requests.

Milieu teaching involves the application of behavioral teaching procedures in naturalistic, conversational settings (Hart & Rogers-Warren, 1978). Research has demonstrated that milieu teaching is effective in teaching a range of productive language skills to individuals with mental retardation and other language-related disabilities (Kaiser, Yoder, & Keetz, 1992.) A range of language responses (e.g., single words, adjectives, simple utterances [one to four words], compound sentences, specific requests, general requests) in both verbal and nonvocal modes have been taught. Milieu teaching positively affects general language skills as measured by changes in complexity of utterances and vocabulary diversity (Hart & Risley, 1975, 1980; Kaiser, 2000; Kaiser & Hancock, 2000; Kaiser et al., 2000; Rogers-Warren & Warren, 1980; Warren et al., 1984). Generalization across settings has been reported for some subjects in each study in which it has been assessed (Alpert & Kaiser, 1992; Alpert & Rogers-Warren, 1985; Cavallero & Bambara, 1982; Halle et al., 1979, 1981; Hancock & Kaiser, 1996; Hart & Risley, 1974, 1975; Kaiser et al., 2000; McGee, Krantz, & McClannahan, 1985; Miranda-Linne & Melin, 1992; Warren et al., 1984). Finally, for children with initially low levels of responsiveness and initiations, milieu teaching has resulted in increased levels of these specific social communicative behaviors (Halle et al., 1981;

Hancock & Kaiser, 1996, 2002; Hart & Risley, 1980; Kaiser et al., 2000; Mobayed et al., 2000; Rodi & Hughes, 2000; Warren et al., 1984).

There is considerable evidence that children's initiations, responses, participation in conversation, and requesting using trained utterances can be systematically increased using milieu procedures (Charlop & Carpenter, 2000; Charlop & Walsh, 1986; Farmer-Dougan, 1994; Haring, Roger, Lee, Breen, & Gaylord-Ross, 1986; Haring et al., 1987; Hemmeter et al., 1996; Matson, Sevin, Box, Francis, & Sevin, 1993; Schwartz et al., 1988). Studies that have measured broader effects on language development (Alpert & Rogers-Warren, 1985; Hart & Risley, 1975, 1980; Hemmeter & Kaiser, 1994; Warren & Bambara, 1989; Yoder, Kaiser, & Alpert, 1991) report modest changes in more global measures of language development. In two studies (Kaiser, 2000; Kaiser & Hancock, 2000) comparing applications of milieu teaching by parents and therapists of preschool children with significant language disabilities, results indicated that children in both the parent- and the teacher-implemented conditions made and maintained significant gains in most measures of language development. These findings support the value of involving family members in the use of milieu teaching.

Children with autism increased their verbal communication during the milieu teaching interventions when implemented by either parents (Kaiser et al., 2000) or therapists (Hancock & Kaiser, 2002), and the results for children with autism did not differ from those of other children (Kaiser, Hancock, Nietfeld, & Delaney, 1996; Kaiser et al., 1998). These results, along with those of additional studies (Charlop & Carpenter, 2000; Hamilton & Snell, 1993; McGee et al., 1992, 1999), suggest that milieu teaching may be successful in improving the communication skills of students with autism. There has been much discussion on the outcomes of intensive didactic intervention on the functioning of children with autism (McEachin, Smith, & Lovaas, 1993); however, findings to date do not establish that didactic training is better than more naturalistic approaches to language intervention (Green, 2001; Gresham & MacMillan, 1997; Matson et al., 1993), and at least one study found that milieu teaching techniques resulted in equal retention, greater generalization and equal or greater spontaneous language use than didactic training (Miranda-Linne & Melin, 1992). To date, there is evidence that milieu teaching and EMT procedures can increase the language and communication skills of students with autism.

Implementing EMT

Implementing EMT requires more than skill in using each of its three components. Assessment of child skills, selection of targets, structuring the setting to promote naturalistic teaching, and evaluating both the implementation and the student's progress must be addressed to ensure that this instructional strategy is effective.

Data Collection and Evaluation

Effective milieu language teaching is data based. Many aspects of the process may be monitored. At a minimum, it is recommended that data be kept on the following dimensions:

1. *The number of milieu teaching episodes per day and the targets taught in these episodes:* A total of 20 to 25 episodes per day is a reasonable teaching base. Typically, students will have a small number of targets (two to five), and there should be at least five opportunities to teach each target. If students are not learning quickly with this number of opportunities, it is important to determine if more concentrated practice is needed to acquire the targeted form of communication. Massed trial practice can be used to shape sign production, acquire skills for operating an electronic device, or practice discrimination skills that form the conceptual bases for word meanings but is not usually sufficient for establishing the functional use of the communication form.

2. *The number of student initiations across the day or during selected activities:* An increase in the number of student initiations is often one of the primary effects of EMT. Initiations typically are defined as directed intentional communication that occurs in the absence of an adult verbal stimulus (e.g., a request). Noting the content of student initiations helps to assess progress; select activities, materials, and consequences; and establish new targets.

3. *The responsiveness of the student to EMT procedures:* Responsiveness can be measured by counting the number of appropriate student responses to questions, mands, models, and delays. For example, a teacher could determine the number of times a student responded to 10 different questions across the day. Responsiveness to 65% to 70% of the EMT procedures should be considered adequate if each episode ends positively and contains appropriate models of the target behavior.

4. *Use of the target skills by students outside of teaching episodes:* This indicates a level of unprompted generalizations of the target skill across forms, people, and settings.

Each of these dimensions can be monitored using a simple tally sheet. Data sheets can be sticky notes or index cards attached to a lesson plan. An activity-specific data sheet cues the teacher when and how to prompt and provides space for data collection. Sticky notes on the student's communication book, wheelchair, or desk can be used for simple data collection. While daily monitoring is ideal, systematic sampling of different activities across several days yields a more balanced evaluation than does casual monitoring across an entire day. Non-data-based EMT is likely to be highly erratic and, like any such approach, may prolong the use of ineffective strategies, depriving students of critical learn-

ing time. Monitoring is especially important when several students are being targeted for EMT. Table 5–7 is a sample data sheet used to collect data for Kristi across three school settings.

How to Use EMT

EMT can be either used as a primary language intervention approach or combined with direct teaching one on one to facilitate generalization and promote further acquisition. When used as a primary intervention approach, EMT should be applied systematically in routine interactions with the student, in small groups, and at any other time a need for language use can be specified. Skilled teachers can use EMT within the context of classroom and daily living activities without disrupting them.

TABLE 5–7
Sample Data Sheet for a Student

Student: Kristi			
Setting	**Occurrences of target responses**	**Prompts used**	**Student response acknowledged**
Target 1: greet peers "hi"			
Arrival	///	MQ, MQ, MQ	
Breakfast	/	M	+
Target 2: request assistance "help"			
Arrival	/	S	+
Departure	/	S	+
Target 3: "more"			
Breakfast	//	TD, TD	+ +
Lunch	/	TD	+

Setting: Specify activity when response occurred.
Occurrences: Use slash (/) for each time child uses target response.
Prompts: (Record a symbol each time a prompt is used). M = model, MQ = mand or question, TD = time delay.
Acknowledge: + = target response was acknowledged by adult or peer + either with the corresponding prompt or S+ for adult/peer acknowledgment of spontaneous target response without a prompt.

TABLE 5–8

EMT Planning and Data Collection Form for Two Preschool Children in an Activity

Activity: PlayDoh Date: 8-1-03	Materials of Interest 1. 2 cans of PlayDoh 2. 4 cookie cutters 3. 2 rolling pins		Basic Arrangement 1. Cookie cutters on tray 2. Lids on PlayDoh 3. Rolling pins on shelf		
Child	**Communication target**	**Environmental arrangement**	**Milieu procedure**	**Child response**	**Comments**
Margaret	Sign "help"	1. Opening PlayDoh (assistance)	Model	Signed "help"	Only one model
	Point to preference	2. Present two cookie cutters (choice making)	Model with physical assistance	Initiated point	Did not need prompt
	Sign "want more"	3. Small portion of PlayDoh (small portions)	Model "want more"	Signed "want more"	Needed two models
	Sign shape of cookie cutter	4. Present two cookie cutters (choice making)	Time delay and model "want star"	Signed "more"	Time delay, two models, then physical guidance for "star"
Mary	Verbalize "help, please"	1. Opening PlayDoh (assistance)	Incidental teaching	"Help, please"	Mary is requesting
	Verbalize "want ____"	2. Present two colors of PlayDoh (choice making)	Incidental teaching	No response	Consistently nonverbal
	Verbalize "want pin"	3. Roll PlayDoh without pin (assistance)	Incidental teaching	"Want pin"	Models are effective, mands are not
	Verbally request PlayDoh	4. Small portion of PlayDoh (small portion)	Time delay	"PlayDoh"	Exaggerated time delay to elicit response
	Point to cookie cutter	5. Present three cookie cutters on tray (choice making)	Time delay	Points to cookie cutter	Exaggerated time delay to elicit response

Teaching procedures used: model, mand model, time delay, and incidental teaching.

Planning classroom activities and routines around EMT opportunities ensures that training will occur. Routines provide extra support to students who are learning language because the context is familiar and the expectations for communication are clear. Table 5-8 is a completed EMT planning sheet used to organize the classroom activities of two preschool students.

Activity-based instruction (Bricker & Cripe, 1989) is similar to EMT except that it includes a range of social, motor, communicative, and cognitive skills. In activity-based instruction, materials are selected and settings arranged to facilitate active child engagement, provide opportunities for learning language and other skills, and promote natural opportunities for incidental teaching. Another highly effective strategy is to embed EMT into instruction on academic, work, or independent living tasks. Communication integrated with teaching of other skills further ensures that the natural functions of communication are being learned.

Michael is learning to ride the bus from his home to his job training site. His job coach prompts him to use his Dynamyte to greet the driver, to respond when other passengers ask him questions (e.g., "How are

you? Where are you going?"), and to thank the driver as he gets off the bus. These communication skills are functional and well integrated with other daily living skills: waiting for the bus, getting on, putting money in the coin receptacle, watching for his stop, and checking for his belongings before departing the bus.

Communication goals may be embedded in tasks that teach several skills simultaneously. For example, teaching signs during grooming helps Kelly acquire situation-specific language.

In the grooming sequence, Kelly practices washing her face after lunch. The teacher uses time delays to prompt Kelly to sign for soap, towel, finished, and, if needed, help from the teacher. Initially, the teacher modeled by pointing to the photos, providing the verbal label, and prompting Kelly to imitate, but now she focuses her attention on Kelly and waits for Kelly to request the needed objects.

Table 5–9 shows communication targets and EMT procedures for three students during lunch. These students routinely enter the lunch room, ask for specific foods, make a choice of drinks, move to a table, and ask to sit next to a peer. Each student has three communication targets, appropriate for aspects of their established routine. Note that for Kristi, who is just learning to use

her VOCA, pointing to communicate is taught along with the sign "eat" to specify her food choices because she does not have specific food labels yet. Similarly, Jamie, who uses a picture book to communicate, is encouraged to point, vocalize, and attempt "please." Data can be collected on the lesson plan sheet using the columns immediately adjacent to where the target is listed. Social goals, such as looking at peers, getting peers' attention before communicating, and using "please," are taught concurrently with the target communicative form.

Assessment

When EMT is proposed as an intervention strategy, assessment serves two general purposes:

1. To describe the student's existing communication skills
2. To gather a database for developing treatment goals and intervention strategies

Performing an Environmental Inventory

The purpose of an environmental inventory is to identify the settings in which students need communication skills. Since almost every setting requires such skills, the first step of the inventory is to list the settings where a student spends the majority of his or her time. First, settings are identified (e.g., home, school, church,

TABLE 5–9
EMT Prompts and Communication Targets for Three Students During Lunch

Students		Date: 10-25-04						Total correct
Lunch contexts		Order food		Order drinks		Ask to sit with peer		
Jamie	Prompt	Model		Mand-model		Model		
	Target	Point + "eat" (sign)	+	"Juice" or "milk" (sign)	−	"Sit" (sign) + look at peer	+	2/3
Martin	Prompt	Time delay		Time delay		Mand model		
	Target	"I want + _____" (three-word request)	+	"I want + _____" (three-word request)	+	"(Name), sit here."	−	2/3
Kristi	Prompt	Mand model		Mand model		Model		
	Target	Show picture	+	Show picture	+	Show picture + vocalize to get attention	+	3/3

+ = correct response; − = incorrect response; NR = no response.

TABLE 5–10
Environmental Inventory for Communication Opportunities: Taking the Bus to School

Activities	Communication demands/functions	Possible training site	Possible teacher	Comments	Target forms
Getting on bus	Greet driver	Yes	Mom or sibling	Mom willing; sibling may be	"Good morning"
Greeting driver	Ask social questions	No	No one, driver too busy	Check for generalization from other social talk training	
Greeting riders	Friends greet, ask social questions	Yes	Normal peer or sibling	Two classmates are willing and ride the same bus	"Hello" + (name) "I'm fine" "I'm ____"
Ride to school	Varied questions, can comment on environment	Yes	Normal peer or sibling	Two classmates	Three words context appropriate; also yes or no
Getting off bus	Say good-bye to driver and passengers, greet teacher or aide who meets the bus	Maybe	Aide who greets students at school	Could coordinate with Mom on greeting	"Good-bye" "Hello" + (name)

transportation vehicles); then specific activities (e.g., eating, helping with chores at home, ordering and paying in a restaurant) within each setting are listed and particular communication demands identified.

Table 5-10 is an environmental inventory that describes communication opportunities during a ride to school each morning. The setting (bus to school) is identified, and five discrete activities during the ride are indicated. For each activity, general communication opportunities are listed, and a potential teacher is identified. An intervention plan requires that specific forms and functions of language be delineated and potential teachers identified.

An environmental inventory should be based on direct observation of the student in the potential teaching settings plus informal interviews with significant others. Interviews are especially helpful in deciding where to teach and in clarifying whether information gained during direct observation actually represents the student and the environment. Table 5-11 summarizes a plan for intervening to teach a student to greet the driver and peers during the student's ride to school.

Assessing Student Skills

Two general classes of assessment information are related to student skills. The first is a comprehensive overview that describes cognitive functioning, social skills, motor skills, and communication abilities, a topic

that is beyond the scope of this chapter. The second type of assessment examines students' actual performance of communicative behaviors in the settings identified through environmental inventory. This section focuses on the second type of assessment information. (More information is available in chapter 4.)

Functional Communication Skill Assessment

Assessing functional communication skills involves observing students in the activities identified in their environmental inventory and answering the following five questions:

1. *What do the students find interesting in this setting?* To answer this question, observe the students and note the people, objects, and events to which they attend. Determine if and how the students initiate socially to the people in the setting and if they are responsive to particular people.

2. *What communication functions do the students exhibit in this setting?* Seven basic communication functions should be considered: greetings, protests, requests for objects, requests for attention, requests for assistance, commenting, and answering (Table 5-12). Settings in which adult-initiated interactions are infrequent may offer few opportunities for answering and commenting. Note both whether opportunities occur and how the students respond to those opportunities.

TABLE 5–11
Using EMT to Teach Greetings with Multiple Teachers on Bus to School

Student: Tommy			Trainer responsible: Teacher aide with sibling	
New training _____		Date: January 10–30, 2004	Generalization training: √	
Activity	**Trainer**	**Language targets**	**Procedures**	**Data/monitoring**
Greeting driver	Sibling	"Good morning" + eye contact, smile	Sibling *models*, verbal praise for success, one corrective model, driver responds positively	Sibling records on note card for teacher aide who summarizes and gives sibling feedback
Responding to driver	Sibling	"Fine" in response to "How are you?"	Sibling *models*, prompts if needed, acknowledges	
Greeting friends	Sibling	"Hello" + (name)	Sibling *models* (say "hello" to your friend), *models* if needed expands, and acknowledges	
Responding to friends	Sibling	Varies: Reply "hello" Answer "fine" Answer "yes" or "no"	Sibling *models* appropriate reply, uses delayed modeling, expands, and praises	
Getting off bus	Teacher's aide	"Good-bye" "See you"	Aide *models*, prompts if needed, acknowledges	

3. *What forms do the students use to express these functions?* Communication functions can be expressed verbally and nonverbally. As described in chapter 4, students with severe disabilities often have idiosyncratic ways of expressing functions. For example, a student may throw objects in protest rather than nod or say, "No." Kristi, who has a limited verbal repertoire, uses a single gesture to indicate requests for help, for objects, or to invite joint play. Understanding a student's idiosyncratic communication forms is sometimes difficult but always worth the time invested in observation and analysis because current communication forms are the beginning point for teaching more elaborated language.

4. *What communication skills in the student's repertoires can be the base for building new language skills?* General information about students' skills gleaned from the review of existing language assessments can help determine the beginning skills to be taught with milieu methods. For example, the test results on Kristi's picture identification or on Michael's one- and two-word vocabulary should be added to their respective assessments of communication performance in natural settings.

Kristi's teacher reviewed her records and prepared a list of pictures she had been taught in the past. Using this list, the teacher constructed a probe or test in *which Kristi was given two opportunities to use each picture on her VOCA in response to planned presentations of objects or events. Any pictures that Kristi mastered in the probe or test setting were then assessed in everyday settings. Information collected in natural settings indicated whether Kristi spontaneously used her VOCA to request or initiate interactions or whether she used her VOCA in response to questions (e.g., "What do you want?") or mands (e.g., "Tell me what you want to do next.")*

Discrepancies between tested performance and naturalistic performance are ideal beginning points for milieu teaching interventions to promote generalization. The milieu method teaches skills slightly in advance of the students' current functional repertoires. Often, this requires generalization training to transfer already learned forms into their functional contexts. Language goals may include enlarging the student's vocabulary, extending the number of different forms used to express an already mastered communicative function (e.g., greetings), and teaching new ways to use and combine existing skills. Language skills that already have been acquired receptively but are not yet in the productive repertoire are also potentially excellent targets.

Michael understands many more labels than he uses spontaneously; these labels would be good targets in

TABLE 5–12
Seven Basic Communication Functions

Functions	Possible forms
Greetings	Waves Eye contact "Hello" "Name"
Requests for assistance	Gesture to come Giving object for which assistance is needed Taking the adult's hand and directing the adult to the task Crying "Help" Use of the adult's name
Request for object	Pointing Attempting to grab the object Taking the adult's hand and directing it to the object Verbal request: "Give me," "Want that" Naming object
Requests for information	Echoic imitation "What?" Eye contact plus quizzical look Showing object (requesting name or function of object)
Protests	"No" Pushing the adult away Crying Turning away from the adult or peer Throwing objects
Comments	Echoic imitation Pointing to the object Showing the object to the adult

simple *two-word phrases with already mastered verbs (e.g., go library, go gym, go homeroom).*

5. *What social communication strategies are used by the students?* To answer this question, students must be observed interacting to identify when they are socially responsive and what basic interactional skills they already have. EMT procedures teach and strengthen interactional skills as well as communication skills.

Combining Environmental Information and Student Assessments

The final step in assessment is to combine information gathered about the environment and students' skills in order to design a teaching plan. The teaching plan should specify the following:

1. The mode(s) for student communicative responses (e.g., verbal, sign, symbol system, or a combination of these)
2. Specific communication targets described in terms of both linguistic form and communicative function
3. Where and when teaching will occur
4. How the teaching environment should be restructured to include EMT interactions
5. Who will do the teaching
6. What assistance the teacher may need to use EMT strategies
7. Whether supplemental instruction is needed in addition to EMT and when this instruction will be provided

The student communication mode(s) and specific training targets should be derived primarily from student assessments with the communication team's consensus, but targets and mode(s) should also be determined by the characteristics of the settings. For example, if no one in a student's most frequented settings has knowledge of signs and if the student's significant others are unwilling to learn a signing symbol system, a communication board with pictures may be a more useful mode of communication. Many students will use multiple modes of communication.

The first training setting should be one in which the target skills will be most functional, but it should also be one in which milieu intervention is relatively easy to apply. Identification of teachers who can apply the milieu techniques effectively is essential. Often, new instructors need support to begin intervention. Assistance in identifying interactions for teaching and training specific language targets and instruction in modeling, manding, time delay, and feedback should be part of the trainers' preparation. Continued feedback to teachers is also needed if the intervention is to be effective.

Some skills may need intensive practice in the communication setting. For example, when teaching a student an initial set of signs or to associate pictures with objects, places, and activities, massed trial practice may be useful for training the basic motor skills involved in producing the response. Intensive instruction and EMT can proceed concurrently. Trainers can determine if more intensive teaching is needed by monitoring student performance and noting the actual number of EMT trials that students are receiving and their progress toward criterion performance. If the number of trials is low or students are not acquiring a specific target form after a reasonable length of time (e.g., 3 weeks of 10 trials each day), then massed trial instruction may be added to facilitate acquisition while continuing milieu teaching to ensure generalization to functional use. Other considerations include the symbol system taught, the functionality of the specific student's targets, and the adequacy of implementation of the milieu procedures.

To meet the goal of functional language, the effectiveness of intervention must be assessed at frequent intervals in natural settings. If students' functional communication repertoires are not expanding during intervention, adjustments in teaching tactics and target skills should be made. A sort of bottom-line question should be posed at 3-month intervals: What does this student communicate effectively now that he or she was unable to communicate 3 months ago? Assuming regular teaching sessions, even students with severe disabilities should show progress toward more functional skills after 3 months of training.

Generalized Skills Teaching

One of the strengths of EMT is that it is designed to facilitate generalization. Multiple exemplars (e.g., several linguistically similar forms that serve the same function) in functional communication contexts and naturally occurring reinforcers make the generalization of newly trained forms likely. When students have several appropriate forms that communicate their needs and wants effectively, they are likely to use them. However, when planning a milieu intervention, it is still important to consider the generalization of language training.

Language generalization occurs at several levels. Using a specific communication function (e.g., requests) or form (e.g., adjective–noun combinations, such as "red ball") across individuals and settings is an important but relatively simple type of generalization. Formation of a generalized concept, such as "ball," "cup," or "go," without either overgeneralizing (i.e., child says "goed" for "went" or refers to all red, round things as "ball") or undergeneralizing (i.e., child uses "ball" only when she sees a red, round ball but not when she sees a football) the word representing the concept is a more difficult type of generalization. The most complex type of generalization is generative language use (i.e., spontaneously initiating novel, meaningful word combinations in varied situations).

Generalization is an aspect of the learning process. Learning may be characterized as consisting of four overlapping levels or stages. First is the acquisition level, where students learn the basic response or skill (e.g., the word "ball" is associated with a spherical object). Language teaching typically is concentrated on this level. Simple form–object and form–event relationships are taught, and new skills are introduced as soon as students evidence associative learning. At the second or maintenance level of learning, students learn to routinely use the skill. They practice the skill in one or two functional contexts until appropriate use of the skill is well established and dependable. Next is the generalization level, when students begin to use the new response under a variety of conditions. They may overgeneralize or undergeneralize use of the response as they explore its potential functions and discover its essential attributes and delimiters. This level of language learning frequently has been ignored in language teaching, although many students with severe disabilities need help "fine-tuning" their use of forms. Finally, the fourth level of learning is characterized by competence, or fluency, in using the learned response. At this level, students approximate adult competence in use of the response. Students know when to use and not use the response. The response is used generatively—it is integrated with other communicative responses in the students' repertoires. This level of language learning is the desired outcome of intervention but typically has been overlooked.

> *Carter is beginning to learn some three-word phrases (e.g., "give me some," "play new game"). He typically uses his newly learned phrases in one of two ways: he either undergeneralizes and uses the phrase only in the exact circumstance it was learned or overgeneralizes and uses the phrase across many settings and contexts, some of which are not appropriate. Carter may say "give me some" when requesting popcorn from his mother but not when requesting other foods or requesting comic books from his friends. EMT may be used to prompt Carter to apply his newly learned phrases to a variety of appropriate contexts.*

Initial acquisition, maintenance, generalization, and fluency are influenced by a number of variables that relate to the nature of the training, environmental support for trained language, and the criteria for mastery of the trained responses. Variables that relate specifically to training outcomes include (a) what is taught; (b) who teaches; (c) how functional, reinforcing, and consistent the consequences for communication are; (d) where teaching occurs; (e) how the content is organized; (f) what criteria for learning are applied; and (g) how responsive students' environments are to new learning.

What Is Taught?

Both the forms of communication (e.g., words, sentences, signs, use of picture, responses using a communication device) and their functions (e.g., greetings, commenting, questioning, requesting) must be learned if new skills are to be used. Simply put, the content of training must be functional for students, and they must have experience using the content in a functional manner during training.

New forms should reflect communicative functions that students have already acquired. For example, since

Michael already requests objects (e.g., milk, his favorite CD), a new form of requesting (e.g., "give me"+noun label) can be taught easily. New forms for training should be only slightly more complex than the forms that students currently use to express a particular function. Conversely, when teaching a new function, such as requesting information, it is easiest to begin with an already known form, or to teach the function with a single, simple form.

Who Teaches?

The simple answer to this question is everyone. As many people as possible who come in contact with students regularly and are willing to be either spontaneous teachers or trained teachers should be involved. Responsive conversational style as well as use of the four milieu teaching techniques can enhance the natural abilities of teachers, therapists, and parents to promote communication in context. The milieu methods have been learned and effectively applied by teachers and other professional staff, paraprofessionals, and parents. EMT is a particularly feasible approach because training can be incorporated easily into routine activities throughout the day. Parents and significant others can be effective in facilitating generalization through their use of the components of EMT.

When family members are willing, they can also teach new skills appropriate to settings outside of schools (Kaiser et al., 2001). Family members are especially important for ensuring that students maintain newly learned skills. These people may use EMT across the range of daily interactions to prompt functional use of forms that students have already learned. EMT procedures implemented in a naturalistic and conversational style should promote the functional use of students' skills without changing conversations into formal teaching interactions. Research comparing parent-implemented and therapist-implemented EMT found that young children with disabilities, including children with autism, showed greater language growth over a 6-month period after intensive intervention when their parents implemented EMT than when it was implemented only by a therapist (Kaiser et al., 1998). Parent-implemented training may be especially important for students who require intensive intervention over long periods of time and practice in specific social contexts. (Table 5–13 shows adaptations of EMT procedures for teaching students with autism.)

TABLE 5–13
Adaptations of EMT for Students with Autism

Environmental arrangement
- Select and arrange materials and the setting to minimize interfering behaviors
- Select high-preference materials
- Change materials before student loses interest
- Develop specific procedures for managing the child's interfering behaviors

Responsive conversational style

- Define limits to following the child's lead and interest (do not follow inappropriate or stereotypic behaviors)
- Establish patterns of turn taking and shared engagement with materials before introducing prompts
- Repeat and expand student's communication attempts
- Use imitation of student's actions (mirroring) to maintain engagement
- Match affect, volume, and pacing with the student's
- Expand nonverbal behavior toward appropriate play and use of objects

Milieu teaching

- Abbreviate the sequence of milieu prompts in order to maintain the child's focus of attention
- Use choice mands with visual choices
- Model targets alone ("Ball") rather than "Say ball" to reduce inappropriate echoing of the prompt ("Say")
- Use time delay to promote verbal initiations

How Are Students Reinforced?

To be generalized, language must come under the control of a breadth and range of naturally occurring consequences. To the greatest extent possible, only student-selected, naturally occurring reinforcers should be used in training (e.g., preferred activities, toys, or materials). If this is not possible initially with some training targets, then systematic introduction of naturally occurring consequences must be a central part of the training process. Consequences should always include continued positive interaction with teachers, meaningful comments related to students' responses, and expansions of student's utterances. These types of consequences are the typical natural results of everyday language use.

Where Does Teaching Occur?

Language should be taught in settings where communication naturally occurs: at home, on the playground, in the lunchroom, in the community, during academic activities, in the hallway, on the bus, during family outings, and in all the daily routines in which language is functional. With normally developing children, parents and teachers rarely set aside a particular time for specifically teaching language or other skills. There are too

many other things to be done. Language is taught informally in the course of typical activities, such as eating, dressing, toileting, bathing, and transitions between activities. In general, the same model should apply for students who have severe disabilities. In the classroom and in community instruction, it is important to integrate language learning into the teaching of other skills within which the use of language normally occurs.

Responsive Environments Enable New Learning and Generalization

One way to program for generalization is to introduce a new skill into its natural community of reinforcement (Stokes & Baer, 1977), that is, to allow the student to experience the naturally occurring positive outcomes of communication. As students acquire new skills and their behaviors change, natural environments must respond in ways that support those changes. During normal development, adaptation naturally occurs in mother–child interactions. Mothers are aware of their children's improved skills because they are in close contact with the children and expect them to change (Newport, 1976). When students have severe disabilities, adults sometimes lose the expectation that the students will change. In busy classrooms, teachers may not have much time to notice a student's attempts to comment using newly learned signs, pictures, or words. Thus, potential conversational partners may fail to respond differentially when change and growth do occur. Peers, teachers, and parents can become more responsive when they have information about changes in the students' communication. When these people respond to new forms and provide consequences for their use, they help students generalize and maintain new skills. Again, providing opportunities for students to use new forms is an important step toward ensuring maintenance.

Michael's and Kristi's parents should be provided with regular updates on newly learned words and pictures. In classrooms, demonstrations of new skills can help peers and teaching staff members recognize new communication forms.

Kristi is given the opportunity to use the new pictures she has learned on her Stepper™ in a large-group activity. Michael is invited to show his friends pictures on his DynaMyte and to label these pictures with his newly learned words.

Each of the preceding variables (what to teach, who teaches, where teaching occurs) should be directly addressed in designing an individualized communication training program for a student. Generalization should

be assessed on a weekly basis. Parents should be asked to note the use of new forms, and their help in promoting generalization should be sought. A simple report form, such as the one shown in Table 5-14, can be used to both assess generalization and prompt adults to facilitate language use.

Table 5-15 is a generalization planning worksheet developed to monitor and plan for generalization. The basic strategy is to plan training to include multiple, functional exemplars; to probe for simple generalization across persons, settings, and objects; to monitor generalization observed in functional contexts; and to remediate any observed problems in generalization. The worksheet should be updated on a weekly basis and shared with everyone involved in the students' training. Sharing data and brainstorming innovative approaches to support generalization and maintenance should be a collaborative team activity.

Designing an Optimal Teaching Approach

In the following paragraphs, we apply EMT strategies to Jordon.

An Application of Milieu Teaching

Jordon is a 5 year old boy. When he was 4 months of age, Jordon contracted cerebrospinal meningitis and was hospitalized for a period of 5 weeks. As a result

TABLE 5–14

Report Form for Assessing Generalization

Student: Kristi		Date: March 3, 2005		
Person reporting: Sharon (Mom)		Mode: Sign		
Target	**Status**	**When was target used? How often?**		**New context**
1. Help	Kristi has this one really well at school	Opening jar, one time; trying to get toys from sibling, three times		Trying to get arm in coat
2. Candy	Kristi's favorite	Lots of times! She really likes to try this request		None
3. Potty	Maintaining use of this word as a request	About five times (always appropriate)		No, she uses it by herself appropriately
4. Hug	Just started training this word	Not seen		Build a routine with Mom and Dad
5. _____				

Comments and suggestions: I think "hug" will need prompting. Kristi doesn't know how to ask for hugs yet. I may be missing some things she signs because her signing is not precise and I sometimes don't recognize her gestures as specific signs.

TABLE 5–15
Generalization Planning Worksheet

Student: Michael		Trainer: Martha (teacher)			Date: 1/30/05		
	Initial training criterion met (date and %)	**Generalization probed**			**Spontaneous use observed**		**Further training needed? (date, plan, person responsible)**
Form		**Setting (%)**	**Trainer (%)**	**Stimuli (%)**	**Prompted (no, and occasion)**	**Unprompted (no, and occasion)**	
Photo + label (help, book, finished)	10/14/04 100	100	100	85	One time (book) in response to time delay by teacher	Three times (help): 1. When he couldn't reach his jacket 2. When he wanted teacher assistance with his backpack 3. When a peer took his paper	"Finished" will be trained at home beginning 2/12/05. Mom and Dad will build into mealtime routine in morning and evening.

of the meningitis, Jordon experienced significant brain damage, which resulted in hemiplegia of the left side and severe mental retardation. Jordon lives at home with his mother, his 12 year old sister, and his maternal grandmother. He attends a regular kindergarten class from 9:00 a.m. to 3:00 p.m., Monday through Friday. Jordon is seen by the school's speech and language clinician twice each week for small group language instruction. Both the speech clinician and the special education teacher consult with Jordon's kindergarten teacher. Late afternoons are spent at home with his grandmother and his sister, when she arrives home from school. Jordon's mother comes home from work around 6:00 p.m. Weekends are generally less structured. On Saturday mornings, Jordon usually attends a young children's story hour at the local library. Jordon also spends time on other activities, such as going to the grocery with his mother, going to the playground with his sister, and accompanying his grandmother as she does chores around the house.

Jordon has very little "language." He vocalizes and/or points to request; smiles and sometimes produces a string of syllables in response to adult attention; and dependably waves "hello" and "goodbye" with his right hand. He responds inconsistently to peer initiations and protests to peers, but does not initiate contact, vocalizations, or smiling to peers.

Jordon's special education teacher, his regular kindergarten teacher, his SLP, and his mother form a planning team that focuses on his communication needs. This team follows a series of steps in developing a functional language training program for Jordon that uses EMT strategies.

Gathering New Information
First, functional communication skills that will give Jordon more control over his physical and social environment are identified by conducting an environmental inventory in the settings in which Jordon spends the majority of his time. For these environments (his kindergarten class, playground, and home), the following information is determined:

1. The major activities that occur within each environment:
   - Kindergarten class—large group, small group, snack or lunch, and gym or recess
   - Playground—swings, riding push toys, and slide
   - Home—meals, bedtime or story time, trips in the car, and play with favorite toys
2. Basic communication skills that will help Jordon function more independently and that will facilitate increased participation in activities
3. The individuals in each environment or activity who would be logical milieu teachers and their current skills
4. Whether the materials available and the arrangement of the environment are optimal for promoting Jordon's initiations and choice making and facilitating the use of EMT procedures

Information needed to complete the environmental inventories for Jordon's classroom activities is readily available. His mother describes his home activities. Jordon's special education teacher and his SLP divide the responsibility of observing Jordon at school and at home after school. For each environment, they obtain information about strategies currently being used to teach language, the responsiveness of teachers to Jordon when he shows interest in something or attempts to communicate, and opportunities for Jordon to control his physical and social environment.

Second, interviews are conducted to get information from significant others as a basis for planning a functional communication program. Five questions are posed:

1. What does Jordon find interesting in this setting?
2. What communication functions does he exhibit in this setting?
3. What forms does he use to express these functions?
4. What existing communication skills can be the basis for building new skills?
5. What social communication strategies does Jordon use in this setting?

The special education teacher interviews the teacher and teaching assistant in the kindergarten class, the physical therapist, and the peer tutor who works with Jordon. Jordon's mother interviews his grandmother, his sister, and the story-time coordinator at the Saturday morning library program. The interviews are designed to obtain specific information about the existing environmental demands for Jordon to communicate, the social and communicative behaviors exhibited by Jordon in each setting, and the minimal skills that Jordon needs to improve his ability to interact and communicate with others in the environment. The planning team uses the interview data to verify, clarify, and augment their observational data and to gain insight into the ability of significant others to identify and foster Jordon's communicative behavior.

Third, in addition to taking into account environmental characteristics and demands, Jordon's planning team specifies child characteristics essential to consider in developing an individualized, functional communication training program. Test results (including the results of diagnostic testing) and informal observation provide relevant information about Jordon's receptive language and expressive communication skills, motor development, and sensory abilities. Reports from teachers and significant others provide information about his social interaction strategies, preferred activities, and engagement with the physical environment:

1. *What does Jordon find interesting?* Jordon's interests vary by setting. At home, he likes to look at books alone or with an adult or his sister, to be pushed in a swing, and to ride the merry-go-round on the nearby playground. He likes to ride in the car. He also likes to look at mechanical things, such as the vacuum cleaner, the coffeemaker, and the blender when they are operating. He enjoys meals and especially likes having a snack with his sister when she arrives home after school. He seems to enjoy story time at the library as long as he can see the pictures. At school, Jordon does not seem interested in many of the classroom activities (e.g., large group, going to most centers, working independently on preacademic tasks). He does like to look at books, watch and manipulate trucks and cars, and be pushed on the swing during outdoor time. The physical therapist reports that Jordon seems very interested in mechanical toys (e.g., a windup top, a toy truck with a turning cement mixer, race cars that move on a track).

2. *What communication functions does Jordon exhibit?* At home, he dependably greets his family and protests when he does not get his way or does not want to do something. He sometimes requests objects and assistance. At school, Jordon demonstrates these same functions (i.e., greetings, protests, requests) but seems less consistent. For example, he greets his physical therapists and SLP but does not always greet his classroom teacher and never greets peers. He does protest when peers take toys or interfere with his activities.

3. *What forms does Jordon use to express these functions?* In all settings, Jordon vocalizes to greet others (except peers). He reaches for objects, looks at adults, vocalizes to request, and vocalizes cries and sometimes tantrums to protest. Jordon spontaneously produces a variety of one-syllable sounds but does not yet use them to signal specific functions. His mother reports that he can wave good-bye with his right hand with minimal prompting. He waves good-bye at story time and with familiar adults if his mother prompts him.

4. *What existing skills can be the basis for building new skills?* Jordon can take turns nonverbally (e.g., alternating putting objects in a basket, pushing a car back and forth) and vocally (e.g., making sounds when an adult imitates him). He is able to do picture-to-object and object-to-picture matching, and he is working on a program that teaches him to point to an object after presentation of its verbal label. He can also imitate motor gestures with his right hand (e.g., wave "hi," touch his head). He responds to the word "no" by stopping whatever he is doing. Testing has shown that Jordon has good visual and auditory functioning. His motor development limits both his mobility and, to an extent, his engagement with objects, toys, and peers. He basically does not use the left side of his body; rather, his left hand is tightly clenched and his arm drawn upward. He can sit independently for long periods and can pivot around in a circle. He is able to roll from one place to another but typically relies on prompting to do so.

5. *What social communication strategies does Jordon use?* Jordon gets attention from his mother, his sister, his grandmother, his teachers, and his physical therapist by visually following the person until he can establish eye contact. On making eye contact, Jordon smiles and sometimes produces a string of sounds. He can also vocalize and reach for objects and coordinate his attention by looking at an adult, reaching for the object and vocalizing, then looking back at the adult. He smiles and turns toward adults when they speak to him. He responds to his name and to familiar words and simple phrases (e.g., his sister's name, car, eat, potty, time to go) with appropriate anticipatory responses (e.g., looking around for his sister, vocalizing and smiling when it is time to go in the car or eat). He will occasionally respond to peers by taking a toy they offer. He will protest to peers but does not initiate eye contact, vocalizations or smiling toward peers.

Planning the Functional Communication Program

Fourth, Jordon's team plans his functional communication program by considering the data on child performance and learning characteristics in light of the data obtained from the environmental inventories. They begin by determining target responses that are slightly above Jordon's current level of functioning and that are functional across environments and activities. Se-

lected training targets include "more," "help," and pointing to one of two pictures to choose one of the two represented objects (i.e., choice making). The team feels that many natural opportunities to teach each of these targets will occur across the primary activities and environments.

His team next considers the communication mode to be used in teaching each response. A review of Jordon's expressive modalities indicates that he spontaneously produces a variety of sounds but does not imitate sounds. He uses his right hand to point to things that he wants and also for picture–object and object–picture matching. He has virtually no use of his left hand, placing limitations on the repertoire of signs he can ultimately produce. Because he already shows some degree of skill using pictures, Jordon's teachers decide that his primary communication system should involve a picture communication board, but they will always include models of verbal responses.

In summary, three beginning goals are selected for Jordon:

1. Sign "help" (modified)
2. Sign "more" (modified)
3. Indicate choices by pointing on a communication board

The next step in planning Jordon's communication program is determining how and when to teach these goals. Appropriate vocal stimuli (words) will be paired with pictorial stimuli (pictures representing concepts). Vocal imitation training will be given at the same time he is taught to use signs and pictures. Initially, concrete pictoral stimuli should be used. This poses a problem for teaching the more abstract concepts of "help" and "more." The team decides to teach Jordon to express these responses by producing modified signs that will accommodate his physical disability. Verbal imitation training of "help" and "more" will accompany the respective sign training.

The third goal, indicating choice, uses the communication board. Initially, two pictures are presented. Beginning with two pictures is appropriate because Jordon already understands that pictures stand for objects and actions. As Jordon becomes more proficient in using the communication board, additional pictures will be added gradually. The pictures on the board vary and are functionally related to the activity at hand. Once Jordon indicates his choice, he is given access to that material.

In their fifth step, the planning team discusses the techniques they will use to train the target responses. Several EMT procedures are selected.

Modeling Procedure Initially, modeling would be used to teach "help" and "more" at times when Jordon appears to need help or want more of something. The team agrees that they will attempt to give him the opportunity to express each function himself before modeling the appropriate (modified) sign. For example, when Jordon correctly imitates each sign 80% of the time, the teachers will interchange use of the mand-model and time delay procedures (rather than the model procedure) to elicit responses. (Attempts by Jordon to indicate "help" or "more" that are followed by the model, mand-model, or time delay procedure technically represent applications of the incidental teaching procedure, i.e., a child's request followed by the model, mand-model, or time delay procedure.) In addition to collecting performance data on sign production, the team collects data on vocal imitation training that accompanies each nonverbal training trial. The mand-model, time delay, and incidental teaching procedures are used to teach Jordon to make choices using the communication board. An example of how each of these techniques is applied for this purpose follows.

Mand-Model Procedure The mand-model procedure is used when Jordon indicates a choice in response to his teacher's presenting two alternatives.

After Jordon has learned to respond by imitating his targets (help and more) during the model procedure, the mand-model procedure is introduced. When it is Jordon's turn during music group, the teacher shows him the bells and the tambourine. She then places in reach his communication board that shows a picture of each of these objects and asks, "Which musical instrument do you want?" If Jordon does not respond or if he makes an incomplete or unclear response, she prompts by presenting a model of the correct response (i.e., demonstrates a clear pointing response to the picture that Jordon appears to favor), or she physically prompts Jordon to make a clear response. The teacher then verbally expands his nonvocal response (e.g., "You want the bells") and provides a verbal model that is for the situation and his skill level (e.g., "bells"). Following the model procedure to train "bells," he is given the bells to shake.

Delay Procedure The delay procedure is used to support Jordon in learning to initiate use of his communication. Delay will be introduced after Jordon has some success using targets in the model and mand-model procedures.

In free play, when Jordon visually expresses interest in a toy, the teacher presents his communication board displaying pictures of the toy of interest and another toy. The teacher looks at Jordon for about 5 seconds but says nothing (delay). If Jordon points to either picture, he receives the corresponding object. A point to the "wrong" picture (i.e., Jordon shows displeasure on receiving the object) or an incomplete or unclear response results in a mand (tell me what you want) or model prompt (teacher signs an option) with or without a physical prompt, as necessary. An appropriate verbal model is presented before delivering the chosen toy.

Incidental Teaching Procedure The incidental teaching procedure is used on occasions when Jordon requests a material or activity. It can be introduced at any point in training because it embeds the model, mand-model, or time delay procedures as needed to support Jordon's use of his targets.

If Jordon points to the record player, the teacher presents his communication board, displaying pictures of the record player and something else. She then uses the mand-model (what do you want?) or delay procedure (waits 5 seconds while looking at Jordon but says nothing) to elicit a pointing response. Verbal and physical prompts are presented as needed. Before giving Jordon access to the record player, the model procedure is applied to elicit an appropriate vocal or pointing response.

As a sixth step, several additional tasks are completed in developing Jordon's communication training programs. The team writes task-analyzed instructional programs, including levels of prompts, vocal imitation training procedures, and criterion performance levels for each communication objective. Procedures for data collection and data sheets also are developed. The members of the team agree to do EMT whenever naturalistic opportunities occur and especially in the context of other kinds of skill training. Data are collected daily on a minimum of 10 trials for each objective. However, training occurs during other naturalistic teaching opportunities throughout the day. The teachers decide to use certain situations as training settings and other situations as generalization settings. In school, Jordon's communication goals are trained formally during small-group sessions in both his early intervention class and his kindergarten class, during snack, and at recess. Probes for generalization are conducted during large-group sessions, lunch, and gym. Jordon's environmental inventory indicates that his mother and grandmother are willing to use environmental arrangement strategies and the EMT procedures. Jordon's early intervention teacher, who has had previous EMT experience, plans to provide EMT training by visiting Jordon's home once each week for 2 months. Periodic posttraining visits will be made to Jordon's home to assess the family members' use of EMT and to provide feedback and additional training as necessary.

Seventh and finally, the team considers whether didactic communication training should be conducted in conjunction with the naturalistic communication training. The consensus is to implement only the naturalistic training procedures initially. Jordon's vocal imitation skills are monitored carefully, and if the anticipated rate of acquisition is not achieved within 4 months, the issue of concomitant didactic training on vocal imitation skills will again be considered.

Summary

Teaching functional language is a curriculum goal that requires support from a variety of persons in the larger ecosystem in which instruction occurs. EMT strategies are selected and purposefully embedded into the social interactions of activities and across settings. Training needs to be more frequent and dispersed than can easily be managed by speech clinicians who see individual children for two or three sessions each week. Thus, language teaching is a responsibility shared by school staff and family members and cannot be taught separately from other skills if it is to be functional. Assigning responsibility, providing necessary training, facilitating access to appropriate training settings, and sharing information are essential aspects of allocating resources for functional language training. The development of problem-solving strategies through team collaboration is necessary with functional communication teaching because problems undoubtedly arise when such broad-based instruction is undertaken.

Suggested Activities

1. Observe a student with disabilities for a period of 1 to 2 hours. Note the ways in which the child attempts to communicate and the ways in which the adults in the environments respond. From these observations and your notes, identify at least five opportunities to teach a functional language skill. Describe the context, the skill, and the procedure you would use to teach the skill.

2. One of the most important skills that a teacher must master is clear communication about communication. Review Michael's case study at the beginning of this chapter. Then role-play, explaining his skills, his needs, and the basics of milieu teaching to Michael's homeroom general education teacher. This exercise works best in teams of three: (a) one person explains, (b) one person plays the general education teacher, and (c) one person evaluates the interaction and gives feedback. Switch roles and use what you learn from one another. Summarize what you have learned after all three people have role-played.

3. Consider how to create a classroom that is a "context for conversation." Choose a type of classroom that reflects the age and most appropriate options for students of interest to you. Include the following: (a) how teachers will interact with students, (b) the classroom schedules, (c) the physical design of the classroom, and (d) training for teaching assistants and peers. List five simple things that you might do to promote communication in the classroom.

References

Alpert, C. L., & Kaiser, A. (1992). Training parents as milieu language teachers. *Journal of Early Intervention, 16*(1), 31–52.

Alpert, C. L., Kaiser, A., Hemmeter, M. L., & Ostrosky, M. (1987, November). *Training adults to use environmental arrangement strategies to prompt language.* Paper presented at the annual meeting of the Division of Early Childhood, Council on Exceptional Children, Denver.

Alpert, C. L., & Rogers-Warren, A. K. (1985). Communication of autistic persons, characteristics and intervention. In S. F. Warren & A. K. Rogers-Warren (Eds.), *Teaching functional language* (pp. 123–155). Baltimore: University Park Press.

American Speech-Language-Hearing Association (ASHA). (1991). Report: Augmentative and alternative communication. *Asha 33* (supl. 5), 10.

Anderson, S. R., & Spradlin, J. E. (1980). The generalized effects of productive labeling training involving comment object classes. *Journal of the Association for the Severely Handicapped, 5,* 143–157.

Angelo, D. H., & Goldstein, H. (1990). Effects of a pragmatic teaching strategy for requesting information by communication board users. *Journal of Speech and Hearing Disorders, 55*(2), 231–243.

Beukelman, D. R., & Mirenda, P. (1998). *Augmentative and alternative communication: Management of severe communication disorders in children and adults.* Baltimore: Paul H. Brookes.

Bricker, D., & Cripe, J. (1989). Activity-based intervention. In D. Bricker (Ed.), *Early intervention for at-risk and handicapped infants, toddlers and preschool children* (pp. 251–274). Palo Alto, CA: VORT Corp.

Cavallero, C. C., & Bambara, L. (1982). Two strategies for teaching language during free play. *Journal of the Association for the Severely Handicapped, 7*(2), 80–93.

Charlop, M. H., & Carpenter, M. H. (2000). Modified incidental teaching sessions: A procedure for parents to increase spontaneous speech in their children with autism. *Journal of Positive Behavior Interventions, 2*(2), 98–112.

Charlop, M. H., & Walsh, M. E. (1986). Increasing autistic children's spontaneous verbalizations of affection: An assessment of time delay and peer modeling procedures. *Journal of Applied Behavior Analysis, 19,* 307–314.

Charlop, M. H., & Trasowech, J. E. (1991). Increasing children's daily spontaneous speech. *Journal of Applied Behavioral Analysis, 24,* 747–761.

Farmer-Dougan, V. (1994). Increasing requests by adults with developmental disabilities using incidental teaching by peers. *Journal of Applied Behavior Analysis, 27*(3), 533–544.

Frost, L. A., & Bondy, A. S. (1994). *The picture exchange communication system training manual.* Cherry Hill, NJ: Pyramid Educational Consultants.

Frost, L. A., & Bondy, A. S. (1996). *The picture exchange communication system training manual.* Cherry Hill, NJ: Pyramid Educational Consultants.

Gee, K., Graham, N., Goetz, L., Oshima, G., & Yoshioka, K. (1991). Teaching students to request the continuation of routine activities by using time delay and decreasing physical assistance in the context of chain interruption. *Journal of the Association for Persons with Severe Handicaps, 16,* 154–167.

Gee, K., Graham, N., Sailor, W., & Goetz, L. (1995). Use of integrated general education and community settings as primary contexts for skill instruction for students with severe, multiple disabilities. *Behavior Modification, 19,* 33–58.

Goldstein, H. (2002). Communication intervention for children with autism: A review of treatment efficacy. *Journal of Autism and Developmental Disabilities, 32*(5), 373–396.

Green, G. (2001). Behavior analytic instruction for learners with autism: Advances in stimulus control technology. *Focus on Autism and Other Developmental Disabilities, 16,* 72–85.

Gresham, F. M., & MacMillan, D. L. (1997). Autistic recovery? An analysis and critique of the empirical evidence on the early intervention project. *Behavioral Disorders, 22*(4), 185–201.

Halle, J. W., Baer, D. M., & Spradlin, J. E. (1981). Teachers' generalized use of delay as a stimulus control procedure to increase language use in handicapped children. *Journal of Applied Behavior Analysis, 14,* 387–400.

Halle, J. W., Marshall, A. M., & Spradlin, J. E. (1979). Time delay: A technique to increase language use and facilitate generalization in retarded children. *Journal of Applied Behavior Analysis, 12,* 431–440.

Hamilton, B., & Snell, M. E. (1993). Using the milieu approach to increase spontaneous communication book use across environments by an adolescent with autism. *Augmentative and Alternative Communication, 9,* 259–272.

Hancock, T. B., & Kaiser, A. P. (1996). Siblings' use of milieu teaching at home. *Topics in Early Childhood Special Education, 16*(2), 168–190.

Hancock, T. B., & Kaiser, A. P. (2002). The effects of trainer-implemented enhanced milieu teaching on the social communication of children with autism. *Topics in Early Childhood Special Education, 22*(1), 39–54.

Haring, T. G., Neetz, J. A., Lovinger, L., Peck, C., & Semmel, M. I. (1987). Effects of four modified incidental teaching procedures to create opportunities for communication. *Journal of the Association for Persons with Severe Handicaps, 12,* 218–226.

Haring, T. G., Roger, B., Lee, M., Breen, C., & Gaylord-Ross, R. (1986). Teaching social language to moderately handicapped students. *Journal of Applied Behavior Analysis, 19,* 159–171.

Hart, B. M., & Risley, T. R. (1968). Establishing the use of descriptive adjectives in the spontaneous speech of disadvantaged preschool children. *Journal of Applied Behavior Analysis, 1,* 109–120.

Hart, B. M., & Risley, T. R. (1974). Using preschool materials to modify the language of disadvantaged children. *Journal of Applied Behavior Analysis, 7,* 243–256.

Hart, B. M., & Risley, T. R. (1975). Incidental teaching of language in the preschool. *Journal of Applied Behavior Analysis, 8,* 411–420.

Hart, B. M., & Risley, T. R. (1980). In vivo language intervention: Unanticipated general effects. *Journal of Applied Behavior Analysis, 12,* 407–432.

Hart, B. M., & Rogers-Warren, A. K. (1978). Milieu teaching approaches. In R. L. Schiefelbusch (Ed.), *Bases of language intervention* (Vol. 2, pp. 193–235). Baltimore: University Park Press.

Hemmeter, M. L., Ault, M. J., Collins, B. C., & Meyers, S. (1996). The effects of teacher-implemented feedback within free time activities. *Education and Training in Mental Retardation and Developmental Disabilities, 31,* 203–212.

Hemmeter, M. L., & Kaiser, A. P. (1994). Enhanced milieu teaching: Effects of parent-implemented language intervention. *Journal of Early Intervention, 18,* 269–289.

Humphries, T. L. (2003) Effectiveness of pivotal response training as a behavioral intervention for young children with autism spectrum disorder. *Bridges: Practice Based Research Synthesis, 2*(4), 1–10. Available at http://www.researchtopractice.info

Hunt, P., Alwell, M., & Goetz, L. (1988). Acquisition of conversation skills and the reduction of inappropriate social interaction behaviors. *Journal of the Association for Persons with Severe Handicaps, 13,* 20–27.

Kaiser, A. P. (1993). Functional language. In M. E. Snell (Ed.), *Instruction of students with severe disabilities* (4th ed. pp. 347–379). New York: Macmillan.

Kaiser, A. P. (2000, June). *Research on parent-implemented early language interventions.* Paper presented at the Symposium on Research in Child Language Disorders (SRCLD), Madison, WI.

Kaiser, A. P., & Hancock, T. B. (2000, April). *Supporting children's communication development through parent-implemented naturalistic interventions.* Paper presented at the 2nd Annual Conference on Research Innovations in Early Intervention (CRIEI), San Diego.

Kaiser, A. P., Hancock T. B., & Hester, P. P. (1998). Parents as co-interventionists: Research on applications of naturalistic language teaching procedures. *Infants and Young Children, 10*(4), 1–11.

Kaiser, A. P., Hancock, T. B., McLean, Z. Y., & Stanton-Chapman, T. L. (2001, October). *Building social communication skills during peer interaction: Kidtalk for Peers.* Paper presented at the Head Start University Grantees Meeting, Alexendria, VA.

Kaiser, A. P., Hancock, T. B., & Nietfeld, J. P. (2000). The effects of parent-implemented enhanced milieu teaching on the social communication of children who have autism [Special issue]. *Journal of Early Education and Development, 4,* 423–446.

Kaiser, A. P., Hancock, T. B., Nietfeld, J. P., & Delaney, E. (1996, December). *Adapting enhanced milieu teaching for children with autism.* Paper presented at the meeting of DEC International Early Childhood Conference on Children with Special Needs, Phoenix, AZ.

Kaiser, A. P., Hester, P. P., & McDuffie, A. S. (2001). Supporting communication in young children with developmental disabilities. In D. Felce & E. Emerson (Eds.), *MRDD Research Reviews* (Vol. 7 (2):, pp. 143–150).

Kaiser, A. P., Ostrosky, M. M., & Alpert, C. L. (1993). Training teachers to use environmental arrangement and milieu teaching with nonvocal preschool children. *Journal of the Association for Persons with Severe Handicaps, 18*(3), 188–199.

Kaiser, A. P., Yoder, P. J., & Keetz, A. (1992). Evaluating milieu teaching. In S. F. Warren & J. Reichle (Eds.), *Causes and effects in communication and language intervention* (pp. 9–47). Baltimore: Paul H. Brookes.

Koegel, L. K., Koegel, R. L., Harrower, J. K., & Carter, C. M. (1999). Pivotal response intervention. I: Overview of approach. *Journal of the Association for Persons with Severe Handicaps, 24*(3), 174–185.

Lennox, D. B., & Brune, P. (1993). Incidental teaching for training communication in individuals with traumatic brain injury. *Brain Injury, 7*(5), 449–454.

Matson, J. L., Sevin, J. A., Box, M. L., Francis, K. L., & Sevin, B. M. (1993). An evaluation of two methods for increasing self-initiated verbalizations in autistic children. *Journal of Applied Behavior Analysis, 26,* 389–398.

McCathren, R. B. (2000). Teacher-implemented prelinguistic communication intervention. *Focus on Autism and Other Developmental Disabilities, 15*(1), 21–29.

McEachin, J. J., Smith, T., & Lovaas, O. I. (1993). Long-term outcome for children with autism who received early intensive behavioral treatment. *American Journal on Mental Retardation, 97,* 359–372.

McGee, G. G., Almeida, M. C., Sulzer-Azaroff, B., & Feldman, R. S. (1992). Promoting reciprocal interactions via peer incidental teaching. *Journal of Applied Behavior Analysis, 25*(1), 117–126.

McGee, G. G., Krantz, P. J., & McClannahan, L. E. (1985). The facilitative effects of incidental teaching on preposition use by autistic children. *Journal of Applied Behavior Analysis, 18,* 17–31.

McGee, G. G., Morrier, M. J., & Daly, T. (1999). An incidental teaching approach to early intervention for toddlers with autism. *Journal of the Association for Persons with Severe Handicaps, 24,* 133–146.

Miller, C., Collins, B. C., & Hemmeter, M. L. (2002). Using a naturalistic time delay procedure to teach nonverbal adolescents with moderate-to-severe mental disabilities to initiate manual signs. *Journal of Developmental and Physical Disabilities, 14*(3), 247–261.

Miranda-Linne, F., & Melin, L. (1992). Acquisition, generalization, and spontaneous use of color objectives: A comparison of incidental teaching and traditional discrete-trial procedures for children with autism. *Research in Developmental Disabilities, 13*(3), 191–210.

Mobayed, K. L., Collins, B. C., Strangis, D. E., Schuster, J. W., & Hemmeter, M. L. (2000). Teaching parents to employ mand-model procedures to teach their children requesting. *Journal of Early Intervention, 23*(3), 165–179.

National Research Council. (2001). *Educating children with autism.* Washington, DC: National Academy Press.

Newport, E. L. (1976). Motherese: The speech of mothers to young children. In N. J. Castellan, D. B. Pisoni, & G. R. Potts (Eds.), *Cognitive theory* (Vol. 2, pp. 177–218). Hillsdale, NJ: Lawrence Erlbaum Associates.

Oliver, C. B., & Halle, J. W. (1982). Language training in the everyday environment: Teaching functional sign use to a retarded child. *Journal of the Association for the Severely Handicapped, 7*(3), 50–62.

Ostrosky, M. M., Kaiser, A. P., & Odom, S. L. (1993). Facilitating children's social communicative interactions through the use of peer-mediated interventions. In A. P. Kaiser & D. B. Gray (Eds.), *Enhancing children's communication: Research foundations for intervention* (Vol. 8, pp. 7–43). Baltimore: Paul H. Brookes.

Rodi, M. S., & Hughes, C. (2000). Teaching communication book use to a high school student using a milieu approach. *Journal of the Association for Persons with Severe Handicaps, 25,* 175–179.

Rogers-Warren, A. K., & Warren, S. F. (1980). Mand for verbalization: Facilitating the display of newly-taught language. *Behavior Modification, 4,* 361–382.

Romski, M. A., & Sevcik, R. A. (1992). Developing augmented language in children with severe mental retardation. In S. F. Warren & J. Reichle (Eds.), *Causes and effects in communication and language intervention* (pp. 113–130). Baltimore: Paul H. Brookes.

Schwartz, I. S., Anderson, S. R., & Halle, J. W. (1988). Training teachers to use naturalistic time delay: Effects on teacher behavior and on the language use of students. *Journal of the Association for Persons with Severe Handicaps, 14,* 48–57.

Stokes, T. F., & Baer, D. M. (1977). An implicit technology of generalization. *Journal of Applied Behavior Analysis, 10,* 349–367.

Wacker, D. P., & Reichle, J. (1993). Functional communication training as an intervention for problem behavior: An overview and introduction to our edited volume. In J. Reichle & D. P. Wacker (Eds.), *Communicative alternatives to challenging behavior: Integrating functional assessment and intervention strategies* (Vol. 3, pp. 1–8). Baltimore: Paul H. Brookes.

Warren, S. F., & Bambara, L. M. (1989). An experimental analysis of milieu language intervention: Teaching and action-object form. *Journal of Speech and Hearing Disorders, 54,* 448–461.

Warren, S. F., Gazdag, G. E., Bambara, L. M., & Jones, H. A. (1994). Changes in the generativity and use of semantic relationships concurrent with milieu language intervention. *Journal of Speech and Hearing Research, 37*(4), 924–934.

Warren, S. F., McQuarter, R. J., & Rogers-Warren, A. K. (1984). The effects of teacher mands and models on the speech of unresponsive language-delayed children. *Journal of Speech and Hearing Research, 51,* 43–52.

Warren, S. F., & Rogers-Warren, A. K. (1983). Setting variables affecting the display of trained noun referents by retarded children. In K. Kernan, M. Begab, & R. Edgerton (Eds.), *Environments and behavior: The adaptation of mentally retarded persons* (pp. 257–282). Baltimore: University Park Press.

Yoder, P. J., Kaiser, A. P., & Alpert, C. L. (1991). An exploratory study of the interaction between language teaching methods and child characteristics. *Journal of Speech and Hearing Research, 34,* 155–167.